The Bouncer Smith Chronicles

A Lifetime of Fishing

By

Captain Bouncer Smith
As Told to
Patrick Mansell

The Bouncer Smith Chronicles

A Lifetime of Fishing

BY

Captain Bouncer Smith
As Told to Patrick Mansell

ISBN 978-0-9898738-3-3

Dedication

This work is dedicated to all those who recognize that the oceans' resources are limited and who fish with conservation in mind; for those who show respect for the great creatures we encounter, use discriminating gear, and support those organizations that work for more sustainable fisheries throughout the world.

Table of Contents

Preface

Have you heard the expression "Don't try this at home"? I could say that about some of the risky adventures described in this book. Don't venture out into insanely heavy seas. Don't let a lightning storm sneak up on you. Don't lock down the drag on your reel so that the only possible outcome is a broken line. Many of the most important lessons I have learned in my years as a sportfishing guide have been learned through experience; and some of them have been costly.

One lesson I want to pass on to the now and future generations is this: that was then, and this is now. In this book I describe the catching and killing of many wonderful, beautiful fish. Back in the day, in order to win a tournament, or to acquire a trophy mount, we had to take the fish into the boat and back to the dock. A great number of fish that were not eaten were harvested just the same. Many years ago there was little information about fish stocks and stressed out fisheries. Most stocks of fish were in such great abundance that such matters were not a concern.

But that has all changed. Commercial fishing interests have had a devastating effect on stocks of many fish species. Of particular concern are the fishing industries of a number of foreign flags. Some abusers of the ocean resources are terrible examples of blatant disregard for this precious commodity. The finning of one hundred million sharks per year, the slaughter of whales in the South Pacific, and the indiscriminate taking of by-catch through purse seine nets are raping our oceans.

But ocean conservation is everybody's responsibility. You can't tell me 50,000 registered pleasure boats in the South Florida area, with such a large percentage of those boats dragging hooks through the water, are not having an effect on fish stocks. Awareness of this problem, and action to reverse the trend, is of utmost importance. Today I wouldn't think of killing a sailfish or a tarpon. We don't need to take them for mounting as the modern technology in trophy mounts relies on no part of the fish to make a perfect replica. We don't eat them, so we don't kill them. More and more tournaments are conducted without the need for weighing, so the fish do not have to end up on the scales at the docks. And many more tournaments allow only circle hooks, thus increasing the odds of healthy releases.

I have learned a lot about ocean conservation over the years. We kill only what we will eat, and since I like my fish fresh, not frozen, that means we kill very few fish. And I do not sell fish to the restaurants or fish houses, so my take is miniscule.

There is an expression something to the effect of "We are borrowing the earth from future generations," and I believe that. This planet belongs to our kids and their kids, so I feel it necessary to advocate for strong, and wisely crafted fishery management regulations.

When The Billfish Foundation, and other ocean advocacy groups went to work on finding a reasonable approach to a very weakened swordfish population, workable regulations were put in place. Over two decades the swordfish population has come back, and we now can target them conservatively without having to feel guilty about occasionally taking one.

That was then, and this is now. We have learned so much. We have realigned our priorities. I feel as carefree as ever about my approach to sportfishing, because I know that not only am I following a path of conservation as I set out everyday for new fishing adventures, but I am also setting an example by loudly advocating for fishery awareness, and an approach to catch and release that leaves most of the fish I catch for future generations to enjoy.

Tight lines.
Captain Bouncer Smith

Introduction

My fishing career started more than sixty years ago when offshore and backwater fishing was a family event with my parents, sisters, brother, and friends. Since the first time a rod twitched in my hands, I was hooked, pun intended. Living in South Florida since 1956, I have been exposed to more opportunities to catch magnificent fish than imaginable. There has never been any doubt that I would make a career out of fishing; it is the only thing I ever wanted to do. And now, after more than a half century as a fishing guide, I have never for a minute lost my enthusiasm. Of course some of my adventures have been very challenging, but the spirit is alive in me now as much as it was all those years ago.

I have spent something like 17,000 days on the water, give or take a couple thousand, so you can only imagine how many stories there are. And the numbers of fish my clients and I have caught is incalculable. I can only say it has been a fulfilling career and a brilliant one.

Some of my stories are humorous, others are heartwarming; and some may seem like foolish adventures. Anyone who spends five or six decades on the water can expect to see some crazy stuff.

Being at the top of the sportfishing business has allowed me to meet some wonderful people. A few are popular and famous. Some have unimaginable challenges they bravely endure, and some are ordinary fishing enthusiasts just like you and me. It takes all kinds of people to make up this world, and I've been exposed to every one of those types.

I write about family, friends, and clients. I mention people who have helped me, and stood by my side along the way. The list of those people in my life, to whom I owe so much, goes on and on. I only wish I could feature them all, but that would be impossible. So for those who know me, and whom I would call a friend, and to those who have helped me in my career and in my life, just because your name may not appear here, does not mean you are ignored or forgotten. The appreciation for all my friends and supporters over the years burns white hot within me.

Over the years I have had to slow down somewhat. I now take most Sundays off, and only take out night charters a half dozen times a month. But I still fish one or two charters most days, and every bait I let out is done with the same care and precision I would use if I were in a tournament. I want my clients to have the best possible experience with me. I want them to remember their time fishing with me as a positive experience with lessons to be remembered for those times they fish without me.

Nothing thrills me more than to have a client contact me to tell me they bought a kite because they learned that technique from me and adopted it for themselves. I love to hear that this fisher has switched over to circle hooks, or another now carries sabiki rigs on board because they realize the important place live bait has in the overall scheme of fishing. And most importantly, hearing that a client has a new found appreciation for ocean conservation, and a respect for these limited resources; this thrills me the most.

So, sit back and strap yourself in. Be prepared to read of some wonderful, and unique, and occasionally tragic fishing experiences. This is the life I've lived and continue to live. I hope my experiences interest you, amuse you, and educate you. It's A Lifetime of Fishing for all to enjoy.

Sharks

Mako Ate Sailfish

Blakely Smith and his party were from Virginia. They had fished with us several times before, and they were pretty good anglers. It was a perfect spring day, light winds, a good strong north current, a nice color change, and good fishing action. We had caught a couple of sailfish and several really nice dolphins. Later in the day we caught enough dolphin that we were tagging and releasing ten, twelve, fourteen-pound dolphins. We hooked this one sailfish that was giving us a normal fight, putting on a good show, and doing some jumping.

Blakely was videotaping from the bow of the boat. The fish went back underneath the surface and swam toward the stern of the boat. It was probably fifty to seventy-five feet off the stern corner of the boat when this huge boil started coming up in the water. My first mate, Abie Raymond, hollered, "Something's chasing the sailfish."

Blakely Smith activated his camera just in the nick of time. A 500-pound mako shark came shooting into the air with our seven-foot sailfish crossways in his mouth. As it flew through the air we could hear a crunch over the sound of everybody hollering. There were more expletives flying than imaginable. The sailfish was still on the line when the mako hit the water. The angler started bringing it to the boat, and here came half a sailfish. Abie stuck it with a kingfish gaff to hold it next to the boat when the mako came up behind it again.

Then Abie ran to get a shark rig. That morning we had been straightening up the boat, and we came across this shark rig and discussed whether we should break it down and put the components away, or leave it put together. We decided we should leave it together for the time being. Abie grabbed our bottom rod and tied the shark rig on. While he was doing that, the mako came over and grabbed what remained of the sailfish. By now I was holding the gaff, but the shark was shaking the sailfish so hard that he ripped it right off the gaff. Fortunately the sailfish was still on the hook, so the angler pulled it back to the boat and I gaffed it again. While the mako was still circling, Abie cut off a chunk of the sailfish and put it on the shark rig. Sure enough, the shark ate it a moment later.

We put what was left of the sailfish carcass in the boat and continued fighting the mako. We had a harpoon on the boat, flying gaffs, big gaffs; we had a lot of hardware. While we were fighting the mako we decided that we didn't want to kill it. There was one guy on the boat who said we should, but the majority won and we decided against it.

It put on a great fight. It did some jumps right up next to the boat. We could have easily attempted to harvest it. We took video and got a good fight out of it. We called another boat and asked if they wanted to harvest it. This was a guy who sells a lot of fish, but he passed on it too. So after a good fight, it eventually broke the wire and swam away.

Talk about publicity! Abie's posting of the mako shark jumping with the sailfish in his mouth got over a million hits. I don't know how many hits my posting got. And there's no telling how many hits Blakely Smith got with the original. But we do know that we were barraged with phone calls from magazines and TV shows and Shark Week. Everybody wanted to buy the video from us. We had to tell them that we didn't take the video and it's not ours, it belongs to our good friend up in Virginia.

What an experience that was. Like I said, it was a great day, lots of dolphins, plenty of sailfish, and the event of a lifetime. But so far beyond that, to have it videotaped made it the beyond imaginable event of a lifetime.

6

Thresher Shark

As my career has gone on in fishing, which now is over fifty-two years, one of the last fish on my bucket list was to have somebody catch a thresher shark on my boat. But my luck was not good when it came to catching a thresher shark. I had heard about people catching them from time to time while fishing for swordfish, but it had never happened for me. In the New England states, up in Cape Cod, they have the Oak Bluff Shark Fishing Tournament every year, and one of the primary species they catch up there is thresher sharks. One of my clients, Steve Nichols, invited me up to fish the tournament. I jumped at the chance.

I was at the airport, leaving for my trip, when I got a phone call from a gentleman from England for a swordfish charter in Miami. I apologized to him, but explained that I was going out of town. My boat was in the yard for engine maintenance, and I couldn't help them. He asked if I could recommend somebody. I told him to try Steve Huddleston. After I got off the phone with him I called Steve and said, "Hey Steve, if you're taking these guys out, keep in mind that my mate, John, doesn't have any work while I'm out of town. He may want to go with you."

So Steve Huddleston and John took out this charter from England to go for swordfish, while I went to Cape Cod to target thresher sharks. And I'll be darned; when they went out swordfishing they just got the baits out and got a big hookup. Steve and John, and their charter from England, caught a 350-pound thresher shark. I went to Cape Cod to fish for thresher sharks, and only caught makos and blue sharks. It was real abuse on my psyche, but I was happy for them.

Several years went by, and I still didn't have a thresher shark. I was on a charter with a completely different group from New England. We were bouncing around, live baiting, bottom fishing, and just trying to catch anything. It was a slow day. We had a big strip of kingfish down on the bottom trying for a big grouper in deep water. And lo and behold, we came up with a beautiful thresher shark. A beautiful fish, one of the most beautiful fishes in the ocean, it has large eyes and appears a greenish blue at the surface. The tail is bigger than the body. This thresher shark jumped twice. It was just a magnificent creature. We took a bunch of pictures. I even got a picture of it jumping, and we sent it on its way.

Only eight days later I took out a charter from Germany to do some bottom fishing. His name was Gregor. We had a great day. We caught amberjacks by vertical jigging, and big jack crevalles, and big kings. We set up on a wreck and had a shark rig baited with a Spanish mackerel. We ran it way inshore of us before we stopped on the wreck, so it would be way out of our way and we wouldn't have to worry about it.

We were just settling in to bottom fishing and the Spanish mackerel on the shark rod had a hit. Gregor grabbed the rod and fought the fish. We had no idea what it was, but we thought it was probably a shark. Lo and behold, after almost fifty years of trying to catch a thresher shark, it was my second thresher in eight days. Another beautiful specimen over 300 pounds; and again those beautiful colors, and those big eyes, and the huge long tail.

I went from no thresher sharks in my whole career, to two in eight days; and it was a huge thrill. Since then we've caught several more thresher sharks while swordfishing. They'll always hold a dear spot with me because they're magnificent fighters, beautiful fish, and just one of the ocean's oddities.

700-Pound Dusky Shark

In the mid 1970s Phil Conklin was working for me on the *Good Time IV* that was owned by Billy Miller. It was just after Christmas when we had an afternoon charter. The charter consisted of a father, his two sons, and his nephew. He had promised each of the boys a mounted fish for Christmas, so they were out to catch fish to have mounted.

We ran to a wreck called *Lotus* and dropped down with the youngest son. He soon came up with about a twenty-five pound

8

amberjack and we put it in the boat. Now the father was fired up, and the son was all excited about having it mounted. But we wanted to catch a bigger amberjack, so we ran down to the *Versailles* wreck and dropped on it. Here the nephew caught another amberjack, maybe twenty-five or thirty pounds. But that wasn't as big as we wanted. We wanted a really big amberjack, so we left there and ran down to the *Dry Dock* to catch a fish for the older son.

This was nearly fifty years ago and the rigging was a lot different than it is today. We were using a 12/0 Penn Senator on a seven and a half foot solid glass rod. On that we had .040-Monel solid wire that was about 100-pound test. That was tied off to a snap swivel, and tied to the swivel was a triangle made out of a coat hanger with a sinker on one corner and a snap swivel on the other corner. The leader went through the snap swivel, through the third corner, and out to the bait. The leader was number ten piano wire, about 200-pound test. Then we had two 10/0 triple strength Mustad hooks, 9174s to be exact. That was baited with a blue runner.

We dropped on the *Dry Dock* but weren't getting any bites, so I told my mate, "Let's try something different. Let's rig up a 100-pound monofilament leader." So he went into the cabin to make that rig, and while he was in there we got a strike. The oldest son, who was already being recruited by colleges as a football lineman, was a big, strong young man. He got the strike and sat in the chair, as I inched ahead with the boat. He was fighting the amberjack and everything was going pretty well. Then half way to the surface the rod jerked like crazy. It was the most powerful impact imaginable on a rod and reel. With that monel wire there is no stretch whatsoever, so the impact of the strike went all the way up the line, through the rod, and into the poor kid's shoulders. It really jarred him.

He took a few more cranks and the rod slammed down to the covering board, and the line took off screaming. By now Phil was in the cockpit orchestrating things while this fish ran out 150 yards of Monel wire like it was in free spool. It was just peeling line off the reel. Then the fight began. Bear in mind that this kid was really big and strong. Phil coached him on pumping up and winding down. He was in a fishing chair, not a fighting chair, so his feet were on the deck. He did a really good job, fighting and fighting, and by now we decided it was a big shark.

We called Billy Miller who owned the boat, but this day he was running a boat called *The Rave*. We didn't have a gun on the boat. Normally back then we would use a bang stick. Billy came over to assist us. We were driving to the north and the shark was swimming thirty feet off the side of the boat. Billy was backing up with his bang stick in the rod holder. Then he spotted a cobia swimming with the shark, so instead of giving us the bang stick so we could get the shark, they pitched a bait to the cobia and took the time to fight it. After that they backed up and gave us the bang stick. We worked the shark into range and gave him a shot. Normally when we hit a fish with a bang stick it pretty much stops. When we hit this monster with the bang stick, he went straight down out of sight. Then he turned around and came up and shot into the air right in the middle of the transom. Unbelievable! And then he was done.

We put a rope on him and towed him back to the dock. The taxidermist came to the dock to pick him up. They left the shark on the truck all night, and the next morning they took the truck, and the shark, to a truck scale and weighed it. Then they dropped the fish off at the taxidermist and went back and weighed the truck again. The fish had weighted 660 pounds. After all night lying in the truck draining fluids, we were confident calling it 700 pounds.

There was a question about what the dad was going to mount. It meant a lot to us because there's a commission on every mounted fish. He went to Pflueger Taxidermy and discussed getting it mounted. Jerry and Jesse Webb, the owners of Pfluegers, met him there, and showed him and the two boys all around, and explained a little about how taxidermy was done. They took them out to the back landing where the shark was laying on a concrete deck and had one of the employees cut the shark open. It had eight baby sharks in it. It also had the head half of our forty-pound amberjack in its stomach.

In the end the father mounted the twenty-five pound amberjack for his young son, the thirty-pound amberjack for his nephew, and the 700-pound dusky shark for his older son. And then, just to make the whole room more complete, he mounted the head half of the amberjack to go in front of the shark, and the eight baby sharks to go behind it. Fortunately he was a contractor and was in the process of building an addition on to his house, so his addition became a museum with this 700 pound shark, and the head of the amberjack, and the babies, and then somewhere in the room went the two amberjacks that the son and nephew caught. It was certainly a trip to remember.

I had a lot of good times back then, fishing with Phil Conklin and working for Billy Miller. A great group of guys.

Tiger Shark

Once in a while we do win a marathon battle. We were on a convention charter one afternoon out of the Castaways. Phil Conklin was my mate. We had gone out and caught some live bonitos and put them in the live well for bait. We were ready for a full day. Unfortunately one of our anglers got sick and we had to run back to drop him off, but then we came back out.

We put out live bonitos in about 100 feet of water right in front of the Haulover Inlet. We were rigged for catching sailfish, but we would have welcomed a kingfish, or anything that would give our anglers a good fight. We were using relatively light leaders; sixty-pound wire with forty-pound line. We got a good strike and the fish headed off to the east, just screaming line, tearing out drag. So we headed offshore after him. He headed farther and farther east and we were beginning to think he would never stop. We continued to chase this fish offshore and finally it turned to the northeast.

We fought and fought this monster still not knowing what it was. We hooked that fish at 4:00 in the afternoon and at 8:00 at night we had still not seen it. At 9:00 we still hadn't seen what we were fighting, and one angler had been in the battle the entire time. At 11:00 that night we finally saw it. It was a tiger shark.

11

We agreed we were going to take the fish back to shore, which was the 'in' thing to do at the time. We were rigged for sailfish or kings, and this was a 500-pound shark. Near midnight we finally got a shot at him with a bang stick, hit him, and got the gaff in him so we could tie him off and secure him to the boat. At 1:00 in the morning we got back to the dock with our 513 pound tiger. What a monster!

I still regret this fish and so many of the others that we took so we could have mounts made. Today we take their pictures and have fiberglass replicas made; but back then taxidermists used parts of the fish in creating mounts, so many died back then that today would be released. That tiger shark went on the dock in infamy like so many other great fish of that time. I only wish we had it all to do over again so I could put all of them back for another day.

Ouch!!!

No book would be complete if there were no stories of hooks in my fingers, or my appendages, or other places in my body. Over the years I've been stuck plenty of times. Some have been very minor and I've been able to push them through, cut them off, pull them out, or yanked them out with a loop of line. But then there have been a few really tough ones.

The first one that comes to mind happened when we were fighting a big tarpon on fly in Government Cut. We hooked him off the north side of the Cut. He was probably in the neighborhood of 140 pounds. We fought it from the north side of the Cut to the south side, and had it up to the boat numerous times. In a twenty-five foot boat it's hard to get within reaching range to grab the tarpon, measure it, and turn it loose. This fish was a real hog. We had control of it, but we didn't want to harm it, we just wanted to send it on its way.

Before we could control it at the side of the boat, it went from the north side by South Beach to the south side near Fisher Island, and then it swam into the channel. There was a little Boston Whaler trolling by so I waited for his lines to clear. We were a couple of hundred yards behind the Boston Whaler so I started chasing our tarpon across the channel, and I'll be doggone if here doesn't come a double hooked ballyhoo out from under our boat hooked on our fly line. That Whaler had its lines out farther than was reasonable, like more than 500 feet. Who does that? We maneuvered around to where I could grab the ballyhoo. Right then the guy in the Whaler engaged his reel and jerked on it and drove that 7/0 hook all the way to the bend, right into the

13

side of my right hand. We ended up breaking off the tarpon. I taped up my hand and we called it a day. I had to have a doctor extract the hook from my hand and give me a tetanus shot.

Another time, probably the worst time I ever got hooked, was back in the days when we had to harvest a fish to have it mounted. We were in the Bahamas and had a marlin lure with two 12/0 hooks in it. We hooked the boat owner's first ever sailfish, a really big one. He brought it up to the boat and I stuck him with a gaff and pulled him in the boat. I grabbed the bill and tried to pin it in the corner. He shook his head and drove a 12/0 hook down deep into my inner thigh. Then he shook his head and yanked it out. Then he drove it in again and yanked it out, and then he did it again. My thigh had an area the size of a grapefruit that was purple with three big holes in it that took weeks to heal up. That one was painful.

I was fishing in the Ft. Lauderdale Billfish Tournament with some very good friends, Al Hower, and the Webb brothers, Jerry and Jesse. We were trolling for sailfish on an inboard/outboard. We were using big ballyhoo which I had rigged myself on single hooks with wire leaders. The first thing in the morning we caught a barracuda and boated it. I took the hook out and took what remained of the ballyhoo off the hook. I was going to put another ballyhoo on the hook and put the line back out. Well, somebody decided to help me and unsnapped the leader from the snap swivel. I had the hook in my hand in the process of putting the ballyhoo on it and the next thing I knew I was stretched across the motor cover on this inboard/outboard boat. The 140-pound test, number eight piano wire leader, had slipped off the boat and into the propeller. The hook was in the side of my ring finger on my right hand between the tip and the first joint, and sticking out back past the second joint. The wire was in the propeller going thump, thump, thump, thump, thump, stretching me across the motor cover. Fortunately the wire finally broke. My finger was bent and the point of the hook was just barely sticking out of the joint closest to the palm of my hand. I turned to Al and said, "You've got to push this through."

Al replied, "Ain't no way! You're going to the hospital, Boy."

So I turned to Jerry Webb. Same answer. So they took me over to Broward General Hospital where I went into a treatment room.

The doctor finally came in and said, "OK, lay back."

So I laid back and looked up at the clock on the wall. The doctor said, "OK, this is going to prick a little bit." He shot my finger up with a painkiller and started working on my hand. I could feel him bumping the other fingers. As I was lying there, forty-five minutes ticked by. He finally handed me the hook and asked, "Is this what's bothering you?"

The hook had gone right through the middle of my tendon, so he had to cut from where the hook went in, all the way to where it came out, and then carefully remove it without doing any more damage to the tendon, and then sew it all up. He bandaged it up, and the end of my arm looked like a baseball. Then he sent me on my way.

A terrible side effect was the tetanus shot. The next day I went fishing with the guys in the tournament. I couldn't really do anything but shoot the breeze, but I was there anyway. I had a reaction to the tetanus shot and laid down in the bow of the boat. I told them that if I died, just throw me overboard, but don't dare go home until the fishing day is over. I lay there just sicker than a dog all day long. I was sick all the next day too, but finally got over the reaction to the tetanus shot.

Now I couldn't work because my right hand was in a bandage, so I helped my dad in his machine shop. Then I broke my ankle. So now I had a bandage on my hand and a cast on my ankle, which made for an interesting Thanksgiving. On top of all that, trying to take a bath with all these bandages, I slipped in the bathroom and knocked the sink off the wall and knocked the porcelain off the top of the bathtub. As if my poor wife, Ruth, didn't have enough to deal with already, the septic tank backed up. She had to dig up the drain field until they could come in and fix it. What a trying Thanksgiving that was.

Fish to Make a Difference

Clay Barker formed an organization called Fish to Make a Difference. This organization was associated with the Joe DiMaggio Children's Hospital at Hollywood Memorial Hospital. It was founded to take local kids with medical challenges, and their families, fishing. This gave them all an opportunity to forget about the medication, and the hospitals, and all the trials of life, and just go out and have some fishing fun. Some excursions were short because the kids weren't very strong, and some of the trips were fairly long. No matter the length, watching these kids and their families forget about their issues, and just enjoy some time on the water, was very valuable and a lot of fun.

Henry's Snook

Our very first adventure with Fish to Make a Difference was to take Henry and his family out fishing. We started out at about five o'clock in the evening one day in the middle of the summer. It was a good time of year to try for snook. As we went out of Government Cut, we dropped a couple of live baits off the north side of the jetty. Sure enough, on our first pass we got a good strike. Abie Raymond helped Henry get the rod into position. Henry fought the fish, and it put up a great fight. Up came a beautiful twenty-five pound snook. A twenty-five pounder is a very good-sized snook. We made another pass through the same area and Henry's father caught a big barracuda, probably four feet long.

Then we had a little slow time, so in the interest of showing Henry lots of action, we moved out to a productive area called the

16

Bent Range Marker. (It's an old channel marker for Government Cut, but is no longer the property of the U.S. Coast Guard. They had commissioned a salvage company to remove it from the waters. It's such a good place to catch bait, or to target Spanish mackerel, or blue fish, or other types of game fish, that the fishing community started a fund and collected enough money to buy the range marker from the Coast Guard. They paid the salvage fees that were supposed to be paid to the salvage company that was supposed to move it. The range marker was deeded to the Dade County Artificial Reef Program so that we could maintain the existence of this great bait spot.)

So we went to the range marker and began fishing with live shrimp. Henry and his brother caught blue runners, one right after another, that were about a pound apiece. They had an absolute ball, and after a relatively short time, Mom said that was all the physical exercise and excitement that Henry could handle, so we called it a trip. The big snook, and the barracuda with the big teeth, and the really fast action with the blue runners made it a really good trip.

Dolly and Kara Christmas

Over the years my beard has turned very white, and on many occasions I have let it grow out as Christmas approached. I pretend I'm Santa Claus. Even if I'm in an elevator I might lean over and ask a little kid, "Did you brush your teeth this morning, because I'm making a list getting ready or Christmas?" It's funny to see the kids panic about it, or appear really proud and show me their teeth. Playing Santa Claus is always a lot of fun.

This one time Clay Barker had a different plan. He had been informed that there was a little eight-year old girl named Dolly who was very sick. They wanted to make sure she had a wonderful Christmas to finish off her year. Clay arranged for me and a couple of women from Fishing Gals, and ten year old Kara, the Fishing Princess, and her dad, to meet at Dolly's house in Boynton Beach at about seven o'clock at night. Her mother made sure that Dolly was watching TV on the other side of the house when we snuck up. We were told it was safe to park in the driveway and wait.

We rendezvoused in Dolly's driveway. Clay had gotten me an outfit and I dressed as Santa Claus. He had elf hats for everybody, and we all got arms full of presents. Our master photographer, Kevin Dodge, was there to videotape everything. When everybody was in position, I knocked on the door. Dolly was just totally in shock when she and her mother opened the door. Here was Santa Claus standing at her front door. I came in and invited all the elves in with their arms full of presents. There were platters of cake, and sandwiches, cupcakes, and cookies. We were off to a great start for a wonderful evening.

Dolly and Kara and one of the elves built prefab ginger bread houses. I turned to Dolly and said, "Dolly, I think it's time to open the presents." I sat in one chair and Dolly sat in another, and Kara would bring over the presents and hand them to me. I would take hold of it and feel it, and turn it, and shake it a little bit. I'd hold it out to Dolly and say, "Dolly, I think this is a choo choo train."

She said, "No, Santa brings choo choo trains to boys. Girls get dolls and stuff."

Then I'd say, "Well, maybe it's a stuffed bear." And Dolly would say it might be. Then she'd open it and we'd laugh about what we guessed, and what it really was. Then Kara would bring over another present and we'd do it all over again. "I think this is a box of marshmallows."

"No, marshmallows don't rattle," she would say. Each package had something that was on Dolly's Christmas list, and we would spend a few minutes going over each one. We had a great time opening the presents, and then we recorded a Christmas video by the Christmas tree with Dolly and Kara.

After a couple of hours the party was over. We bid adieu and got in the cars and headed home. I was riding back to Broward County with Clay Barker and his wife. In the course of the evening we learned that Kara had heard about Dolly's Christmas party and how sick Dolly was. During the year Kara had heard about a spinning outfit that was

18

available from Florida Fishing Products, and she decided she wanted one. She had told her dad about it, but he said, "I really can't afford it right now, but if you save up half the money, I'll put in the other half." Kara saved all year to buy this rod and reel. But then she heard about Dolly, and she told her daddy that she had a rod and reel that was working, and Dolly really needed to have a super Christmas. She wanted to take the $140 she had saved and buy Christmas presents for Dolly. So, a lot of presents we brought that night were actually paid for by young Kara.

It was such a heart-warming story that we had to get on the ball and get this spinning outfit for her. We weren't able to get it done in time for Christmas, but a short time later we managed to get a hold of Florida Fishing Products and I bought the rod and reel and line and had it shipped to me. When I had everything in my hand, I called Clay Barker and told him he should come down. I told Kara's dad that I had gotten hold of what she had asked for and would he please bring her down to Miami Beach Marina at six o'clock at night. The pretense was that she would be coming down to feed the tarpons.

A friend of my sister and mine by the name of Kris Mercier said she wanted to chip in on the cost, so we invited her down to the tarpon feeding. Kris, Sue, and I went down before the other people got there. I had the rod all put together. We planned it out to where, when they got there, we would feed the tarpon then somehow get Kara over by the boat, and Kris would present her with the rod and reel. Six o'clock came, and Kara and her dad showed up. Clay couldn't make it because he had a really bad bout with the flu.

Dozens of tarpon hung out behind the boat, and we had saved a big bag of ballyhoo for Kara to feed them. And she had a ball. At first when she fed them she was scared to death, but as time went on she was getting braver and braver. Sue was down there on the ground with Kara, helping her to figure out how to deal with these tarpon, and just having a great time. After we were done with that, we moved over to the side of the boat, and arranged for Kris to hand her the rod and

19

reel we had been hiding. This was exactly the rod and reel she had wanted.

Then Kara jumped on the boat and checked it out from bow to stern, and port to starboard. She opened every hatch; checked out everything, and stood at the helm and steered the boat back and forth. She was just so infatuated with the boat that she didn't want to get off. She stayed for the longest time, just playing with the boat, and I promised her that in the near future we would take her out fishing. I don't know why it didn't happen that night, but she still had a really good time, with good times to look forward to in the future.

This was a great Christmas party. It was so great to see this little girl give up her money to buy Christmas presents, and then of course the only right thing to do was to make sure she got her dream outfit as well. It was really a heartwarming Christmas. What a way to go!

Monster Amberjack

Clay Barker decided that one of his pet projects was doing a trip targeting sharks during Shark Week with one of his kids/hospital patients/families. He would take one of these families out fishing with me, and bring along a camera crew. On this trip were the young man and his father, the owner of the new sponsor's restaurant up in Ft Lauderdale, and Clay Barker, Abie Raymond, and me.

We were warned we had to be very careful with this young man. He had a port in his left bicep for taking his medications for his illness. Actually a lot of these kids had to have a treatment before they went on the boat, and would have to get back in time for another treatment.

It always seems that Shark Week falls on nice beautiful weather, and this was no exception. It was a nice calm, flat day, and after an hour or so we got a good strike on the live bait on the bottom. It fought and fought, and we thought we had a shark. But up came a huge amberjack. It was an absolute monster, easily over 100-pounds. The young man was thrilled with that catch. He was just grinning from ear to ear and high fiving everybody. It was really great. This was, and still is, the biggest amberjack I can ever remember catching in my career.

But it was Shark Week and we hadn't caught a shark yet. So we put the baits out again. Only thirty or forty minutes later we hooked up again and the young man fought for a long time. Then the new sponsor from the restaurant fought it for a while. Then the young man fought it again, and sure enough, up came a beautiful 250-pound scalloped hammerhead. These sharks are a brilliant yellow on the back and sides with a white belly; just an absolutely fantastic looking shark. We got it up to the boat and took some great pictures, and sent it on its way.

As a sidebar, almost a year later we had an event to celebrate Fish To Make A Difference, and at that celebration I was given a beautiful trophy of a mounted tarpon, with a half sailfish coming out of the water on one side, and half bull dolphin clearing the water on the other side, all on a beautiful piece of wood done by King Sailfish Mounts. Abie also was given a beautiful trophy honoring him as the Mate of the Year. King Sailfish Mounts gave the young man who caught the hammerhead a beautiful release mount replica of his shark.

King Sailfish Mounts has been very generous over the years in presenting mounts to many of our kids and clients who participated in Fish To Make A Difference. It makes a lasting memory of good times for a youngster and his family at a time when a little fun is so appreciated.

Tuna

My Giant Bluefin Tuna

In 1969 I worked on the *Top Luck* out of the Castaways Hotel in North Miami Beach. *Top Luck* was a forty-eight foot Lemay built in North Carolina. The owner's son, Randy Lacey, Jr., ran a boat called the *Big A*. That boat was legendary in itself, in that it was owned by the mega recording company Atlantic Records, whose partnership with Jerry Wexler had catapulted the label to become the largest record production company in the world. Randy, Jr., asked me to go bluefin tuna fishing with him in Bimini on the *Big A*.

I helped him load the boat, and in doing so created quite a fiasco. I stupidly put the milk on the top shelf of the refrigerator, and put the eggs in the bottom. That was a big mistake. When we left Miami it was really rough. Randy and I were both riding up on the bridge, coming off big seas. We got about half way to Bimini and Randy suggested I go down to make sure everything was OK in the salon. The milk and the meat and everything else on the top shelf had collapsed the shelf down onto the top of the eggs. We had a giant milk and egg mess all over the floor. That was a big mistake on my part. I should have put the eggs on top and the heavy stuff on the bottom. We learn the hard way sometimes. So I cleaned it up and we made our way into Bimini.

We were supposed to fish with Mitch Miller of television fame, *Sing Along With Mitch,* and with Aretha Franklin. But first we were going to fish with Jerry Wexler for giant bluefin tunas. Randy, Jr., and I would watch for bluefins from up in the tuna tower. Randy wore prescription glasses, and at the time, they didn't have side shields for clip on sunglasses, so his vision was limited. I had wrap around sunglasses and could see the bluefins coming along the dropoff. I would point them out to Randy, and then run downstairs. Mr. Wexler would get in the chair and I would run the line out and get him set up. We'd hook a giant bluefin tuna, and it would run out off the dropoff giving Wexler a very hard time fighting it. He was an older gentleman and he moved slowly, so eventually sharks would eat his fish and we'd retrieve a head or a spine and a tail. It was becoming very frustrating.

The bluefin tunas were so thick that we could blind troll. We were using one to one and a half pound silver, wedge-head, split-tail mullets. We'd run a four-ounce egg sinker with a #15 piano wire leader down through the top of the head, out the gills, and through the sinker. Then we'd tie it to a 12/0 super sharp J-hook. Our reels were 12/0 Fin-Nors loaded with 130-pound braid. That was how we blind trolled for giant bluefin tunas. And that is how we baited them when we sight fished for them.

Aretha Franklin was in Bimini as part of our party, but she never showed up at the boat. She was always tired or not feeling well. But Mitch Miller went with us several days. When he was with us we fished for blue marlin, but we had terrible luck. We hooked a couple of blue marlins, but on both of them the snap swivels broke. It was a real bummer of a trip until everybody went home. When the celebrity guests all left, Mr. Wexler said we could stay and fish for another day or two.

I rode up in the tower with Randy, Jr., and pointed out a school of tunas. I'd ask him if he had them. When he said he did, I ran back down from the tower and jumped into the fighting chair. I'd throw the bait overboard and hook the harness to the chair. I would run the bait out, and when the tuna hit, I'd hook him and fight him up to the boat. Then I'd put safety lines onto the rod, jump out of the chair, grab the wire, and pull the hook. It was an adventure that kept me as busy as I can ever remember being in the cockpit, and I'll never forget it.

I sat in the fighting chair just above water level, and looked out to the side. I could see five and six hundred pound bluefin tunas swimming along next to the boat. It was the most amazing thing in the world. It was an absolutely unbelievable trip. I could never thank Randy Lacey, Jr. enough for taking me along, and Randy Lacey, Sr. for giving me the time off for this fantastic adventure.

Yellowfin Tuna

Top Luck ran local half-day trips for split parties. It was $15 per chair and we would take six people out at a time for four hour fishing trips, either eight to twelve, or one to five. We might have four people, five people, or six people, depending on how many signed up for the trip.

In early December a regular customer named Carl came down from Ohio. He was in his mid sixties, and he came onto the boat alone and fished by himself. His wife was in town, but she didn't care to fish but that didn't stop Carl. He would go out every morning on that eight to twelve shift. He was a very likeable guy. He would kibitz with all the clients on the boat. When we headed out from the dock he would come up on the bridge with me. Carl would say, "That couple there from New York would love to catch a sailfish and have it mounted." Or, "That guy with the beard, he'd like to catch some fish that he can eat – he's not going to have anything mounted, but he's just a nice guy. And that other couple, they just want anything. They don't care if it's a sailfish, a shark, or a barracuda. Whatever it is, they just want to have a trophy to hang in their living room when they get done with this trip."

So we headed out on a Friday. It was Carl's last day to fish with us this December. I was running the boat but I'm at a loss for who my mate was at the time; it might have been Jerry Rushmeyer from Montauk, New York. First we went out live baiting off Haulover Inlet. Then we put some blue runners up on the kite, a pinfish on one outrigger, and a ballyhoo on the other outrigger. Carl had been handing off everything that bit on his line saying, "Oh no, let that couple catch it; oh no let that guy catch it."

I told him, "You've got to catch a fish. You haven't caught a fish your whole vacation. You've just been directing traffic."

24

He said, "Well, we'll see what happens." So, we were fishing for maybe a half hour. It was about nine in the morning when the pinfish on the left outrigger popped out. It was on fifty-pound monofilament on a Penn Senator Six-O, custom build Uslan rod. When we hooked the fish it sounded and acted like it was probably a shark. It took a good bit of a run and then went down deep. I gave the rod to Carl.

I said, "Ok, Carl. This is the fish you're going to catch this trip." And the fish was off to the races. Shortly thereafter we hooked a sailfish on the kite. We had to worry about this one because the couple really wanted a sailfish to mount. So we were chasing the sailfish all over the place, completely ignoring Carl and his fish. His line wrapped around the bow, so we cleared it from that. Then his line was up underneath the boat, but didn't cut it off, so we ignored it. Eventually we cleared that, and a few minutes later it became wrapped up around the bow again, and we momentarily ignored that too.

We finally caught the sailfish. Back then, to have a fish mounted, we had to kill it, because they actually used the skin. (It's much better today because now if we want a mount of a nice sailfish or marlin or swordfish, or any valuable game fish or shark, we get a good idea how long it is and take a picture of it in the water. We tag it and release it, and it goes on its way, and it's there to be caught another day. We place the order with Gray Taxidermy, and they make a fiberglass reproduction of the fish. A very good artist will paint up this reproduction, and the client will have this beautiful fish mount to take home. While we and our friends admire that fish, which is a three-dimensional work of art, an exact replica of the fish we caught, we also know that the original fish is back out in the ocean available for catching again. It's really a win/win situation with these fiberglass reproductions, what they call release mounts.)

At any rate, we put the sailfish in the boat, and the couple was overjoyed. We were taking pictures – and ignoring Carl. He was still fighting his fish, but not gaining any line. First it was off the side of the boat, and then it was off the bow. Pretty soon, along came a beautiful hammerhead shark on another line. So now we fought the

25

hammerhead. We were backing down and chasing it, ignoring Carl for the second time.

Carl's line was now up around the bow again, peeling off the reel. We didn't tend to his line when it went under the boat, or around the bow, because we were busy with the hammerhead shark. So, we caught hammerhead and pulled it into the boat – there were high fives, and photographs, and big smiles, and congratulations all around. Then I remember, "Oh yeah, how you making out over there, Carl?"

"Oh, I'm still alive. Still got a lot of line out."

We finally set out to think about Carl's fish. "It's getting kind of late," I said. "It's getting time to go in, so we better get to work on your fish." Bear in mind that we still hadn't seen the fish, so we had no idea what it was. We were presuming it was a shark. It was starting to move slowly westward toward the shore. Carl was pumping and winding and gaining line, because now he was the center of attention. And before long, "Oh my gosh! Look at all that yellow." It was a beautiful yellowfin, or Alison tuna. It had yellow streamers that went from the dorsal fin almost all the way back to the end of the tail, and another that went from the anal fin almost all the way to the tail. It had beautiful blues in it and a gold hue down the middle of the side. It was just the most beautiful fish ever. Before long we got a gaff in it, and it was high fives all around again! We hadn't seen a yellowfin tuna on the Castaways dock in several years; this was the first.

Here's an idea of the impact this fish had: I used to run the boat almost every single day, seven days a week. Randy Lacey would come down in the morning to shoot the breeze with us for a while and say, "Well, I'm going to go down and get coffee and breakfast and I'll see you tonight," or "I'll see you in the morning." Anybody who was hanging around the boat never knew for sure if Randy was going to go to work, if he was going to run the boat and I was going to be the mate, or if I was going to be the captain and somebody else was going to be the mate. But what happened after we caught that fish? Randy was so jealous that we caught an Alison tuna that he ran the boat for two weeks straight hoping for another opportunity to catch one.

Well, we didn't catch one in those two weeks. It was really crazy, here was the first Alison tuna of my whole career, and we completely ignored that fish for two full hours. We wrapped the line around the bow and under the boat, and the fish hung in there, waiting to bless us with one of the greatest catches we could ever ask for.

So that was a great story about ignoring a fish and having it come out well; but believe it or not, it happened again. I was running my own twenty-five-foot Dusky, the one they called the 256. A couple of guys from upstate New York, Bob Evans and Harold Wallace, chartered me. They loved to fish for barracuda, and I knew that my special tube lures would be perfect for that. The tube lures are made out of vinyl surgical tubing in bright colors like orange and green. I would cut a length of tubing about eighteen inches long and run a piece of wire down through it. I'd cut a slit in the middle of the side of the tubing, and in that slit I'd push the eye of a 3/0 treble hook, and then I would go out the other end of the tube. I would slip on a sinker and tie on another 3/0 treble hook. At the front end, where I'd begun inserting the wire to begin with, I would add a bead to the wire, and wrap on a swivel. I would put this on a spinning rod using a fifty-pound leader about four or five feet long.

For barracuda we liked to fish on the shallow reefs off the Fontainebleau Hotel. We'd cast this surgical tubing out and wind it in real fast at the surface. It emulated a needlefish or a hound fish, which the barracudas love to eat. It was a hoot. Back then we were covered over in barracudas. We would wind in that tube, and the barracudas would come up and slam it. The fish might jump, or he might go down deep. He might not fight hard at all, or he might fight like an amberjack, and we thought he was never going to quit. Bob and Harold might spend five or six hours catching barracudas on tube lures.

The way I controlled expenses was to always start the day with three lures that I made myself. As the morning progressed, and they would destroy a lure, they would have to take a timeout while I made them a new one. It gave them a chance to rehydrate or grab a bite to eat. And it gave me a chance to control the pace, because sometimes the fishing was pretty hectic.

It was an absolutely beautiful day, slick glass calm. About noontime I got a call on the radio. "Hey Bouncer, I'm ten miles off Government Cut. There's a tree here and it's loaded with dolphin." So, we decided to head out there. The guy on the radio was confident we'd find the dolphin. He said he'd wait until we got there to make sure we found the floating tree branch. We wound in our tube lures and took off running.

When we got out to this tree, sure enough it was loaded with dolphin. The other captain waved goodbye and went on his way. We had thrown the cast net in the morning, so we had a lot of pilchards. Now Bob and Harold started catching dolphins, one right after another. We were catching them left and right, and throwing them in the fish box. We would pitch out the little pilchards, and hook another one – it was chaotic, exactly the way we liked it.

We were having a ball catching these dolphins. But eventually we had more than enough, and at the same time they quit biting. I threw out another bait, and put the rod in the rod holder. Bob and Harold went up in the bow to eat their lunch, and have some ice teas and waters. I was in the back of the boat cleaning up all the blood and mess. Low and behold, the twelve-pound spinning rod got a bite. So Bob came back and fought the fish while I cleaned. I was just ignoring Bob while we were both busy. I knew what he was doing and figured he had hooked some kind of shark.

Bob fought that fish for thirty minutes. I said, "Yo, Bob, you're having a lot of trouble with that fish. Now that the boat is all cleaned up I guess we should concentrate on it." But there wasn't much I could do. The fish was straight down below us. I made sure Bob had his drag right, and coached him on pumping and winding. After a little while the fish started to scope up on the surface. So I followed it. Suddenly, oh my gosh, here's these big yellow streamers sticking up out of the water, and I can't believe it. I've been ignoring a guy fighting a yellowfin tuna on twelve pound spinning tackle. Thank goodness Bob was a good angler. He fought the fish for another hour and finally, and unbelievably, we got that sixty pound yellowfin into the boat. What a thrill!

Crazy, the first two Alison tunas of my career and I completely ignored them both, acting like they were sharks, and paying no attention. And then we came up with two of the most spectacular catches ever. That's what Alison tunas are like; we never know when one is going to show up.

These two yellowfin tunas were the start of a major fishery. In about 1970 we started catching a fair number of them, and by 1980 the captains in the fleet had figured out that if we fished in October, in four or five hundred feet of water, we could troll, or use live bait, or chum with lots of live pilchards, and we could actually target yellowfin tunas.

Giant Bluefin

On Easter Sunday in 1973 I had a charter with guitar player Steve Cropper and a friend he had invited along. Steve was best known for playing in the band Booker T and the MGs. He also played backup music for Aretha Franklin, and was very influential in *Sittin' on the Dock of the Bay* by Otis Redding. Steve was a pretty lucky fisherman, except when it came to sailfish; then he was very unlucky.

On this day the wind was blowing twenty to twenty-five out of the east and the sea was a mess. I was running a fifty-foot Carolina boat called the *Good Time IV*. We were kite fishing off the north end of Miami Beach on a day where there was no current, a strong east wind, and pretty clean water. A 250 or 300 pound hammerhead shark we had caught was lying in the cockpit of the boat. We took him in because Steve's guest wanted to have him mounted.

Low and behold, we had a strike on a live mullet off the outrigger. It was on a red Penn Senator 6/0 reel with fifty-pound test. The fish took off screaming line to the east, and I took off chasing him. When we began to run low on line, my mate, Phil Conklin, grabbed a 9/0 Penn with eighty-pound test. He fastened the snap

29

swivel from the 9/0 to the harness lug on the red 6/0 and threw the 6/0 overboard. He backed off on the drag of the 9/0 and we continued to chase the fish as it ran toward the east. Our biggest mistake was that back in those days we hadn't learned about running with the fish. We always backed down on our fish. So we were taking heavy water over the stern and into the scuppers. We chased the fish down this way for quite a while.

After a while we caught up with the red 6/0 and brought it back into the boat. Then we started gaining line on the fifty-pound test. Altogether we fought this fish for about six hours. By this time the guest was seasick, and Steve Cropper was totally worn out. Phil had been spelling Steve on the rod when he needed a break, and the rod went back and forth like that. Now we were down to the last 150 feet of line. Steve was winding and Phil was hand lining.

Before long, we saw the fish down in the depths. It was a bluefin tuna, probably around 600 pounds. As it was getting closer to the boat Phil hollered up to me that the line was severely frayed. I certainly did not like hearing that.

We had been sitting still for hours. We hadn't run, and we hadn't done anything to tip us off about the performance of the boat. Now the fish was just fifty feet under the boat. I said, "You guys keep working the fish. I'm running down into the galley to get a big grapple hook. We'll drop it down and snag the fish and pull it up."

I climbed down off the fly bridge, and hurried through the salon. I started toward the galley where the grapple hook was and stopped dead. The counter top, the refrigerator, and the stove were completely under water. The boat was full of water above the appliances down in the galley. I hollered to Steve and Phil that we were full of water.

I opened the engine room hatch, and all that was sticking out of the water were the air intakes on the 300 Cummins engines. The only things visible were two chrome boxes sitting on top of the engines. I grabbed a knife and jumped down between the engines. I closed the seacock on the port engine. Then I cut the intake hose above the seacock so the port engine could suck seawater out of the bilge and pump it out of the boat. While I was doing that, Steve and Phil tried to get the fish up, but it ended up breaking off.

The port engine pumped out about three quarters of the water before it sucked up a cardboard box and overheated and shut down. So, now we were on one engine, and the boat was still a quarter full of water.

The ocean had become rougher, and the outgoing tide made the Haulover Inlet treacherous. We called the Coast Guard for help. They came right away in a helicopter and dropped us a gas powered pump. But, low and behold, it wouldn't start. I don't know if it got water on it when they lowered it down, but it was no use to us. Then they dropped us another pump, and it wouldn't work either.

Near panic and exhaustion, I idled us back to the inlet. When the tide turned and started going in, I slipped into the bay and pulled into the Haulover fuel dock. The dock master brought us another pump and we pumped all the water out of the boat. The boat was saved, but the tuna was gone. Steve was broken hearted that he put so much time and effort into that big fish and then it got away, but we were all thankful that we did not sink and die, or have to be rescued.

The next day we were towed down to Tommy's boat yard where they hauled us out. We had to have both engines and transmissions rebuilt. The boat needed all new wiring, all new appliances, new wallpaper and flooring, mattresses, and everything. Fortunately, when the owner bought the boat a few months earlier, he took out insurance that covered nearly all of the damage. It also covered eighty percent of our lost income based upon the previous six weeks. Right before Easter was the busiest time of the year, so for all intents and purposes, the boss lost no money, and we got our pay. We were really lucky in that respect.

It was kind of coincidental though; one year later I was fishing with Steve Cropper again. We were in almost the exact same spot; the weather was almost exactly the same too, a strong east wing and no current. We had a live mullet out on the right rigger, and here came six giant bluefin tunas riding down a wave. I hollered, "Steve, here they come!"

He said, "What, what?"

I said, "A school of bluefin tuna."

He said, "If they bite, cut the line. I don't want anything to do with them." So, that was a memorable day with giant bluefin tuna.

Three Double Headers

In 1979 I went in partnership with Al Hower on a twenty-foot Seabird. The yellowfin fishery was developing at the time. Larry Able was a client I would sometimes teach how to fish on his boat, or we would fish on my flats boat. Larry handled the incorporation of my business, and when I asked him what I owed him, he said, "Well, the first time the yellowfin tuna show up you can take me fishing."

I said, "You got it."

I called him up around the last week of October and said, "Hey, Larry, the yellowfin tunas are biting pretty good."

He said, "I'd love to go, but I'm busy this week."

I think I called him almost every week, reminding him that the yellowfins were biting, and each time he would say that he was busy and couldn't make it. Week after week this went on. Finally about the first week of December I reminded him again, and he finally said, "OK, I can make it this weekend."

Larry brought his friend, Richard, and we headed offshore in the Seabird trolling ballyhoo. We were in four or five hundred feet of water off Haulover Inlet and hooked a double header and brought them into the boat. They were typical yellowfins, thirty or thirty-five pounds.

We wanted to make good time heading south, so we decided to troll at high speed. We made special lures for high-speed trolling out of the turnbuckle off 9/0 or 12/0 Penn Senators. We put a skirt on the back of the turnbuckle and made a trolling lure out of it. It was probably an inch and a half long, and weighed about an ounce. We put a wire leader through it, and tied a hook on the back end of it. We could troll them pretty fast. And I'll be a son of a gun if we didn't catch another double-header of yellow fin tunas.

We got down to the Miami Sea Buoy and caught a couple of small live bonitos. We put them out hoping we might spice up our catch with a wahoo or sailfish. There's no telling, but we know that when we put out baby live bonitos, odds are something's going to bite. We would already have the other rods rigged with an 8/0 or 9/0 j-hook on a number six leader wire. We'd wind the bonito in on the spinning rod, unhook it, hurry up and hook it through the upper lip with that j-hook, and then drive along using these live bonitos for bait. We had to drive at over a mile an hour to keep the bonitos from suffocating.

So I headed offshore with two live bonitos until we got into almost 400 feet of water. And I wouldn't have believed it! Another double-header of thirty to forty pound yellowfin tunas. This was on a trip that was postponed for close to eight weeks, and when we finally went out we caught three double headers of yellowfin tunas. Talk about getting lucky, that was a trip beyond belief.

We found out that we could go out to 500 feet of water on an east wind and start chumming with little pilchards. We'd fix big pilchards on the kite and the flat lines, then put another bait sixty feet down. Meanwhile we'd chum with live pilchards and drift back toward shore. Very frequently we'd be blessed with yellowfin tunas, anywhere from twenty-five to nearly one hundred pounds. It was so consistent that people would charter me to go to fish specifically for yellowfin tunas.

In 1989 Florida Sportsman called me up and asked if I would write an article on how to chum for yellowfin tuna with live pilchards and monofilament leaders in four or five hundred feet of water. They ran the article in November of 1990 right when the season should have been rolling. But the yellowfins never came back, and we've never had yellowfin tuna fishing like that again.

That being said, here's a little sidebar: every once in a while someone will still catch a yellowfin. In 2017 a couple of guys out of

Haulover Inlet in a private boat with no pressure to satisfy a charter, went out a couple of different weekends and duplicated our method. They fished thirty or forty pound fluorocarbon leaders and small circle hooks. They went out to 400 feet of water and chummed with live pilchards. Two or three times they were successful in catching yellowfin tunas. Those fish are still coming by with some regularity, but nothing like the good old days.

I took a day off to go to the boat show, and Abie Raymond heard that a couple of yellowfin tunas had been caught. He was the one running my boat that day and told his charter, "Let's go out there and catch some yellowfins." They went out, chummed with the live pilchards in 400 feet of water, and caught one. My boat has targeted yellowfin tunas by that method in the last ten years, but I haven't had much luck at it. But I'm happy for Abie, emulating this fishing from years ago, and making it work.

Big Eye Tuna

Back in my early days of chartering out of the Castaways Charter Dock I fished a lot with Tommy Morrison. Tommy had a friend named Dom Siano who was a really nice guy. I had known Dom for a long, but we never fished together. First he fished with Tommy, then he was up in Ft. Pierce, so we didn't see much of each other. But we stayed in light contact, and several years ago he decided he should come down and go fishing for swordfish with me. He wanted to learn my daytime swordfishing techniques.

It turned out to be a daytime/nighttime swordfish trip. We went out in the middle of the afternoon and stayed in the evening so I could show him both methods. It was our first trip and we were going to use two lines for swordfish. We used the Hooker electric drive attachment on a Penn International eighty. The reel was filled with sixty-five pound braided line, and that was spliced to 150 feet of 300-pound test. Fifty feet from the braid there was a mark on the monofilament line that holds a long line clip in place attached to a ten or twelve pound lead. At the end of the 300-pound mono is a large swivel from which is tied a five-foot bait leader, followed by a skirted bait. The bait could be a bonito belly, or a bonito strip, or squid. Some captains use mullet, and mackerel, and ladyfish. The important thing is it's some kind of bait with a skirt over it to improve the hydrodynamics. It is very important that it doesn't spin.

Back at this time we were letting the second bait down to 1,500 feet. We had a marker on the line 1,500 feet from the sinker where we would attach a big orange bullet float. We would let that line go out behind the boat a couple hundred feet. So, now we had a line going straight down and a line going down from a buoy 200 feet behind the boat.

We were all sitting there watching the rod that was straight up and down, and kind of ignoring the float. This was the very first time we used the line with the float, kind of an experiment. We were told if it got a bite it would do different things. It might pop up and lay flat on the surface, or it might pull under water, or it might go east or west. We had the drag on the up and down reel in the strike position. On the rod with the buoy we were just using one-third drag, so we would know if it got a bite.

Somebody was messing with the reel and put it up to strike. After about thirty minutes, we heard POW, and the line was broken on the buoy rod right at the spool. We wound up the other line. We strung the line on the broken line through the guides, and drove over to the buoy. We didn't know what we were going to find there. We knew that something went wrong, but the buoy was still floating like always. We picked up the buoy and hurriedly connected the line on the reel to the line on the buoy. We took the buoy off and Abie started to bring up that bait. He said, "I must have a whole bunch of weed on here" as he was winding up with the Hooker electric drive. Then he said, "No, there's a fish on here I think."

I think it was Dom Siano's son who got on the rod. We took the motor off and he began to hand crank. It fought really well, but after it came up, probably after thirty or forty minutes, the rod started to throb like there was a tuna on it. And before long, up came this beautiful 250-pound big eye tuna. We gaffed it and put it in the boat. That day we got the big eye tuna, and a couple of dolphins.

We raised a white marlin on a ballyhoo that we liked to drag behind the boat while we sword fished. But the marlin wouldn't eat. Nor did we catch a swordfish that day. But seeing a white marlin behind the boat, and catching a 250 pound big eye tuna and a couple of dolphins, we had no grounds to complain. What a beautiful fish that was.

Today, when we get to the site, we head north and run out 100 feet of line until we come to the marker where we attach the sinker. We continue going north at trolling speed. We then run out another 500 feet of line and take a tight U-turn and drive back until the line is going straight down. We let the line run full speed all the way to the bottom. We lock up the reel and wind the sinker 100 feet off the bottom to try to prevent hanging up.

After that line is in place, we duplicate that setup, but we use two pounds less of lead. We drive at a slow rate of speed just to keep the first line straight up and down fighting the current. With the second line, the bait streams out to the north until we come to the marker for the weight. We clip on a longline clip to a five-foot section of 300-pound test followed by the smaller sinker. We let that line go down at half speed. It takes a while, but when we are within a couple hundred feet of the bottom we let it go down faster until it hits the bottom. It stops for a second, and we engage the reel and wind the bait 100 feet off the bottom. Because the current is running north, we drive into the current to keep the lines straight up and down. The second line angles to the north just a little bit because of the smaller lead and the current pushing it back a little more. This keeps the two baits separated. That's how we fish it today.

Recipes for Yellowfin

And talk about some good eating. It's real simple to prepare yellowfin tuna. Start by bleeding the fish by pulling out one of the gill rakers. If at all possible, stand the fish vertically head down to let the blood drain out. Chill it down, skin it, filet it, and make certain not to get any fresh water on it. Pat it dry and store it in zip lock bags. It's best to let it sit for three days, as cold as possible without freezing it. After three days, pat it dry again, and cut it in ultra thin strips. Make up a bowl of soy sauce and a platter with a little wasabi. Each person then should mix the wasabi and soy sauce to his/her own taste, then dip the tuna in the sauce and enjoy.

Mario Cote Tuna Steaks

The best tuna steaks I have ever eaten were prepared by a friend of mine, and fellow fishing guide, named Mario Cote of Hollywood, Florida. We were invited to his house on a Memorial Day weekend. Mario marinated half inch thick slices of tuna in sesame oil, and then pressed them in sesame seeds. He had a black iron skillet on an outdoor grill. When it was red hot he would drop these oiled, sesame seed coated tuna steaks onto the skillet. He'd grill one side, flip them over and grill the other side. I don't think they were on the pan for more than a minute, maybe two on each side. They were beautifully charred on the outside and pink in the middle. Medium rare would be the best description. Remember, a cast iron skillet on a hot fire. Again sesame oil, sesame seeds, and then just a couple of minutes on each side of the half inch thick tuna steaks, and that is one delicious meal.

Key Biscayne

Terry was off from school for the day so he and I went out fishing. We were down off the south end of Key Biscayne, the area called Mashta Point. We were slow trolling with live mullet for bait. The tarpon were rolling and it wasn't long before a nice fish, about 120 or 130 pounds, crashed on the mullet. Terry swung into action. This tarpon took off running, headed right for the seawall about 200 yards away. It looked like he was going to crash right into the wall, but as he approached it he turned to the southeast and shot parallel to it. As he proceeded along the seawall he went under a couple of the docks behind the houses.

There was a narrow finger pier, just one row of pilings with some planks on top of them. Then there was the main pier, which was probably eight or ten feet wide with plenty of pilings. This formed a slip for a homeowner's boat. Beyond that were more pilings before opening to the bay again.

I pulled up to the little finger pier and clipped my anchor ball onto the rod and threw the rod and reel overboard. Then I pulled on the line so the tarpon would want to run. The anchor ball went under the finger pier and stopped. With no pressure on the line, the tarpon stopped fighting. I had to pull up into the slip between the finger pier and the main pier and agitate the tarpon again to get him moving to the other side.

While I was doing this, the gardener, and the maid, and the lady of the house all started yelling at me that I was trespassing, like I was some kind of criminal. Terry was panic stricken because he didn't want to see us get into trouble. In my maneuvering I did crack a little piece of molding on the boat that was docked at the end of the pier.

As I had planned, the tarpon towed the anchor buoy away from the dock. We pulled around and picked up the rod, and Terry went back to the fight. We got the tarpon up to the boat, unhooked it, and sent it on its way.

We idled back toward where we had been fishing, but by now the lady of the house, and the maid, and the gardener, and a police officer were all standing out on the main pier. I have big letters on the side of the boat, so I'm not hiding from anybody. I pulled up to the side of the dock and the officer asked, "What did you have on?"

I said, "We had a nice tarpon."

He said, "Did you know law of Key Biscayne, or the waters of South Florida?"

I said, "I'm not sure what you mean."

He said, "Well, the law says that the owner's property extends out to the farthest improvement they made. So the farthest dock or piling is still their property. To come inside that, is technically trespassing. Do you fish here a lot?"

I said, "I do."

"Do you catch a lot of tarpon?"

I said, "Sure."

"Well, you can't come in and trespass on peoples' property, even though you're in the water. It's against the law. So you have to refrain from doing that. Do you catch anything besides tarpon here?"

"Yeah, we caught a giant barracuda here last year. If you fish with crabs here or even pieces of crab, you can catch an occasional permit or bonefish right off the dock."

The officer was not the least bit nasty, just trying to do his job and help avoid conflict. "You have to stop aggravating my residents. So please refrain from coming inside their docks to fight your fish. Other than that, enjoy yourself. I see you have a young man there and you're having a good time. We'll hopefully keep peace in the neighborhood."

"You bet, Officer," I said.

"Oh, by the way," he asked, "do you fish for tarpon anywhere else? Do you always use mullet for bait?"

"No we sometimes use shrimp, and crabs, and pinfish, and mullets. And we fish with artificials too."

"OK, well don't bother my residents and enjoy your fishing, and have a good day."

We drove off into the sunset. This Key Biscayne law enforcement officer seemed uncomfortable to be under the duress of having to warn us about invading these people's private property in the act of having some fun fishing. During the course of this discussion I gave the officer and the lady of the house one of my business cards.

I never heard from the owner of the house again about the little quarter inch crack in his molding. But I can imagine him coming home from work and his wife complaining about this guy who was invading their property and damaging the boat. I can visualize him looking at the card and responding, "The guy's a fisherman. What's he doing that upset you?" It was just a conversation that I imagined in my mind.

But all's well that ends well. Terry caught a nice tarpon and we had a fun day at Key Biscayne.

Mahi Mahi (Dolphin fish)

To begin with, mahi mahi (the Hawaiian name meaning 'very strong') are called by a number of different names: mahi, dolphin, dolphin fish, or Dorado. When it comes to dolphins, one thing we always do is to pay attention to the birds. A couple of things we've learned over the years: first of all, big dolphin swim against the current, so if we see a frigate bird or even a couple of dolphin birds, which are actually sooty terns, working to the south, like they might be working a fish, we don't try to chase them down from behind. We wind in our lines and get around in front of them, to the south, and then put our baits out again and let them catch us. The odds of getting a hookup will be much better. When frigate birds dive, they always go downwind a little bit. So, we don't get upwind of frigate birds. We stay down wind a little bit because that's the way he's going to dive when he finds a fish.

When we see a whole lot of birds it's probably some kind of tuna: skipjacks or black fins. If the birds are going to the north, odds are it's very small dolphin, or blue runners. It's less likely to be dolphin. That's a couple of tips to remember about watching the birds, because they'll flat find the fish.

When a dolphin is chasing flying fish, we're always prepared to run around, because they can move fast. We see them running and jumping, and chasing flying fish at thirty miles an hour. That's as fast as many of us run in the ocean, and keeping up with them can be a challenge.

Here are some tips about using lures when hunting dolphin. When throwing lures for dolphin, everybody on the boat should start off with the same color, whether it's red, or orange, or yellow, or white. If we're in a real big school of dolphins and they stop biting white lures, we will change to another color and often they'll start biting again. If they get tired of that color we can go to another, and keep doing that. If everybody starts off with a different color lure, then the fish will just be done with lures, because they've seen all the colors, and the bite is over with.

When they start to fade away, we'll cast a popping lure and start chugging it real hard. This often fires them up again, and brings them back from quite a ways off. Also, when using a popping plug, I suggest removing the treble hook and putting a nice big j-hook on the back. Now they sell actual lure j-hooks that have a different eye than a standard j-hook does, and it can really make a difference. That big single hook hooks them better and prevents the angler from getting caught on one of the trebles.

Tagged Dolphin North and South

I have been involved in a lot of tagging operations with many of my different mates. One of the most exciting to follow with respect to migration and growth is our tagging of dolphins. Most tagging of dolphins occurs in the spring when they're migrating north with the Gulf Stream. These are relatively small specimens on their northern migration; very few have any size to them.

We tag dolphins throughout the year; some that are ten pounds, a few that are twenty pounds, and have even tagged some that were in the forty-pound range. As we get into the later part of the fall, a lot of the dolphins we tag are heading south.

Here's an interesting observation: we visualize dolphins hatching and forming a school. So they are little baby dolphins, many of which are eaten by other fish. As the bigger dolphins start to get a higher survival rate, fishermen are trying to catch them to harvest them. The bigger they get, the fewer threats they have from predators, but at the same time, they must find more food for themselves, and there is a certain amount of attrition there. The bottom line is that when they get up to sixty or seventy pounds, that's about as big as they get. A lot of them don't survive for that length of time, let alone to reach that size. The eighty or ninety pound dolphin is an extreme rarity.

One time we tagged a lot of dolphin in the later part of the fall. In one school the fish were ten or twelve pounds. We tagged probably about a dozen of them. Over the next three weeks, three of the tags were recovered. One of the fish stayed right around Miami. One of the fish was recaptured up toward Stewart, which is about 120 miles north of Miami on the coast. Another was recovered in Marathon, which is about 100 miles south. Then later on one of them was recaptured in Key West. From that, the dolphin research program recognized that as these dolphins mature, and by the fall and early winter, those that are still in the Straights of Florida, or even up into the Carolinas, will turn back around and migrate along the Florida coast on the edge of the Gulf Stream. That's why every fall we start to get runs of dolphins that are no longer those two and three pound little dolphins, now they're six to fifteen or eighteen pounds.

I tagged a dolphin in July one year that we estimated to be two pounds. Exactly 200 days later, in February of the following year, that two-pound dolphin was recaptured in Exuma Sound in the southeastern Bahamas. It had gone from two pounds to twenty pounds in 200 days and had traveled nearly 400 miles. So, they grow very fast and they are highly migratory.

We had another dolphin we tagged in June that we estimated at five or six pounds. That dolphin was recaptured on the south side of Puerto Rico eighteen months later. That five-pound fish had grown to fifty-eight pounds. So, not only do dolphin fish grow very fast, but they cover a lot of ocean.

Another thing about dolphin is that they are found in all the oceans of the world. Our migration appears to be from the Caribbean Sea, to both sides if the Bahamas, and the Straights of Florida. Some of them go up into the Gulf of Mexico. They go all the way up into New York and east. The vast majority come down the Mid Atlantic Ridge, and come back in from the eastern side of the Caribbean. There are some dolphins that, as we prove with tagging, come right back down into the Gulf Stream to provide us more thrills.

Gaff Shot

Captain Abie Raymond started when he was still in high school, and is still with me today. When he first started fishing with me, we had a father and son out of England as customers. They were Rob and Bob. We were kite fishing on the edge of the Gulf Stream and hooked a big dolphin. Bob, the father, was fighting this fifty-pound dolphin. He got it very close to the boat, and then we were stalemated. The dolphin was ten feet off the side of the boat and no matter what I did, it would stay ten feet off and wouldn't come any closer. It just swam along next to the boat. It was very frustrating. I tried to pull on the leader and he wouldn't budge.

Abie was standing there with a long handled gaff just waiting for a chance to gaff this big dolphin. I was looking over at this big fish, and then I looked at this green kid who had never gaffed a fish this big in his life. I was thinking, 'Maybe this is a time to call an audible. Maybe I should gaff this fish, because I have a lot better understanding of what I should do when I hit it with the gaff.'

So, the fight went on and on with the angler. The fish didn't pull away, and it didn't come closer. It had already done its jumping, and just lay there off the side of the boat. So I said, "Hand me that gaff. Better let me stick it."

I was maneuvering the boat just a little bit. I'd mostly just stand there holding the leader. As I'd pull a little line in, the angler would wind it in. Then I'd pull the fish a little closer, and the angler would take up the loose line again. We did that one more time, and I figured the fish was now close enough. I took the gaff in both hands and hit that dolphin right behind the head. It did a 270-degree turn from parallel to the boat headed to the bow, away from the boat, all the way back around, and back under the boat. It bent the gaff handle, ripped right off the gaff, and got away.

To this day, whenever we get into a gaffing situation, I am never allowed to say anything about Abie gaffing fish, because I've already taught him that we all have the potential to have a mistake on the gaff. It's just a part of fishing.

The interesting thing about it was that when the fish got away, Bob said, "Aw, that's OK. There was no reason for us to kill it anyway." Hopefully that fish lived a few more years to thrill some more anglers. I know we may have done a little damage to his back, but I sure hope he survived. But what a way to teach my mate how to gaff a fish, and I'll never forget it.

Sixteen Pound Test

Bill MacDonald was a great customer of mine back in the eighties. He had a private boat, a Scarab Sport with a couple of Mercuries on it. We used to go fishing all the time. He was a great guy to be around and he lived rather comfortably. For my birthday he gave me a brand new rod, so I paired it up with my new Penn reel and this turned out to be my new sixteen-pound outfit. I wanted to fish sixteen-pound test for a world record class.

One day shortly after Bill gave me the rod he was going out. I was sitting in the tackle shop at Fred Lou Bait and Tackle and Bill said, "Hey, why don't you join us today?"

I said, "Ah, you're going dolphin fishing today. You know all about dolphin fishing, you don't need any help. And you've got a couple of buddies going."

And he said, "No, come on, go with us."

I agreed. So, we started trolling offshore with rigged ballyhoo. It was a very calm clear day in June with no wind. Everything was just beautiful. There were no weed lines, and we didn't find any fish or birds. When we were twenty miles offshore, this brand new rod and reel took of screaming. We had hooked up to a big dolphin. Bill fought the dolphin as it ran around on the top for a while. Then it sounded way down deep. Bill was fighting it, and fighting it, but couldn't get it to come up. He started threatening, "I'm going to tighten the drag."

I said, "No, don't tighten the drag. We set the drag when we started. We know it's set right. If the rod bend is still the same, stick with it. We'll get him up. It's a big fish, and it's going to take a while." So the fight went on thirty or forty minutes, and finally the big dolphin came to the top. We hit it with the gaff and pulled it into the boat. And it was a beautiful fish.

We put this big bull dolphin in the boat and headed back to Fred Lou Bait and Tackle to weigh it. It weighed fifty pounds even. It was a new IGFA world record for a fifty-pound dolphin on sixteen-pound test. And sure enough, our line passed muster with the line tester at IGFA.

So Bill MacDonald had a new world record dolphin on sixteen-pound line on a brand new rod, with a brand new reel. It was very exciting for us. That outfit turned out to be very lucky seven months later, in February, on a completely opposite day.

Our angler was Mario from South Miami, and it was the second time we fished on his Boston Whaler. The wind was a little bit rough, and the water was ugly, dirty green. We came to a big weed patch in the middle of all this dirty green water. Mario was using the same sixteen-pound rod and the same reel. I threw a live bait out into this big messy weed patch and we got a good strike. And low and behold, it was a great big bull dolphin. This bull was fifty pounds eight ounces, and it beat out Bill MacDonald's world record by eight ounces. Then we had the world record again. How about that! The same rod, the same reel, on two completely opposite days. I wish I still had that same outfit. I could use some more fifty-pound dolphins today.

Keith Baskette

My nephew, Keith Baskette, lives in Atlanta. He had one of our memorable dolphin trips as well. His mother is my sister, Sue. Keith and I hang out together all the time. He came down several years ago and we headed offshore to look for dolphin. We were running and gunning. That's where we run around looking for birds, or floating debris, or weeds, and then when we see something we stop and fire out some live bait, or pitch lures to see if we can catch something.

Keith loves to throw lures. This day he had an eight-pound spinning rod with a small green and white bucktail on it. We were running around looking for birds, and we saw this big dolphin swimming down the weed line. While I was trying to get a live bait to put on my hook to cast to it, Keith grabbed his eight pound spinning rod with the bucktail, and cast it over in front of the dolphin. And sure enough, he hooked up with it. It was one of his greatest catches ever. He caught a twenty-five pound dolphin on this little eight-pound rod. It was a fish to remember. It put up a great fight and it was really a lot of fun.

As I sit here in my office there's a twenty or twenty five-pound bull dolphin mount staring down at me from the wall. It was caught by my son, Terry. My son and I joined Chico Fernandez, who is a world class fly cast fishing instructor and fly fisherman. His son was on board with us for a day of dolphin fishing off Miami. We went to Newport Pier and caught a bunch of pilchards, and then we ran offshore. We found this really nice weed line. The line was maybe only a half mile or mile long, running north and south, but the dolphin were really thick in there. Chico was teaching our sons how to cast flies to dolphins, and how it was very important to never let the flies lay in the water. If the dolphin swims up to the lure and looks at it, and it doesn't try to escape, they somehow tell the whole school not to eat that lure. So, if there's a false cast, or a tangle, it's important to get the lure out of the water and then make another cast. Leaving the lure in the water will kill that lure for the entire school.

Chico's son and Terry caught a whole bunch of dolphin that day. Terry's biggest dolphin ever was in the low twenties, and as I said, it's mounted on the wall. He caught that on a real light spinning rod. We had a bunch of dolphin up to twenty pounds, and a bunch of schoolies. It was just a short weed line but it was full of fish. It was such a memorable day, fishing with Chico and his son, and my son Terry. It was a thrill to remember.

Poached Mahi
Now, here's a tip about cooking mahi: Keith loves poached dolphin. We cut the dolphin up in fingers a half-inch, by half inch, by three or four inches. We bring salt water to a rolling boil. Then we add the mahi fingers and boil them for ten minutes. While we're boiling them, we melt butter and then serve poached mahi with drawn butter. It's the best faux lobster in the world. It's really delicious. Actually dolphin by any method is great, but we really like that way to make faux lobster out of our mahi.

Swordfish

Herb Ratner

A stiff breeze blew out of the northeast on this special night in 2001. On board my trusty Dusky on this beautifully moonlit night were the president and IGFA Hall of Fame member, Mike Leech, Herb Ratner, owner of 163 IGFA world records, along with my mate Ron Jon Cook, and me. Inspired by Marty Arostegui's first ever sword on fly, Herb was hoping to set a new record in that class. When we reached our spot I put out a squid at 100 feet, and a live blue runner at 200 feet, both on fifty-pound test. We rigged the fly with twenty-pound tippet and set it out in hopes of greater things. Shortly after setting the lines, I heard one of the clickers slowly signaling action. I looked to see which line it was, but the sound was coming too slow to even be certain it was a bite. Just as I was about to relax, the 100-foot line with the squid started screaming. Now there was no doubt: the action had started.

Herb grabbed the rod to begin the fight while Mike cleared the fly. Just then the 200-foot line with the blue runner took off too. Mike handed the fly rod to Jon and took over the new fight. We had a double header, a very rare event in the world of sword fishing. In order to help maintain some semblance of order in the cockpit, Herb moved to the bow to work his fish. Then Jon, Mike, and I got busy with his twitching rod. This was not a long fight, only about fifteen minutes, and Mike brought his fish to the surface. He had caught what appeared to be about a fifty-pound sword. We were momentarily ignoring Herb while we worked the sword, and ultimately released it.

Meanwhile Herb Ratner, still fighting from the bow, had his hands seriously full with his catch. He called back to us, "Hey, did you forget about me?" Actually we had not forgotten about him; we had simply been very busy. Now it was time to focus our attention on what was going on in the bow. Herb returned to the cockpit and continued to fight his fish. This was when we realized that something pretty darned important was happening. Herb was straining for all he was worth. We though we might have a monster on the line; and that was confirmed when the fish jumped for the first time. In the moonlight we could see that this was a special fish, one of record-making possibilities.

The fight lasted for hours. To our delight we were treated to eleven jumps in all. With the moonlight for illumination, it was turning out to be one of our most memorable sword fishing events ever. Herb was a sixty-three year old man at the time of this fight, and he had given it all he had. Standing up, fighting any fish for four hours would challenge the toughest fishermen. But now Herb had hit the wall. I was worried this fight might kill him, and was relieved when he handed the rod to Mike Leach. We all knew this fish was special, a real fighter with some impressive weight. And I know that Herb was still hesitant to hand over the rod. He took his world records seriously, and handing off the rod would of course end any hope of a line class record. And, as luck would have it, had Herb held out for another ten minutes, history might have shined on him. But now Mike had the rod, Herb's fight was over. Mike soon brought the fish to the boat. We estimated it to be about 600 pounds, a magnificent specimen and undoubtedly a record for fifty-pound gear. We photographed it, tagged it, and released it.

As things turned out, the fish took off into the darkness, the photos did not come out, the tag was never recovered, and an exhausted Herb Ratner did not get his record. But this was a night to remember, starting with a double header, successfully landing two swordfishes, and culminating with a sword that was one of the biggest my crew, or my anglers, or I, for that matter, had ever caught. Nothing feels better than helping to create memories for the great men and women I am honored to fish with.

Full Moon Adventure

The 2005 Full Moon Adventure Swordfish Tournament was held in the third week of June. It was a nighttime tournament beginning at early dusk; 'lines in' at 6:00 p.m. In fact, it was not even dusk yet as the June sun does not usually set over Miami until after 8:00 p.m. But the contest goes until 3:00 a.m., when the Committee Boat calls 'lines out'; and the final weigh-in is at 5:00 a.m. With me on my boat this night were mates Pumpkin Eater Steve and Silent John, and two anglers from the Cayman Islands named King Flowers and Buster McLean.

We were on site when the Committee Boat radioed 'lines in.' We dropped our bonito strip to 1,800 feet. I hated to think it may be an auspicious omen for the evening, but we had no sooner hit bottom than we were hung up. Our beautiful fresh bonito strip and the eighteen pounds of paver bricks we used for weight, were firmly attached to something on the ocean floor. We tugged mightily until the line parted. We had fortunately only lost our terminal tackle, so we wound back up and re-rigged.

Again we dropped our rig overboard and waited for it to hit bottom – but it never did. Just when we believed bottom could only be a few seconds away, the line began to take off. Buster took over the rod, but said he believed we were snagged on the bottom again. I saw what was happening and reminded him that the bottom does not run to the north. We were hooked up.

After thirty exhausting minutes of cranking, our paver bricks were at the boat, a sign that the fish was only 100 feet away. Pumpkin Eater unclipped the weights and brought them aboard. We thought our progress had been good, and with luck we would soon be seeing what it was that Buster had been fighting. Within a minute the fish was circling thirty feet under the boat. We were blinded by the glare of the steep angle of the sun, and had to squint to see. Finally Silent John saw the sword and excitedly yelled, "It's as big as a Volkswagen!"

Buster, who had been wearing out his arms fighting this monster exclaimed, "Yeah, a Volkswagen bus!" Having had a peek, we had become even more anxious to boat this fish. So close!

At least we got to glimpse it before it dived back down. Thrilled and excited that we were contenders in the tournament; all we had to do was finish catching this great fish. So much easier said than done. For the next three hours the fish held at between 300 and 400 feet, neither rising nor diving.

I saw on my radar that an approaching thunderstorm would soon be interfering with our plans. Thunder and lightning sprung up around us. This is something mariners hate because of the danger lightning presents. We now had reason to hate it even more: with every bolt of lightning, the fish dove another 100 feet, and by the time the storm passed, it had nearly returned to the bottom.

Now the fight was getting ridiculous. For the next hour and a half everyone took turns cranking the reel. And everyone had worn himself out, with aching arms and backs all around. Finally I had taken to grabbing the line between the reel and the first eye on the rod, and pulling on the line while one of the other guys reeled. This is how we brought the fish up, one foot at a time. And after five hours and fifteen minutes the fish was only thirty feet under the boat. Then fifteen feet, then seven feet. With assistance from Silent John, Pumpkin Eater handled the flying gaff. Buster and King each manned straight gaffs. But this fish was not done. Even with our gaff hooks in it, the boat was dragged backward at trolling speed for several minutes. I stood there with a slack tail rope in my hands shouting encouragement to the four men who did the heavy lifting of bringing the great fish on board.

The last 5 ½ hours flashed through my mind. In the beginning someone was calling every ten minutes on the radio to see what was happening, and for the first two hours I would reply with information about the estimated size of the fish and our 350-foot stalemate. Then for the next 3½ hours we went to radio silence as we fought the fish. People were beginning to wonder what had happened to us. Well, we had been very busy, that's what happened to us. Finally, when the fish

52

was aboard, I reached for the mike, and in an excited voice called out, "Hello, Committee Boat . . ."

The reply, "Hello Bouncer, this is the Committee Boat. How big is it?"

I replied, "She's bigger than my ninety-six inch gaff."

Exhausted, we returned to the dock with our prize. Drew Kettlehut was the weigh master and tournament organizer. At 1:30 a.m. he verified the lower jaw/fork length to be 103 inches, and the weight to be 545.5 pounds.

That fish held the record as the largest sword ever caught in a tournament in the southeast U. S. until August of 2018.

558 Swordfish

Abie and his wife Yudith went to the Pacific Northwest for their early August vacation. I took the boat into Dusky Marine to have new Evinrude G2 300 horsepower engines installed as the other engines had 2,700 hours on them, and we wanted them to be in good shape for the coming season. There was a swordfish tournament taking place out of R.J. Boyle's studio up in Pompano, and I wanted to fish the tournament. So I stopped by R.J. Boyle's shop to see if he had room on his boat for another crewmember. He said, "Sure let's do it."

So, R.J., John Bassett, John Barfield, and I set out on R.J.'s boat *Datsnasty* to fish the tournament. We did a lot of bragging in advance on Instagram and on Facebook about how we were the team to beat. So we put out the word that we were looking for somebody to compete against us.

Twelve boats went out on a Saturday morning in the middle of August. It was a beautiful day; calm, a little bit cooler than normal with lower humidity, and the wind was light out the north. We ran out to where the whole fleet was congregating off Port Everglades. Everybody was set up in about 1,500 feet of water. We set up about a half-mile offshore of everybody just so we wouldn't be fishing in the same water as eleven other boats. We dropped a bottom rig straight down below the boat. We put out another bait, and when it cleared the bottom we attached a double bullet float, and let it way back behind the boat.

We'd been fishing for about an hour. John Bassett and I were facing forward; John Barfield was watching the tip rod off the starboard side, and R.J. was sitting in the chair facing aft. R.J. asked, "Hey, where did the jug go?" We all looked off the stern of the boat and could just see the top of the jug bobbing on the surface. This jug takes eighteen pounds to pull it under water, so there was a lot of pressure on it. The jug was almost completely under water; then it came back to its natural position floating like it had a ten-pound weight on it. So we said, "Well I guess you pulled that one off." And we went back to fishing.

Ten minutes later R.J. said, "OK, there's prize for the first swordfish, so we better get on this swordfish's case. Let's wind in the tip rod. We'll wind in the ballyhoo rod, clear the decks, and we'll see what we've got going here on the jug rod."

"Why, what's the matter?" I asked.

He said, "Now it's floating free. It's not being pulled down at all." I turned around and there was the jug. It was made of double orange bullet floats on a stick, and they were floating flat on top of the water back behind the boat, about 100 yards off. So we cleared the tip rod, and cleared the ballyhoo on the spinner we had set out, hoping for a mahi. We put all the rods in the port forward corner, so the starboard side was completely clear. They set up two harpoons, and John Bassett turned the boat to the north toward the buoys. R.J. fired up the Hooker electric reel to wind in the slack line. We got to the buoys and unclipped them. The bow in the line curved back to the south, so we headed in that direction. The line was slack, and the Hooker reel was winding as fast as it could; and we were getting closer and closer to the fish.

But we didn't see anything, and before long here came the weight. R.J. unclipped the ten-pound lead and laid it out on the deck. The line was still relatively slack, and the Hooker was still cranking. Then here came the first strobe light. R.J. pulled the light off the line; it was just tied on with a bridle band. We were almost to the second light and our gain stopped.

We finally got the fish close enough that he was concerned about the boat, and he started running around on top of the water. John Bassett was now driving, chasing him all over the top of the water, and John Barfield was standing up forward in the bow waiting to get a chance to throw a harpoon. The fish was running around in circles and figure eights; just running around all over the place. Finally it turned to head back down deep. He went down to about 200 feet and stopped; and he just laid there for about ten or fifteen minutes. He shook his head violently, jerking on the rod, and then raced toward the surface. John Bassett, with years and years of experience said, "Oh, I think he's gone."

R.J. Boyle said, "No I think he's still there." The Hooker again was winding as fast as it could, and the line started to scope off the bow. Then the line came tight, and we chased the fish around again. John Bassett was still driving the boat, and John Barfield was up in the bow, waiting with the harpoon. Then the fish sounded back down deeper yet.

Well, the fourth time the fish came to the surface John Barfield finally got to see it, and he said it was a good-sized one. And he also got a throw with the harpoon. Missed. We all saw the fish for an instant before it went back down. Then it came back up and ran around, and it went back deep again. I turned to R.J. and said, "Oh, at least two or three hundred pounds." He didn't answer; he just kind of gave me a funny look.

But it was amazing; this fish would be 200 feet down. It would shake his head up-and-down two or three times, and then charge up to the surface. After almost two hours of these shenanigans, now R.J. was driving the boat, and John Barfield was up on the bow with a harpoon, and John Bassett was in the stern with a harpoon. Finally they got a harpoon in the fish, and the battle was pretty much over. We got a tail rope on and slowly towed the fish backward. Soon it was lying next to the boat. We were all high fiving because we knew this fish was a beast.

R.J. called in to the fleet because we were the Committee Boat. He told them that we had caught a good swordfish.

Then things got more difficult. Like with my previous giant swordfish, I held the tail rope and cheered everyone on while they did all the work. But it was worse this time, because we only had three guys and they were not very big. That other time we had four guys and they were all 250 or better. This time we were on a boat with a flat bottom, so it didn't roll to the side at all. The guys were smaller; the swordfish is bigger, and they were trying to haul this huge fish into the unyielding boat. My contribution was that I was holding the slack tail rope, calling them names, and telling them to get the fish in the boat. It was funny, but finally with lots of grunting, and groaning, and leverage, and pulling, they were able to slide the fish into the boat.

More high fives, more cheering, and we were on cloud nine. Here it was, three hours into the tournament; two hours into the fight, and we had an almost unbeatable fish on the deck. We covered it up with ice and towels. Because we were the Committee Boat we had to stay offshore. So we ran back south to the fleet. We put the baits back out and just drifted and kibitzed, and told jokes. Nobody was worried about catching another fish. And, except for the sword we had lying on the deck, the fishing was really slow. A couple of the other boats had bites, but they didn't catch any of them.

Finally it was just about time to go home, so we wound up the lines and started idling toward the beach. Being the Committee Boat, we still had to stay within radio range of the fleet. The tournament went until three, and at about two thirty we started in. What was really neat, when we got about four miles offshore everybody's phones worked real well, and we started telling our friends we had this big fish. R.J. got on his Facebook page and told anybody who wanted swordfish steaks to meet us at the Hillsborough Marina. We'd be giving away free swordfish steaks a little bit after four o'clock. So we got to the dock and unloaded the fish, and hauled it up on the scales. It had a 101 inch fork length, and 151 inches overall. And, at 558 pounds, it broke the record that I already held for the biggest swordfish ever caught in a tournament in the Southeast United States. The other fish we caught a few years earlier was with no power reels allowed. This tournament allowed power reels, so nobody had much cramping from fighting the fish, but boy they worked themselves to death to get it into the boat.

We weighed the fish and photographed it, and then began cutting it up. People were at the dock with their Publix bags, and their Winn-Dixie bags, all different kinds of plastic bags. Everybody was getting two, three, four, five steaks. John Barfield and John Bassett each took about twenty-five pounds for their personal use. I took eight or ten pounds I wanted to give to a few friends. All the rest of the fish was given away. And we took a huge bill off the fish. It was really an amazing fish.

What an honor it was to fish with R.J. Boyle. He had fished with me many times before, but I had never fished on his boat. I got to meet and fish with John Bassett. It was the first time ever I got to spend time with him, and he shared knowledge about Kingfish all day long. He's a wealth of knowledge and very generous with it. John Barfield has fished with R.J. for years, and it was a pleasure to get to know him. We just had a ball and we won all the prizes. It was a great way to spend an August day. And poor Abie now had to listen to stories of giant swordfish that he wasn't here for.

How to Swordfish + Cooking

When fishing for swordfish, weight, as in sinkers, is very important. At one point we were using paver bricks for breakaway weights. This was necessary because we didn't have a place to cast our own concrete, and the paver weights were convenient to purchase and band together. The downside to paver bricks is that they only give about sixty percent efficiency as opposed to lead. When a ten-pound lead stick is placed in the water, it still weights about ten pounds. Ten pounds of steel in the water weighs about eight pounds. Ten pounds of bricks in the water only weighs about six pounds. So, eighteen pounds of paver bricks in the water equals just about the same as ten pounds of lead. Most of us have begun using the stick leads. When we're going by IGFA rules, we use a downrigger system with a stick lead and a diesel release clip. That clip is a lot like a blacks release clip, only about three times as big, and red in color.

Another thing to be remembered about sword fishing in areas like Miami Beach or Palm Beach is that in these areas there is a lot of current, and baits and leads will drift to the south of where the boat is. In the southeast Florida area the current generally runs to the north. So when we're putting our baits out, we drive to the north, letting out line for about eight hundred feet, and then we turn back south and let our sinker down to the bottom. Now our bait is already south of us, where it's going to end up anyway. If we were to drop our bait to the north of our location, or downstream, and run it out, and then put out our lead and let it go down, after the bait stops dropping to the bottom it will have slid past the lead and end up to the south anyway. Dropping the bait to the north of my location and letting the lead down, the bait will drift past and can easily hang up on the bottom because there is no tow on it. What may also happen, as it has with us many times, the hook will get caught on the line above the lead. So the bait is tangled up the whole time we're on the drift. If we're fishing in a strong current in 1,500 or 1,800 feet of water, we'll drop the bait going down with the current and then turn around and let the sinker drop. This will produce much better results.

And another thing about swordfish: it is against federal law to remove a swordfish from the water that you're not going to harvest, including to measure it. When we measure swordfish for release we have to do it in the water. Fish taken out of the water for photographing have only a fifty percent chance of survival. So, keeping that swordfish in the water while taking pictures and tagging is really a fun thing to do. It's very rewarding to hear that a fish we tagged was later caught and had gained two or three hundred pounds before it was recaptured.

Now, let's talk a little about cooking swordfish. The very best way to cook swordfish is on a grill. It's hard to beat. Mix some salt and pepper and a little bit of blackening seasoning in some melted butter, and brush that onto the swordfish. Then lay that side down on the grill. When the fat starts to bubble out of the meat, flip it over. Baste the upside and leave it on the grill. As soon as fat starts to bubble out between the grains of the meat, that swordfish is done. And it is some kind of delicious.

Swordfish meat can be anywhere from white to pink to orange. The richest swordfish is orange, and we call that pumpkin swordfish. Abie Raymond, who has fished with me for years, finds that in the broiler the pumpkin swordfish is too rich for his taste. But when he cooks it on the grill, where a lot of the fat drips down into the fire, then he finds it relatively peasant. So, get out there, catch a swordfish, cook it up, and enjoy the fun. Tight lines.

Bananas

Yes, we have no bananas; we have no bananas today!

Thank goodness. So, what about all this banana hype? Well, here's the story as I know it. One of the original banana tales goes way back, and can be traced to the Polynesian Islands. In that part of the world only royalty ate bananas. This one time some fishermen on the island stole a stalk of bananas and took them out to sea to eat them. They knew they could throw the evidence overboard and nobody would be the wiser. While they were offshore, a typhoon hit and the fishermen took tragic losses. The way the civilization was, it was natural that the fishermen would live closest to the water, so their families onshore were also devastated. The farmers lived farther inland and were safer, so their families came out OK. The only people effected were those directly involved in the banana heist. So the Polynesians would no longer eat bananas if they were going fishing.

In Europe, in the days of the sailing ships, scurvy was common with sailors. Eventually they realized that it was from lack of produce. When they started to put produce on the ships, if they mixed bananas with their fruits and vegetables, and put them in a sealed container so the roaches and rats could not get to them, it was bad news. When the bananas ripened they gave off methane gas, and everything in the container would all ripen at the same time, and soon it would all start to rot. Without the bananas, the ripening was staggered and one fruit would ripen one day, and something another day, and everything would ripen at a different time. One container might last all week, whereas if there was a banana in there, everything would all be green one day, ripe the next day, and rotten the next day. So, they learned to not put bananas on the sailing ships.

When steam ships came into being, one of the main produces they started to import to America was bananas out of Central America. Getting assigned to a steamer hauling bananas was the worst duty a sailor could have. In loading the bananas they would come on board full of poisonous spiders and snakes which would crawl all over the boat. So banana duty was bad. Bananas have gotten a bad rap on the water all through history.

I was in Islamorada, Florida, fishing out of Bud and Mary's Marina on a flats skiff. One day we didn't have a charter, so I was just hanging around in the marina in the afternoon when the charter boats came in. The *Hawk*, run by Sarge Warner backed in; the mate tied up the boat, and Sarge came down off the bridge. He went into the cabin, and was in there with his clients for a few minutes. Then I heard all this hollering and carrying on, and Sarge came storming out of the cabin with a hand of bananas. He climbed onto the dock, threw the bananas in the garbage can, and headed for Papa Joe's, the bar across the street.

I turned to Sonny Fisher and asked, "What was all that about?"

Sonny said, "Everybody knows you don't bring bananas on a boat. They're bad luck."

I said, "What are you talking about?"

He told me the story. "Well, they had a sailfish tournament down here years ago. Back then the boats were so slow you went straight out to fish. There was no time to go up and down the coast to get to where the sailfish were. So, the boats out of Bud and Mary's fished by Alligator Light. The boats out of Caloosa Cove fished down by Tennessee Light, and the boats out of Whale Harbor fished Conch Reef or Davis Reef. They never intermingled. After several days of tournament fishing, the boats out of Bud and Mary's were leading all the top positions, because Alligator Light was where the fish had been the thickest. On the last day of the tournament, first thing in the

61

morning, the Chiquita banana boat went right through there shoveling fruit overboard, right into Alligator Light reef. Then the sailfish completely shut down in that location. They bit like crazy up at Davis Reef, and the guys out of Whale Harbor ended up winning the tournament."

So bananas were bad luck for fishing in the Keys, and the story spread all over the country. I've been to Alaska and seen signs warning "No Bananas" on the boat. I've seen the same thing in Europe. I was not a believer at first, but only a couple weeks later I was on a charter on my flats skiff, and we were tarpon fishing down at Channel Five Bridge. The fishing was really slow. It got to be lunchtime and one of my customers got out his box lunch, opened it up and pulled out a banana. He started to eat it and then said, "Oh my God. They tell me I can't have any bananas on the boat, and maybe that's why we haven't caught anything." He threw that banana overboard, and in the next forty-five minutes we caught three big snook. After that I was a believer; and we have had other misadventures with bananas on board since then.

One of my best banana stories was hard for a lot of people to believe, but it is the gospel truth. I had two guys by the names Don and Sandy fishing with me the third Wednesday of every month when I was fishing out of Keystone Point Marina. Sandy went to Spain for the month of November, so Don brought Jack with us on this one trip.

We went out into Biscayne Bay. I threw the net once or twice and loaded the live well with pilchards, and ran straight out of Haulover Cut, and anchored up on a wreck in 105 feet of water. I put out two flat lines to look for kingfish, dolphins, and bonitos, or whatever. And I put two lines down on the bottom for mutton snappers and yellowtail. I was chumming with live pilchards. We were not getting any bites at all.

Then along came Dennis Forgione. I had worked with Dennis a lot, out getting business and whatnot. We both had twenty-five foot Duskies. He caught bait in the same place I did. We were fishing with the exact same Penn Fishing Tackle, the same hooks, the same leaders;

everything was identical on the two boats. So everything should have been considered equal, and we should have been catching fish at about the same pace. He anchored next to me even after I tried to tell him not to because there was nothing biting. He was close enough that we could talk from boat to boat. I told him, "I tried to tell you not to anchor here. There's nothing biting."

He hooked on a bait and threw it out, and immediately the rod bent over with a kingfish on it. He handed the rod to a customer and baited another rod. He immediately got another hit and handed it over to the other customer. Now they were catching kingfish as fast as they could. The third guy wanted to get in the game so Dennis gave him the bottom rod. He dropped down to the bottom and began catching snappers. They were just wailing on the fish, and we weren't getting a bite. Same bait, same tackle, same boat, everything was the same. The bait even came from the same school.

We could see they were biting for Dennis like crazy. I told my guys that there was something on the wreck today that's scaring the fish. We were going to wind the lines in and go around the other side of Dennis, and get further from the wreck. I pulled everything up and went around his other side and put the baits back out. Dennis was still catching fish left and right, and we were sitting there twiddling our thumbs.

I said, "Doggone it. Somebody on this boat is wearing Fruit of the Loom." Jack came off the back seat like I had fired a Polaris missile up his rear end. He jumped up, spun around, hands on his hips and said, "What would you say if one of the guests on your boat was from Fruit of the Loom?"

I said, "I'd tell him they ought to change their logo because it has to be bad for business."

He proceeded to inform me that he was the Vice President in charge of sales for Fruit of the Loom, and my opinion about that underwear was a bunch of bull. So, we had an all day discussion about all the bad things that happen with bananas.

I told him about the time we were fishing the Ft. Lauderdale Billfish Tournament and there was a banana on board, and we caught nothing on the first day. On the second day I was getting ready to leave the house at three in the morning. I was going to start by running up the bay to go catch bait, then I was going to run up to Ft. Lauderdale to pick up my charter. As I was leaving the house I saw a banana sitting there, and I decided I would take it along just so I could throw it overboard in case I needed to improve my luck. And if not, I'd eat it.

I got on my boat all alone and went out Haulover Inlet. It was rougher than a cob out there. I went off Bal Harbor and threw the anchor overboard. When I went to put chum in my chum bag, the bag was tangled up in the transom. I reached over the transom to try to free it, but somehow a piece of a hook had gotten caught in my stern line and in the chum bag, and my finger got caught on the hook. I was pinned to the back of the boat. Then all of a sudden the anchor pulled loose and the boat turned. We were drifting toward the beach with me pinned down by the hook in my right hand. And my pliers were on my right hip, so I couldn't reach them to cut myself loose. I ended up reaching down and getting hold of the hook, and ripping it out of my finger.

We were drifting toward the beach and I had to act fast. I ran up and went to pull the anchor, but I could hardly pull it. Then up came up a giant sponge on the anchor. I cleared that and moved the boat over by Haulover Pier, and threw the anchor overboard. I finally got my chum bag clear and put a block of chum in it, and went back by the console waiting for the pilchards to show up so I could throw my net. I saw that banana and threw it as far as I could.

It wasn't two minutes when the back of the boat was covered up with the most magnificent school of giant razor belly pilchards. I filled my live well to over flowing. I went to Ft. Lauderdale, got my people, and went out and had a great day of fishing. We were one of the top boats for the day, but that banana was gone from the boat, thank goodness.

I shared that story and many others with Jack. We only caught one mutton snapper all day, but we returned to the dock and Jack and Don went on their way. And I'll be doggone, in less than a year the banana was gone out of the Fruit of the Loom logo and all their advertising. I pat myself on the back when I think that I, one little fisherman in Miami, helped change the advertising program of a mega company like Fruit of the Loom.

Outdoors Writers and TV Show Hosts

Over the years I've fished with a lot of outdoor writers and TV hosts. Any time I have an opportunity to entertain a writer or TV personality, or anybody who can give me a step up in life, it becomes a great investment in advertisement. Add to that the benefit of becoming friends with these intelligent and worldly fishing enthusiasts, and the entire experience is a dream for a guy like me. That my life's experiences became so much richer is the prize; that my business benefitted is also a tremendous bonus, the appreciation for which I could never fully express. Here are some of these remarkable friends just to name a few:

Steve Waters

Steve Waters is one of the journalists I am closest to. He has been amazingly supportive, and a great friend. Steve has been a sportswriter covering the waterfront for several decades, first for the Ft. Lauderdale Sun Sentinel, and later for the Miami Herald. We went to the Cayman Islands together and have fished together more times than I can count. Steve has written numerous newspaper and magazine articles on me. In fact, he mentioned me in so many articles that his editors told him to quit using my name so much. They were beginning to think I was running a free ad campaign through his newspaper columns. Of course that was just a humorous jibe, but the truth is we have been very close and share a common love of fishing.

Steve got the job as outdoor editor for the Ft. Lauderdale Sun Sentinel in the 1990s. He had contacted me many times for fishing reports, so I invited him fishing with me. We met at Keystone Point Marina in North Miami. We went out into Biscayne Bay and netted a bunch of pilchards on the grass flats, and then proceeded up to Dumfoundling Bay. We got into baby tarpons in the five to fifteen pound range on eight pound spinning rods. It was a really good time.

The fishing was slowing in the bay as radio reports were coming in of numerous kingfish off the Newport Fishing Pier in about 100 feet of water. So I turned to Steve and suggested, "Hey, why don't we catch some kingfish?"

His response was, "Well, I really don't like king fishing, but if that's the best option, then let's go give it a try."

We picked up the lines and went back down the Intracoastal Waterway and out Haulover Inlet. We ran a couple of miles to the northeast and anchored up in the general area where they were reporting the kingfish. We used ten-inch long wire leaders attached to fifty-pound mono leaders on the eight-pound spinning tackle with an eighty-pound Spro swivel. I baited 3/0 hooks with live pilchards. We'd cast them out, and before we knew it, we were catching one kingfish after another.

Steve was shocked. He said, "I didn't know kingfish could be so much fun. I thought they were caught on a fifty to eighty pound outfits with braid, and a planer, and a long leader. First the tackle was too big, and then they got fifty feet from the boat and the planer came up, so the mate had to pull them up to the boat. That way it had all the excitement of pulling up dirty laundry. This is so much more fun."

So that was Steve's introduction to kingfish. It was quite a shocker to a guy who thought he had to use heavy tackle, and then found out he could catch them on eight-pound test.

I took Steve fly fishing for bonitos one time and we anchored right off Haulover Inlet. We were chumming with pilchards and had the bonitos boiling behind the boat. Steve was using a fly outfit that had been given to him by a manufacturer. He threw out the fly and started to strip it when a bonito came up and ate it. It was chaos, and when the dust settled the bonito was gone, the reel was broken, the rod was broken, and the line was broken. We put what was left of that outfit away for the rest of the day. Then we got out my fly outfit and chummed up the bonitos again and hooked one. As Steve fought this frisky bonito, it went up to the bow of the boat and ran around the anchor line.

I told Steve he would have to pass his fly rod around the anchor line. He did as I suggested, but he didn't keep the rod quite far enough away from the anchor line and broke off an inch and a half of the rod tip. Then he tried it again, and he broke off another inch and half. So now the fly rod was in pieces, and the line was still wrapped around the anchor line. I decided that I would have to get over there and help out. Steve held the fly rod while I cut the guide eyes off, then I let the anchor rope out a little bit to where it was originally. I unwrapped the line and gave the rod back to Steve. He proceeded to fight the bonito, but it went out behind the boat and got bitten in half by a barracuda. He pulled in a half a bonito. I turned to Steve and said, "This is not eligible for a worlds record."

He said, "It's not?" as if he didn't know better, but of course he did.

I said, "If you break the rod, and get an assist from another angler, and your fish is mutilated, it doesn't count for a world record." That was one of my memorable trips with Steve; and we had a lot of other great trips together too.

Eric Brandon

Of course, when we mention Steve Waters, Eric Brandon can't be far behind. Eric became Steve's radio co-host and close friend. Eric was a popular show host at Magic 102.7 FM for decades, and at KISS 99.9 FM before starting his fishing host career. Around 2005 he and Steve started The Weekly Fisherman show on 940 AM radio. It runs from 6:00 a.m. to 8:00 a.m., and consists of banter between the two hosts and various captains and divers from Boynton Beach to Islamorada. I have been with them from the beginning, and do an on-air call-in at 6:00 a.m., and usually again at 7:00 a.m.

Eric has two adult sons, and we fish together several times each year. One day in mid December, Eric and Steve were joined on my boat by the owner, the head chef, and the daytime manager of Shenanigans restaurant. We started out trolling for grouper. Baited with single hook rigged ballyhoos under sea witches, we were using sixty-five pound braid, and planers to take the baits down to fifteen feet. We caught five black groupers, a couple of barracudas, and a couple of cero mackerels on small surface trolling lures in twenty-five feet of water. When we got as far south as I wanted to go, I ran six miles offshore. In short order we caught several mahi up to fifteen pounds. We called it a great day and headed home. Flat calm water, sunny skies, fabulous food (provided by the chef) and great people made this a perfect fishing trip.

Eric Brandon's sons were always great to fish with as well. We caught many sailfish and snappers on these trips, and on one particularly memorable one, Eric's son caught one of the biggest tilefish ever caught on my boat: twenty-eight pounds.

Saltwater Sportsman

Saltwater Sportsman is a magazine targeted spot on to the people who I appeal to. I have been a contributor and collaborator to more of its articles than I can remember. The magazine employs featured writers with such names as George Poveromo, Mark Sosin, and Barry Gibson. I have written with, and fished with, and done TV shows with all of them, and have become friends socially with them as well.

George Poveromo's Joke on Me

George Poveromo is another famous TV host and writer I had the privilege of working with over many years. We fished together on many occasions and we caught a line class world record blackfin tuna. George caught it and I was the guy there to gaff it for him. I think it was forty-two pounds and tied the world record on the tackle he caught it on.

We fished in local waters, and made many trips to the Bahamas together. On one occasion George asked me to take a fellow named Chris out. He said that Chris was a new writer for Saltwater Sportsman, and he needed some exposure to big game fishing. So I took him out during the Miami International Boat Show.

He met me at Keystone Point Marina, and I called Paul, the bait man, and asked for a dozen live mullet. I was going to go out of Haulover to catch some pilchards or blue runners, and then come back into the bay and hook up with Paul in thirty or forty minutes, and we'd see what we had. I stayed out in the ocean for an hour while Paul was in the bay, and neither one of us caught any bait. I decided to move down to Government Cut to see if there was some bait down there. I told Paul to give me a holler if he caught any mullet.

I had just gone through the Broad Causeway Bridge when the steering on my boat blew out. I had to idle back to Keystone Point Marina. I called Paul and told him I was going to try to fix the boat, and if he found some mullet to let me know. I went back to the marina and tied up. I asked Billy Carson, the mechanic, if he could help because the hydraulic cylinder on my steering had blown out. He said he didn't have one, so I called Dusky Sports Center. They had one, so Billy took the hydraulic cylinder off the boat I took it up to Dusky. I got the new cylinder and brought it down. Billy installed it, purged the system, got the steering working, and we took off again to go fishing.

By now Paul was able to hook me up with some beautiful silver mullet. We ran down the bay and went out of Government Cut. We put up the kite, and in short order we hooked a massive dolphin, but he got away. Then there was a sailfish on the kite, but he got away too. Then a yellowfin tuna ate the kite bait, and he too got away. Then two more sailfish, and another big dolphin, and they all got away.

Now it was three o'clock in the afternoon. We had steering problems, bait problems, and fish problems. Our problems just wouldn't end. Finally, after three o'clock, we hooked a sailfish and got it up to the boat. We took its picture and turned it loose. Thank goodness, we finally caught a sailfish. Chris said, "That was my first

70

ever sailfish, and it was really great. And George sent you a trophy to commemorate me catching my first sailfish. Where's my carry case?"

I said, "It's in the console."

He said, "Well, pull it out here and open up the zipper. You'll find your prize."

I opened the zipper and said, "There's nothing in here."

He said, "Not that zipper, the other zipper."

I opened it up, and there was a banana! I chased Chris around the boat with the banana ready to beat him to death with it. I threw it overboard and we went home. He said, "Well, we caught my first sailfish."

I said, "Yeah, we spent an hour and couldn't get any bait. We broke the steering, and had to go all over town to get that fixed. We lost sailfish, and dolphins, and yellowfin tunas, and you're saying this is a good day? Think how good it would have been without that stupid banana."

Mark Sosin

Mark Sosin and I have known each other for many years. He had a sterling career as a writer and TV host, and became a member of the IGFA Hall of Fame. Together we created numerous magazine articles and TV shows. We also co-hosted fishing events and national seminars with audiences of thousands. I could never pay proper tribute to all that Mark and I have done together over the years, and the experiences we've had.

Mark has a huge TV audience. In a typical half hour show, there are twenty-two minutes of content, and eight minutes of advertising. People see a twenty-two minute fishing episode, and it looks like they are hooked up the whole time. In fact, we might have a good day, and catch all the fish in one day. But to be safe they always plan three days. It might be hard to catch fish, or there might be a camera problem, or the fish might not bite. There's no telling. But if we plan three days, the odds are we'll be able to shoot a good twenty-two minute show.

71

Mark probably broke the record on one of our scheduled three-day shoots. On the first day we caught some little baby kingfish, not worthy of a TV show. Then it got rough, and because Mark had some strict parameters on weather conditions we could shoot in, we went into the bay. There we caught a nice 120-pound tarpon, but it never jumped. We fished the rest of the day, didn't catch anything, and went home. We came to find out there was a glitch in the camera, and every other frame was black and white, and then the opposites were color. So there was no video, but the tarpon didn't jump anyway. The next day we met at the dock but agreed that it was blowing too hard, so we went home. The next day it was blowing so hard we never left our respective homes.

Long story short, we tried to make this show for eighteen days. Somewhere in the middle we did actually get out and catch a tarpon, but we couldn't catch a second one, and the wind was blowing like crazy, so we couldn't do anything else. Then on the sixteenth, seventeenth, and eighteenth days Mark said that if we didn't make a show on the boat we were going to a tackle shop and do a show there.

As a sidebar, within a year or two he started doing a show every season with Tommy Greene on the dock behind Mark's house. They would show lures, and knots, and equipment. They would do a whole episode every season on the dock. It was very well received, and entertaining. I've watched it many times myself.

Barry Gibson

Barry had just become the editor at Saltwater Sportsman when I met him and his new wife. We fished together on the *Black Duck*, a private boat out of Maryland that was in South Florida for the winter. My long-time friend Jack Plachter was the boat's captain, and his mate was Craig Coke.

I remember one incident when we were out fishing and dropped a live bonito on a wire leader down to a wreck in 325 feet of water. Within five minutes we had a strike, and very soon thereafter we had a jumping sailfish off the bow. That was the Gibson family's first introduction to sailfish. Barry went on to be Saltwater Sportsman's editor for years before returning to Maine to run charters again.

Of course Saltwater Sportsman is a first class magazine of huge influence in its market, and being associated with it, even as a contributor, has been a big boost to my career.

Florida Sportsman Magazine

Florida Sportsman was lead by Karl Wickstrom from its inception. A man who became a legend in sports writing both at that magazine and for the Miami Herald was Vic Dunaway. Vic was very generous with his coverage of me and many of the successful anglers who chartered me. I was a friend of Jim Martinoff who also wrote for the magazine and the Herald, and Jeff Weakley was the magazine's editor for more years than I can count. To all these men involved in Florida Sportsman, who have been so generous with their coverage of me and my charters, words fail to describe my deep appreciation of them not only for their coverage, but for their friendship throughout the years.

Sport Fishing Magazine

I owe a great deal to Dean Travis Clarke, Doug Olander, Glenn Law, Ms. Chris Woodward, and John Brownlee at Sport Fishing Magazine. I have worked a lot with Doug Olander. He and I have worked on articles together, and from time to time he would send me texts, or emails, or call me on the phone throughout my whole career. We have actually learned a lot from each other through this experience.

When talking about Sport Fishing Magazines and Sport Fishing TV, I have to mention John Brownlee. John first fished with me with Frank Mathers of the Woods Hole Institute in Massachusetts. Frank was one of the pioneers in marine conservation, and was one of the most influential people behind tagging. Frank was a gentleman I enjoyed fishing with. I never would have met Frank if it were not for John Brownlee.

John and I have had some great times together. We fished together with Frank and made a TV shoot for Sport Fishing Magazine where John Brownlee was the show host. John was also the speaker for The Billfish Foundation for several years. He seems to pop up everywhere there are good things happening in fishing. In addition to his work at The Billfish Foundation and Sport Fishing Magazine, John was the Editor in Chief of Marlin Magazine, the Executive Producer for Anglers Journal TV, and the Senior Editor for Salt Water Sportsman. Now he is working as the General Manager for Maverick Boats down in Costa Rica This is a great loss to us because we really miss his voice in the South Florida area.

Bob Mehsikomer

One of my most memorable TV trips was with the legendary freshwater fisherman from Montana named Bob Mehsikomer. Bob is an IGFA Hall of Fame Angler, and the holder of thirteen world records. He hosted such popular TV programs as Thunder on The Water, Simply Fishing, Simply Fishing Extreme, and FishnStix TV. He has produced more than 500 TV shows, countless videos, and educated thousands of anglers through his seminars.

Bob had met Mark Sosin in Orlando, and that led to us getting together. He was not local, but he was valuable to me just the same. Bob and his wife came down and fished with me. We caught sailfish, dolphin, tarpon, and tunas together. We made a great show with him, and the popularity of that helped propel my presence in areas outside the South Florida market.

The reason this trip was so memorable was in how quickly we did it. Bob and his wife, and his camera crew, and I went out to record a show that was scheduled for two days of shooting. We went out and put out some baits, and right away caught a thirty-pound blackfin on the downrigger. Blackfin tunas are very colorful and we got some good footage of this fish. Then we ran down by Government Cut and caught a couple of big king mackerels. From there we ran down off Elliott Key, and went over by Triumph Reef, and caught thirty-five pound and forty-five pound dolphins. Then we headed back to Watson Island and caught a big tarpon. By two o'clock we went home.

They said that was all the footage they could use for the show. They suggested we go fun fishing the next day, which we did, and one of the cameramen caught a sailfish. That was the easiest show I ever made, compared to the eighteen-day fiasco with Mark Sosin.

Jim Hardy

Jim Hardy was a long time ago writer for the Miami Herald. He had an impact on my career without even knowing it. Jim would call the Castaways dock and say that he had a nephew in town and he'd like to take him fishing. All the boats would offer to take him out, but just like any other client, they would rent him a couple of chairs (all the boats back then charged so much per chair.)

Connie Myra of the *Connie M II* and the *Connie M III* owned charter boats. She and my boss were good friends, and I'd get to shoot the breeze with her from time to time. She gave me some advice I'll never forget. Connie said those other guys were crazy. Her idea was to take Jim and his nephew up on the bridge. She sold out her other chairs to other anglers, but she would insist that Jim and his nephew ride for free. She knew that Jim, with his big heart and excellent sense of appreciation, might write a half page article for the Miami Herald. The cost of a half page ad in the Miami Herald was a whole lot more than the cost of two chairs on a charter boat. I took that lesson to heart and learned from it. When the opportunity comes to spend the day, or a few hours with somebody in the media, it's going to help business a lot more than that charge for the trip would be.

Sue Cocking

Sue Cocking was with the Miami Herald and other publications. We have known each other for years, and have fished together a number of times. An important influence that Sue had on me was to color my belief that circle hooks were viable for catching sailfish. I was an early skeptic, but in working with Sue I became a believer, and then an early advocate. On one day we caught a swordfish, and then we went on to catch dolphin on fly. I will always fondly remember that day with Sue.

Chip Howard and Sammy Lee each touch my life every year by contacting me for interviews on their nationwide broadcasts. And while I would love to name every sportswriter who ever helped my career, that would be another book altogether. But for purposes of a demonstration of the far reaching work of such national sports personalities as Marty Klinkenberg, Bruce Lawless, and Craig Davis, the following is an episode that actually happened to me several years ago: I was visiting the quaint Swiss styled village of Helen, up in the mountains of North Georgia. Suddenly a man ran out of a store and yelled, "I'd know that voice anywhere. Where's Bouncer? I've heard him on the radio so many times." Not only do they recognize me by my face, but now they can recognize me by my voice. This happens on account of articles that have featured me, and radio shows I have done with people I have known and have become friends with like Paul Castronovo and Mike Ranieri. What a run we had; just ages of doing fishing reports on the AM and FM radio all the way back to 1984. It has been a non-stop run.

The list is endless and I could never hit it all. But I am eternally grateful to all the media people who have helped to make my career over the years. I have no way of knowing just how far my influence might spread, so the best philosophy is to treat everyone, I mean everyone, sports writers, clients, colleagues, and friends, with respect and decency.

Fishing, and working with all these writers and on-air personalities, has not only benefitted my business, but it has been a pleasure to know them, and work with them, and call them my friends. Whether it's taking them fishing, or just talking on the phone for a little while, or helping them write an article about expert tips on different fishing techniques, I have enjoyed it all. Without the outdoor writers and outdoor TV men it would have been much harder to make the career I have had. I can't thank them all enough.

Kids

Charles, Allen, Ryan

Florida Sportsman's Magazine used to have a two-day fishing exposition every year at the Dade County Youth Fairground and other locations; but the Fairgrounds was the most popular one. Around 1990 I was helping out at the Miami Billfish Tournament booth at the Expo. I got there about 9:30 on Saturday morning and was walking to the booth, when I walked past a family looking at one of the exhibits. The family consisted of the mother, father, little girl, and a child with no hair in a wheel chair. As I was continuing on my way, I was thinking how down on their luck that family might have been over the summer. So after I dropped my supplies off at the booth, I went back looking for them. I found the mom and the two kids still at the same exhibit. I pulled out a business card and walked up to the mom and said, "You know, you look like you've been down on your luck a little bit this summer, and I haven't gone fishing in several days. I'd love to take you all out fishing as my guest."

About that time the father started stammering behind me. "You mean you're going to take the whole family out fishing? Wouldn't that be great."

I said, "It would be my pleasure." So as the event continued I found that the dad's name was Allen, and the little boy in the wheel chair was six years old, and his name was Charles. He had had brain tumors and successful surgeries, and he was doing pretty well. So, we figured out that we could go fishing Tuesday morning, just the guys;

Charles and Allen would go fishing with me, and the girls would go to the beauty parlor.

We met at Keystone Point Marina in North Miami. We got on my twenty-five Dusky, and went out into the bay and anchored up on a flat. Allen took a spinning rod with a trout lure up to the bow to try to scare up a trout. Charles and I sat in the back of the boat with a bait catching rig, with a couple of small hooks baited with shrimp, on a light spinning rod. We were targeting predominantly pinfish to use for live bait later in the morning when we would try for tarpon.

Every time Charles caught a small baitfish his smile would beam from ear to ear. We were catching plenty of baits, but there were no trout. When we had enough of live bait I said we should go up and check out the very north end of Dade County, up around Golden Isles and Aventura. So, we packed it in and pulled the anchor, and headed on up the bay. While we were under weigh Allen mentioned several times he needed some pictures for Sue. Well, there were three Sues that I knew of. Sue Cocking wrote for the Miami Herald, and Sue Baker ran the Met Fishing Tournament, and my sister Sue. So I didn't know which Sue wanted the pictures, but it didn't matter right then.

We went on up the bay and into a residential canal where there were some tarpon rolling. We put out some live baits and caught ladyfish, and jacks. We didn't catch any tarpon, but we had a whole lot of fun. After an hour or so of that, Charles began to get a little bit droopy eyed, and Allen said that we probably ought to call it a day. So we headed back to the dock. As they were getting ready to go home Allen said, "Boy, I can't wait to share this story with Susan."

I finally said, "Which Susan are you talking about?"

He said, "Oh, Sue Cocking from the Miami Herald."

I said, "Well, if you're going to tell her a story, remember that the story is about you and Charles, and not about me."

Sure enough the next day Sue Cocking called me and assured me that the story was about Charles and his father, not about me. I was just looking to share a little bit of my good fortune with some other people.

She said, "Well, we'll see what we can do about that." Allen had sent her a couple of pictures of some small fish, but they weren't worthy of the newspaper. But she did run a beautiful article about me taking Charles and Allen out fishing in the bay, and how it was such a relief from all the hospital trips and the worrying of the summer, and how we had a great time.

Soon thereafter Ryan Edelstein, a thirteen-year-old boy, called me up and said, "Hi, my name is Ryan. I fish on the *Reward* all the time. I'm turning thirteen, and I have to do a Mitzvah for my Bar Mitzvah." A Mitzvah is a good deed unrewarded. He said, "I want to take Charles and Allen out fishing. You, and Charles and Allen, and my brother and me. I want to charter you for the day and we'll go fishing together."

I said, "Well that would be great by me, let's see if we can put it together." A couple of weeks later we all got together. It was Charles again, and his father Allen, and Ryan Edelstein, and his brother. We went fishing in the bay and caught some barracudas, and some gag groupers on DOA Terrorize lures. We had a great time, these gag groupers being the highlight of the day. At one point Charles sat with me on the back seat of the boat and we held up a grouper with a DOA Terrorize hanging off his lip. Sue Cocking published that picture of the grouper, and Charles and me, and the DOA lure. And she ran another story about Ryan taking Charles out on my boat, with a brief background of what had already taken place.

This is such a wonderful story. From that picture in the newspaper Charles was sent a whole tackle box full of DOA lures, rods and reels, memberships to all the fishing organizations, and on top of that, Ryan got a check in the mail from an unknown person to refund the money that he spent on the trip.

So Ryan called me up and said, "I needed to do a Mitzvah and this guy sent me a check. It messed up my Mitzvah, so I have a favor to ask of you."

I asked, "What's the favor?"

And he said, "I'd like to take this check the man sent me, and send Charles, and Allen, and the mom, and sister up to Disneyworld for the weekend. That should cover the whole thing."

Well, Ryan got a very discounted rate from Disneyworld because of what he was doing. The family went and had a fabulous weekend. Besides that, paying it forward even more, Marsha and Lenny Bierman, very famous bill fishermen, called me up and said, "We want to take Charles and Allen fishing." And sure enough, we took Charles and Allen out a couple more times catching all kinds of fish. It was such a great snowball effect from 'Let me take you out fishing for a few hours,' to five or six fishing trips, a trip to Disneyworld, and everybody just sharing their good wishes on a family a little bit in need. And that is what I call a perfect fishing trip.

Troy Ross

In 1988 Easter Seals started a program called Catch a Cure. It was a fundraising tournament for challenged children with cerebral palsy and disorders such as that. I was invited to join the Board of Directors. We had our meetings in downtown Coral Gables where Terry Claus ran the meetings.

We held a very successful tournament. There were all kinds of eating fish, and everybody had a good time. Sometime after the tournament we had another meeting and I spoke up. I said, "We had a really good tournament, and we raised some money, but none of the kids who are beneficiaries of this event participated."

Aileen Ross-Gutaw piped up and asked if I would take one of the kids fishing. I said, "You better believe it."

She said, "You're on. My son Troy is going with you in the next tournament."

The following year Troy and Aileen came fishing with me. Troy was a challenge. He had cerebral palsy, and was mentally and physically challenged. But boy, he loved being on the boat. He would stand next to me and whoop and holler about how fast we were going. He would point out ships up ahead, and he would grab the microphone from the radio (I had to keep the radio turned off.) He'd be calling people on the radio, and waving to people on the other boats. Every time we got a bite he would wind the fish in. He may have had physical and mental challenges, but he was very strong. He caught kingfish, and dolphin, and bonitos, and barracudas. We had a ball. Troy and I became good buddies, and as time progressed we got to meet Troy's sister. Her name was Mimi. She also had cerebral palsy and was mentally and physically challenged.

My son, Terry, was probably six or seven years old at the time. Terry, and my wife, Ruth, and I would get together with Troy and Mimi and their mother, and a man who was coming into their life. We would go bowling, and play putter golf, and just had some great times together. Terry found it somewhat difficult. He asked why we spent time with people like these. I explained that it was an opportunity to give back to the community, and to share some good times with people who were a little bit different, but still loved what they were doing.

Troy and I fished that tournament for several years. Unfortunately that tournament ceased to exist after Hurricane Andrew, which hit about a week after their last tournament. For a little while I stayed in touch with Troy and Mimi and their mom, and her boyfriend. Then they moved to California and I didn't hear anything from them for years. A year ago or so their mother called me and said they were being challenged with life, but they were surviving out in California.

Boy, the trips I had with Troy were so much fun. It didn't matter what he caught, he was so thrilled with every catch. He loved to get on the radio and call all the boats, and point out all the traffic. Trips like that were just so rewarding, to see the brilliance in his eyes as he enjoyed the outdoor life and being out on the boat and the whole experience. I know I got more out of it than Troy did. It was wonderful times.

Make a Wish Tarpon

The Make A Wish Foundation contacted me about taking a young man swordfishing. This was in the days when swordfish were only targeted at night. Sherman Huffman was my mate at the time. We were going to meet the people on a Monday night. I went to the tackle shop to grab a couple of things just before the party was about to arrive. I came back down to the boat, and the people had gone down to the deli to get some drinks. Sherman said, "Bouncer, we can't take these people swordfishing. It just won't work."

Soon the people came back. The Make A Wish boy was about thirteen years old, a typical fun loving kid. He had his little sister with him who was probably ten years old, and his mom, and his grandparents. The grandparents were probably in their seventies at the time. The grandfather had lung cancer and was very ill. The young boy was also very ill, and the mother was pretty worn out from raising two kids, one of which was very sick. They were in pretty tough shape to go swordfishing.

I recommended that swordfishing might not be too good because it was windy, and there was a decent chance of rain. It would be a very long boring night. Maybe some tarpon fishing would be more appropriate for their group. They said, "OK, let's do whatever you want to do. Let's go tarpon fishing."

We went out Government Cut in my thirty-three foot Dusky, and pulled over by the south jetty and put out a couple of live shrimp. In relatively short order we hooked a tarpon. This tarpon obviously knew his chore in life, because with this thirteen-year-old boy fighting the fish, and Sherman helping to hold onto the rod, the tarpon jumped and stayed up on the surface. He put up a really good fight, but not too much. We brought him up to the boat and took a picture of him swimming in the water. When Sherman was trying to grab him for another shot, the hook popped out of the tarpon's mouth. He was on his way, but we had successfully caught a tarpon.

Grandpa was a little miffed that here we were fishing, and the fish we were targeting were not good to eat. We had no intentions of harvesting a tarpon. We told him we were using live shrimp for bait, and there was always a chance we would catch something that was good to eat.

We went back over to the jetty and put the baits out again. We were drifting down along the edge of the jetty when we got a really good strike. We were fighting the fish, but it wasn't jumping. I was thinking it might be a nice snook. That would be perfect. They could eat a snook for dinner.

That fish was really fighting hard, but it was not coming to the surface. Lo and behold, grandpa came up with about a fifteen or eighteen pound black grouper. That was the only time in my life I've ever targeted snook or tarpon and ended up with a black grouper. It was perfect, because grandpa wanted a fish to eat, and now he had it. One or two drifts later we hooked another tarpon and mom fought this one. We brought it up to the boat and took some nice pictures of our Make A Wish boy with the tarpon, with Sherman in the picture of course.

So now we had pictures of the tarpon, and grandpa with the grouper. Little sister didn't catch a fish, but she loved when we ran around real fast. Every time we got done with a fish we would have to run back into position. I'd run around at twenty-five or thirty miles an hour and she'd be thrilled with that.

Then we put out the baits one more time and caught a mutton snapper that was probably five or six pounds. Then we saw a heavy rainstorm coming, so we high tailed it back to the dock. I suggested to Mom that we weren't going to fish all night and that we had no charter in the daytime the next day. Maybe they could come back in the morning and go fishing again. Everyone in the family was in agreement with that. We iced down their grouper, and they went on their way just about the time the skies opened up and it poured down rain.

They met us again in the morning, and what a beautiful morning it was. Slick glass calm, no wind, and not a cloud in the sky. We tried to catch live bait in a couple of spots but couldn't find any. We went to the Miami Sea Buoy and caught some frigate bonitos, otherwise referred to as speedos, for bait. Everything loves to eat them: sailfish, dolphin, kingfish, wahoo; the whole gamut loves the live speedos. For that matter, a dead speedo on the bottom is like offering filet mignon to a mutton snapper. It's a very popular bait.

We put out the speedos and were slow trolling around, but the fishing was slow. We finally got a strike. Sherman dropped back on the fish and got a hook in it. Now we had a nice sailfish on. The Make A Wish boy was sitting on the back seat so we put a fighting belt on him. Grandpa was sitting with him, cheering him on. We got the sailfish all the way up to the boat and Sherman took the leader. He was trying to pull him over to take a picture but the fish was too spooked. It took off on another run of almost 300 feet.

The boy turned to Grandpa and said, "Grandpa, I don't think I can wind it in again. Maybe you could take over for me." So, he gave the rod to Grandpa, and it was just the most memorable fight. The boy would tell Grandpa, "Pull up on the rod. Now wind down Grandpa. Wind it quick." Then, "OK. Stop Grandpa. Pull up on the rod; pull up on the rod. Now wind down quick Grandpa. You're doing a great job."

During this whole fight this boy coached his seventy something year old grandpa on how to fight the fish. They joked about the fact that Grandpa and his grandson were racing to see who would go to heaven first, because they were both so sick. The two of them were sitting on the backbench, strategizing on how to fight this fish. The mother was standing next to me behind the grandfather and grandson, and trying to take pictures.

I said, "You've got to go around there and go back by the motors and get a picture of your two boys. They're never going to be happier than they are right now." She got the most precious picture of grandfather and grandson in the heated battle with this sailfish. We got the sailfish up to the boat and took beautiful pictures of grandpa and grandson and Sherman holding up this sailfish. It was just the most spectacular catch to go with all the fish they caught the night before. After we caught that fish and headed back to the dock, Sherman fileted the grouper and cut it into grouper fingers. We took it up to Monty's and they fried it up.

The little girl said she doesn't eat fish so we ordered her a hot dog. But I don't think she ever touched the hot dog, because once she had a piece of those grouper fingers she was hooked on fish.

It was just a fantastic event for the whole family. They caught all these tarpon, the black grouper, the mutton snapper, the sailfish, and the speedos; and ate the grouper for lunch. The whole trip was just spectacular. It was a blessing to be sharing that trip with them.

Tarpon

Tarpon Tangles

The rod twitched. Hans flinched. The rod started to bend and Hans started to rise. The rod bent double, and Hans rushed to get the rod from its holder while keeping the rod tip up. Hans had arrived from Holland at noon. He cleared customs at the airport, and grabbed a taxi over to Miami Beach where he checked into a sparkling hotel. With his fishing trip scheduled for 5:00 p.m., he had plenty of time to get a rental car, and grab a sandwich for lunch on South Beach before driving to meet me. He watched beautiful people stroll the sidewalk. In the background he could see four boats drifting just outside the swim buoys. He was envious because he knew those boats were loaded with anglers who had probably already caught tarpon today, and were just basking in the warm beautiful South Florida sun while dreaming about those fish they had caught. Two things kept Hans' spirit up: first, he had been catching tarpon for fifteen years, and secondly, he knew that in a couple of hours he would be out there himself catching tarpon under the neon glow of a Miami Beach evening.

The fish ran hard, and line screamed from the reel that Hans held in front of him. He knew that at any second the silver king would burst through the surface of the water and throw itself skyward. Here he came! The spotlight lit its silver six-foot side as this gallant fighter of the sea jumped to escape the resistance he felt in his jaw. It splashed down, hardly disappearing below the waves, and rose again from the sea.

His large eye glowed red in the minutes Hans had the fish along side. With a quick pat on its side the fish spooked and surged away. The sudden pressure on the fifty pound leader being held by the guide was all it took to free this giant. The leader was broken. The light wire hook would disappear from the tarpon's jaw with no ill effects, and the angler's arm would stop hurting in a few minutes.

Hans would reflect on this tarpon trip as he drove to Joe's Stone Crab for a late evening business dinner meeting. He had caught three fish from sixty to over one hundred pounds in three hours. World-class big game fishing was only one hundred yards from a metropolitan area with over two million people.

Every evening from Thanksgiving to Memorial Day finds a couple dozen boats scattered up and down South Beach fishing for tarpon. Some days there will be twice as many boats. These charter boats and private boats entertain residents as well as travelers with some of the best big game fishing in the world. If we sneak a peek into the log/tournament entry books of one of these guides we will find addresses of anglers from South Africa, England, Germany, San Salvador, Holland, Italy, Argentina, Venezuela, Ireland, France, Israel, Colombia, Mexico, Canada, Australia, Belgium, Russia, Japan, and even a few from our United States. They come to Miami Beach to fish, or vacation and fish, or take care of business and fish. But they leave talking about fish caught in Miami Beach that weigh up to 200 pounds and are caught on trips with over ninety percent success rate. That is a catch rate that is almost unheard of in sport fishing.

Then and Now

Tarpon are near and dear to my heart. I love catching them. There are so many ways to catch tarpon – live bait, whether it's live shrimp or mullet, live crabs, live pinfish, or live grunts. Every season or location has a best live bait for tarpon, but they can almost always be caught on live bait. They can also be caught casting plugs, mirror lures, rattletraps, or x-raps, and all the different brands of plugs and bucktails. And then one of the most popular things to do is to catch tarpon on fly. Another technique less mentioned, but just as good, is using soft plastics for tarpon. Then when all else fails, they can also be caught on dead baits.

Tarpon fishing is a lot different now than in the good old days. We started off using j-hooks, with at least eighty-pound, and sometimes as much as 120-pound leaders. When the j-hook got caught inside the tarpon's mouth, the leader would rub back and forth across the lips, and they could chew through it. When we used plugs, we'd use a real short heavy mirror lure, and we would retrieve the plug just by winding. When we felt a thump we would drop the rod tip toward the fish, and then wind and come tight on it. With the mirror lures we had to use an even heavier leader because those fish were almost always hooked down in the throat. It was bad for the tarpon, and for us too for that matter. These plugs had two not so little treble hooks on them, and they were frequently down in the tarpon's throat. It made it nearly impossible for the tarpon to eat because his throat would be blocked. It made it hard on us because we'd have to use a tool to reach down in the throat and get the hooks out. So, it was a bad situation that we have since remedied.

As time progressed we changed over to using circle hooks with live bait. With the circle hooks we could go to fifty-pound mono leaders because the leader and the shank of the hook was always outside the tarpon's mouth. With the circle hook every tarpon is hooked in the lip. We can use a lighter leader, the bait can swim better, and it's harder for the fish to see the leader. We caught a lot more fish when we switched over, and it became a win/win situation. By the same token, on the plugs, whereas we used to drop back when they ate the hard plastic plugs, I went to tying a circle hook to the end of my leader. Then I take fifty-pound wax thread that knots really easily and I tie my mirror lure. Then we changed to rattletrap, then to x-rap. Whatever plug we're using, even bucktails and rubber shrimp, we tie the eye of the lure to the bend of a 7/0 VMC circle hook. We can cast the lure and wind back. We feel the thump, keep right on winding, and the fish is hooked. Again, every fish gets hooked in the lip on the circle hooks, and our catch rate on plugs went from one out of ten bites, to eight out of ten bites. The same thing is true with our live baits. We went from about a fifty percent catch rate with j-hooks, to an eighty percent catch rate with circle hooks. Circle hooks at the leading end of the bait really made a big difference.

More recently we have yet another change in tarpon fishing. I have tarpon fished from Islamorada to Ft. Lauderdale since the sixties. In 1976 I had one hammerhead shark come after a tarpon that was hanging on a stringer off the back of my boat in the Keys. That's the only shark I ever had come after one of my tarpons. We pulled that tarpon into the boat so the shark couldn't get it. We were keeping it anyway to have it mounted. Back then we never had an issue with sharks. Now every time we hook a tarpon we fear that a bull shark or big hammerhead is going to come out from under the boat and bite our tarpon in half. The worse thing that can happen for a guy who loves tarpon is to have sharks attacking his fish.

We used to fight all of our tarpon till it would roll over, belly up. Then we'd take a nice picture with them. We'd swim them forward with the boat, get them swimming real well, and send them on the way. Now we've had to change. When we hook a tarpon, we hope to get numerous jumps, and when we get close to them, we try to get a picture of them swimming or jumping next to the boat. Then we grab the leader to break them off. We want to make sure that when that tarpon is released it is swimming strong enough to get away from the sharks. If we wear them down to where we can grab them by the jaw and hold on for a picture, there's just too much of a chance of a shark killing that tarpon. I think of tarpon as a valuable resource. Their numbers are dwindling; the recoupment for the future is low partially because of land development, but also the shark populations are way up, so there are many more tarpon being killed by sharks.

We have to do everything we can to preserve these wonderful game fish for the future. So, a quick fight, a quick release, and some great memories far outweigh watching a shark eating this beautiful game fish.

For years I tied up at the Haulover drift boat dock. I would tie my boat up to one of the pilings and cast big chunks of kingfish, or ladyfish, or bonito, or whatever kind of fish I had. I would cast them out into the bay. We would sit there and relax, and pretty soon the drag would be screaming, and we'd have a tarpon in the area of 100 to 200 pounds. I hope for that possibility again with responsible management of the tarpon fishery.

Mark's Biggest Tarpon Ever
Mark Sosin, a very famous outdoor writer and television producer and host for years, caught the biggest tarpon ever, fishing with me inside of Haulover Inlet. This fish weighed close to 200 pounds. What a behemoth! And we caught that one when we were tied up to a piling using dead bait. We used to fish from that position quite frequently. As the drag went screaming out, we would untie from the piling, fire up the engines, and chase the fish down. We chased them all over the bay, and everybody would stop to watch us fight them. We'd get them up to the boat and turn them lose, and then go back to try to catch another one.

Al Hower
One of my most memorable tarpon trips was right outside of Haulover Inlet. I was fishing with Al Hower. We ran down from Ft. Lauderdale and were drifting with live shrimp. This was in October, back in the good old days when there were a lot more tarpon, and they were showing up a lot earlier. We were drifting with shrimp. We would start out in about twenty feet of water and drift right up to the swim buoys, and then go out and make another drift. In the course of the day Al caught nine tarpon over 100 pounds, probably averaging 120 pounds apiece. After nine tarpon he was wiped out. I said, "Al we can't go home until we catch a tenth fish." Bear in mind that every one of these tarpon he caught was a thirty-minute to an hour knock down drag out fight on twenty-pound tackle.

He replied, "Well, if we're going to catch ten, then you're going to have to catch the tenth fish." So I set up another drift. I got a bite and grabbed the rod. The tarpon came up jumping, and he jumped, and jumped from where he started jumping in a big semi-circle, back toward the boat, and close to the boat. He jumped right next to the boat and stopped. He pulled backwards on me and then rolled over and surrendered. I probably had that tarpon on the line for twenty or thirty seconds and then it was lying up next to the boat.

Al moaned and groaned all the way home about how he fought those nine tarpon, all of which gave him a tough fight, while my tarpon took seconds to land and was totally whipped.

Sixteen in Three Hours

People ask me what was the most tarpon you ever caught on a trip. The most we ever caught on ocean tarpon, which is a lot different than catching fifteen-pound bay tarpon, but my most ever ocean tarpon was sixteen. It was during the Miami International Boat Show, which is in February. We were fishing in Government Cut. I had two guests who were in the sport fishing industry. It was a trip that I traded for a magazine ad. I had a brand new mate, a young guy named Yancey Perkins and it was his first trip. He was a wonderful person, a great personality and a lot of fun to spend time with. We went out to the end of the south jetty of Government Cut and rigged with live shrimp. About six feet from the hook we would double over the leader. We would slide the leader through the hole in a two-ounce egg sinker. When the loop of the leader came out the other side of the sinker, we'd stick a piece of rubber band in that loop and pull the rubber band snug up against the sinker so it would stay in place. The sinker would stay on while we were fishing, but if a tarpon pulled real hard, it would straighten out the leader and the sinker would break away. We wouldn't have to worry about a sinker swinging around while we were fighting the fish.

We watched the depth finder and sure enough we marked some fish. We stopped the boat and started to drift through the area, and hooked a double header. Both guys on the boat caught tarpon. We went back in, marked the fish, dropped the baits in and hooked another double-header. It was a most amazing night. After three hours, the anglers couldn't lift their arms anymore. They begged for mercy, so we went home. We caught sixteen tarpon in three hours in Government Cut on live shrimp. Those fish averaged sixty or seventy pounds each.

Dumfoundling Bay

I mentioned that bay fishing is a lot different that ocean fishing. I should emphasize that bay fishing for small tarpon was a lot different. We would go up into Dumfoundling Bay in the very north end of Dade County. There was a basin up there that I used to go to when I was in high school. It had a grass bottom about three or four feet deep. Builders came along later and developed Turnberry Isle and Williams Island, and all those properties on the west side of the Intracoastal Waterway. They went into Dumfoundling Bay and dredged half of it thirty to fifty feet deep. They dug up all that fill, filled in the mangrove swamps, and created the City of Aventura.

We used to go up in there with live pilchards or finger mullet. We would find a school of tarpon rolling on the top. We'd hook a tarpon on a live pilchard on a little spinning rod and fight them up to the boat. There next to the boat we'd have this tarpon on the line, and there would be four or five more tarpon swimming with it. So, we'd flip a pilchard out on another rod and hook another tarpon. Then we'd release the first tarpon. Now the second tarpon was getting tired; he'd be next to the boat and we'd flip out another bait; and we had occasions where we caught over thirty tarpon. Just like catching schoolie dolphin where we keep one fish in the water and keep hooking more. Well, that's how we would catch tarpon in Dumfoundling Bay. Talk about a hoot; those fish were great on six to eight pound test.

It's kind of a segue into another phenomenal tarpon story.

Six Pound and Twenty-Pound Outfits

I had a client by the name of Bob Tenaka, who used to manage shopping centers, like the Mall at 163rd Street, and the Northside Shopping Center. He worked for a big conglomerate that owned a bunch of shopping centers. Bob would come to town once in a while to check up on their properties. We were going up to Dumfoundling Bay, or right adjacent to it at Little Maul Lake. We were catching these small tarpon, five to maybe thirty pounds tops. Bob was in the habit of bringing his own six-pound outfit, and using my six or eight pound gear. Most of the time he went tarpon fishing with me was in the fall, but this one time he made reservations to go with me in February. When he showed up at the dock, I was rigging the twenty-pound outfits with Penn Internationals on fiberglass rods. But Bob showed up with his six-pound test and asked, "What are you going to do with those things?"

I said, "We're catching some big tarpon now. They're not quite right for your six-pound test."

We got the rods rigged, along with his six-pound outfit and ran down to Government Cut. Before dark the tarpon had been showing up off of the south jetty. Those fish were running maybe up to forty or fifty pounds. So we made a drift and caught a Spanish mackerel using a blue runner for bait. We made another drift and caught another Spanish mackerel and a jack crevalle. Bob said, "Wait a minute, these fish are small, let me use my six pound rod." So we rigged the six-pound rod and he caught a couple of jack crevalles with it. Then it started to get dark and the big tarpon were starting to show up off South Beach. So we wound everything up and went over to South Beach, and I started baiting up twenty-pound outfits. He asked, "Well, what about my little six-pound outfit?"

I told him, "I don't think it's heavy enough for this spot. So let's put the twenty pound outfits out and see what happens." So, we put the twenty-pound outfits out and started to drift. We probably drifted for fifteen minutes and BANG! We got a strike. We were using live shrimp. Back then we were using 3/0 j-hooks, hooking them crossways to the horn, and we used eighty-pound monofilament leaders. We hooked this nice tarpon, so I cleared the other two lines and in five minutes the tarpon was right next to the boat. But it was on a fifteen-foot leader, and probably fourteen feet of leader was still off the rod tip. It was just right straight down.

So Bob asked, "If that's all there is to this, why do we have to use such heavy tackle?"

I said, "I don't think the battle is quite over yet." Sure enough, the fish took off fighting again. It had already jumped once, so I knew it was a big one, but I didn't know how big. We got into hand-to-hand conflict with this fish, and three hours later we had that tarpon up to the boat. According to the length and girth formula, which was: the length times the girth, times the girth, divided by 800, it came out to 230 pounds. They have a new formula now and all the fish are heavier on the new formula. So this 230-pound tarpon may have been pushing 250 pounds. But the bottom line was, it was a three-hour fight, and we're real glad it wasn't on the six-pound test. We let it go to catch another day. It was quite a thrilling trip. And this segues into one more story with the same guy.

Once Bob got into the springtime tarpon fishing he loved it, but he always liked to cast lures whenever he could. So, sure enough we were out there one night drifting with live shrimp. The fishing was slow. Some shrimp began to show up in the water, and we started getting a few bites. Soon the shrimp were pouring out of the inlet and the tarpon were going crazy. They were busting shrimp all around the boat. There were explosions, and oh man! We gotta cast for these fish! So I dug into the tackle box and pulled out a brand new artificial shrimp, still in the package. I gave it to the mate and told him to tie it onto the guy's line. He tied it on, and the guy cast the artificial shrimp out. He would cast it in and BANG! He had a tarpon on, but it jumped and came off. He was still winding in on the same cast and he got another hit. And this one jumped off too. He got the shrimp back to the boat and cast it off again, and then another bite. This one jumped off too. He cast again and got another bite that also jumped off. I said, "We better check that hook on that rubber shrimp."

He wound it in and handed the shrimp to the mate and the mate said, "Oh my God." The mate handed it to me. I had taken it out of the package and handed it to the mate. The mate tied it on and handed it to the angler. And the angler cast it out. The hook had a piece of vinyl tubing over the point. So, no matter what, we wouldn't have been able to hook a fish on it. Imagine all those casts with the vinyl tubing over the hook. There wasn't much hope for us on that one. That was a crazy mistake on my part that time.

A Whale by the Tail

Did you ever have a whale by the tail? I had a charter out of Ft. Lauderdale on the boat called *Doctor's Orders,* and we were on our way home from fishing off Haulover Inlet. We headed down to the south to get some hot sailfish action, and were rewarded with three sails and a big hammerhead. It had been a terrific day.

We headed north and were just past Hallandale, when we saw a whale shark swimming on the surface. As we slowed down to take a look, we saw several cobias swimming with him including one that was probably in excess of eighty pounds.

We put out a live blue runner and tried to drag it past the whale shark to see if we could get a cobia to eat. And don't you know, we hooked that whale shark right in the tail. He wasn't panicked in the least. It probably had no idea it was hooked, but the angler holding the rod was almost knocked out of the fighting chair with every sweep of its tail.

It went WHUMP! The angler would go flying out of the chair. Whump, and he'd go flying out again. It was a funny sight. We got as close as we could to the fish and cut the line and sent him on his way, hopefully no worse for the wear, but that was definitely having a whale by the tail.

The Happy Hooker

In the late 60s I had a couple of customers from Jackson, Mississippi, who would come down once a month to go to Bimini for a few days. We were on a fifty footer out of Haulover Inlet. Whenever they came down they always brought some ladies of the evening. The ladies were not allowed to have a stitch of clothes on if they were far enough offshore to not see the dock. All day, everyday, running around in their birthday suits. Other than that nothing went on, just good scenery.

They made friends with a fellow named Pat from New Jersey. He came down a day early and asked my customer if he would send the girls down to keep him company on the boat. Xavier Hollander had just come out with a book entitled The Happy Hooker. So here we had these two beautiful young women out fishing with us and they were reading The Happy Hooker. They got a hold of our flying gaff, which is a twelve inch hook with a sharp point on one end and a straight bar on the other end. They posed for Pat au natural on the fish box on the back of the boat, and had a good time as they posed with the gaff (hook) and the Happy Hooker book.

Sam Caraway came out of Haulover on an afternoon trip and we were fishing live bait for big smoker kingfish right in front of the inlet. He put the nose of his boat so close he could almost step from his boat onto ours as he observed the girls posing. It was really crazy.

And I'll have to admit that as a young man, I was totally consumed by this performance going on, as was my great captain, Randy Lacey. We went to the Bahamas with these girls, and our clients. We'd run along in fifty or sixty feet of water along the dropoff in

Bimini, with snow white sand bottom, the water looked like a swimming pool. What memories of fishing with those guys; and those were some pretty girls.

Sailfish

The beauty of a sailfish! The fin on the back of a sailfish, what we call the sail, is three or four times as high as the height of the body. It is brilliant bright blue with black polka dots and black shading. The bill on most sailfishes is about eighteen to twenty-four inches long. The majority of the bill is rough like a file would be, but the last third of the bill, as it approaches the mouth, is smooth. That helps the bill to push down on food and lead it right into the fish's mouth. They have a very deep forked tail. The tail on a five-foot sailfish is probably twenty inches from top to bottom, but it is thin like two knife blades running at thirty-degree angles from the base of the tail.

On the belly of a sailfish there are two feelers that extend out. These are the ventral fins. They're about eighteen inches long and extend out below the fish so that when he is feeding along the bottom he can keep track of how close he is to the bottom. These are also sometimes used in steering. They look like two black sticks hanging down, but the fish has the ability to spread them so they actually look more like long, skinny fins.

One of the other interesting things about a sailfish is that the dorsal fin actually folds down into a flap on the back. There's a layer of skin and flesh that extends up, and the fin disappears into this layer so that the fin gives no resistance in the water. The pectoral fins on the side of the fish also have depressions they lay into. This is a common situation in some ocean fish, so those fins completely disappear. When the dorsal fins and the ventral fins, and pectoral fins are gone, the sailfish is a missile capable of swimming seventy miles an hour.

The sides of the sailfish change color with the attitude of the fish. If a sailfish comes up and he's trying to catch a baitfish, he appears black in the water on the back and on the fins. When they are completely at rest, and calmly traveling in the ocean, they're a very pale greenish blue, almost the same color as whatever water they're swimming in, and they cannot be easily seen. When they're in fighting colors, they're brilliant blues, not only in the dorsal fin, but also on the back; and the tail and pectoral fins look like a blue neon lights at times. It's unbelievable how much ocean fish can vary in color just by their attitude at the moment. Sailfish really light up when they are excited and putting on bursts of speed.

Captain Ronnie Hamlin and Tim Choate Circle Hooks

Today a person would be hard-pressed to find a tackle box outfitted for ocean fishing that didn't have circle hooks in it. It was not long ago that circle hooks were not real popular. They were used for deep dropping and for long lines. Eventually it became mandatory to use circle hooks for bottom fishing in the Gulf of Mexico. Everybody on the Atlantic side was using j-hooks. We caught a lot of sailfish and other kinds of fish, and we were proud of the ones we released. We knew that they would bleed for a while, but we believed they would recover from the damage of the j-hooks.

I was at the Miami Beach Rod and Reel Club when the two guest speakers were Tim Choate and Captain Ronnie Hamlin. They came to the Rod and Reel Club to talk about using circle hooks for billfish. Tim Choate was a founding member of The Billfish Foundation, a notable conservationist, and an early advocate for the use of circle hooks. Ronnie Hamlin, known among the sportfishing enthusiasts as Captain Hook, was one of the foremost bill fishermen in the world, having caught upwards of 30,000 billfish in his life, and the owner of many world records. He too was early to catch on to the benefits of circle hooks.

The two men had worked with Eric Prince to prove that sailfish caught on j-hooks frequently died from injuries within a day or two from the time they were released. Conversely, sailfish caught on circle hooks had a ninety-seven percent survival rate. They demonstrated that using circle hooks was the future of catch and release so we could have greater fishing in the future.

I listened. I knew that many of the sailfish that were caught on j-hooks bled a lot, and that bothered me. I was interested in trying these circle hooks. Ronnie told me that I should use Eagle Claw 7/0 circle hooks. I went to the tackle shop and saw that 7/0s were much bigger than the hooks we used on our live bait, so I bought 5/0 circle hooks instead.

Then I took Rob Cohen and his son out fishing a few days later. We hooked a double header of sailfish on these 5/0 circle hooks, and both of them came off. I was disgusted. Here was a valued customer with his son; his son's first ever attempt to catch a sailfish, and we lost it because of those dumb circle hooks. I threw the whole box of circle hooks overboard, put out the j-hooks, and caught some more sailfish.

Now I was bothered. Every time I caught a sailfish and it bled, I just knew that I needed to try circle hooks again. But I had tried them, and they had failed. I was thinking I couldn't let my customers down by not catching fish, but these j-hooks are killing the fish. What was I going to do?

One day we hooked up to a little white marlin, maybe twenty-five pounds. This beautiful fish jumped and carried on. It was all lit up, and it was beautiful. We got it up to the boat and I grabbed the leader and pulled. I felt a pull in the leader and blood just poured out of this little white marlin; just solid red running down both sides of the fish. It swam in the water, but I knew it was going to die. I cut it loose and watched it more sink out of sight than swim out of sight. That was the coup de gras. I just had to figure out these circle hooks.

Not too long afterwards I was running down the beach in the morning, and everybody was catching sailfish. I called up Steve Waters from the Ft. Lauderdale Sun Sentinel, but he couldn't get away. I called up Sue Cocking from the Miami Herald and told her the sailfish were biting red hot, and asked if she could go out in the afternoon. She said, "Sure."

I decided we would go out and test circle hooks again. I now had 7/0 Eagle Claw, non-offset circle hooks. We fished a j-hook and a circle hook on the flat lines, and a j-hook and a circle hook on the kite. At the end of the afternoon we had caught six sailfish on the circle hooks and five sailfish on j-hooks. The only sailfish we lost was on a j-hook, and that was because the leader broke. At the time I just thought it was: oh well, the leader broke. Happens all the time. I learned later that it could have happened because the j-hooks catch down inside the fish, and they can fray the leader off on the raspy surface of their bills. It turned out that using j-hooks increases the leader damage when catching fish. So then I went around telling everybody that we caught more fish by using circle hooks than using j-hooks.

We did more and more experimenting with circle hooks. I fished with Eric Prince and did a bunch of tagging studies on sailfish. We were involved in a study on circle hooks and j-hooks, and we proved again and again that circle hooks were very efficient at catching sailfish. With circle hooks almost every sailfish was hooked in the corner of its mouth, and the survival rate would be much better. I became a champion of circle hooks.

I caught a swordfish on a j-hook and cut it open. The j-hook had come through the belly of the swordfish and ripped the liver to shreds. It was evidence of a fish swallowing a j-hook, and then being severely damaged by the hook down in the internal organs. But when a fish swallows a circle hook, and the hook gets caught in the gullet, the hook will be turned back on itself, and can do no more damage.

The bottom line is: we proved that circle hooks is the way to go, and I am an extreme proponent. I can't say how many heated discussions I have gotten into trying to get people to switch to circle hooks. It even almost came to blows with my fellow committee members on the Miami Billfish Tournament. I said we needed to go to circle hooks. Fortunately, with Joan Vernon as my partner in crime, we finally got the Miami Billfish Tournament to switch to circle hooks.

This inspired the Ft. Lauderdale Billfish Tournament to switch to circle hooks. This inspired the National Fisheries Service to make circle hooks mandatory in all billfish tournaments in the Atlantic Ocean and the Gulf of Mexico.

Now everybody fishes with circle hooks. They are perfectly happy with them and most guys wouldn't want to give them up. Circle hooks are good for the future of fishing, and I am proud that I was a good follower of Captain Ronnie Hamlin and Tim Choate. Nobody could ever thank those two enough for what they brought to the angling world.

Heather's Sailfish

It has been fifteen years or more since I met Heather Harakvey. Heather and her father, Jeff, fished with me on numerous occasions. Jeff was very involved in the IGFA, and his daughter was using her fishing accomplishments to show dedication to something as a youth growing up, as a way of improving her chances for college admission. In addition to that, Heather absolutely loved to fish.

When I first started to fish with Heather, she wanted to catch world's records on just about any kind of tackle. And we did catch several world records with her. I think we caught one for grouper; and I know we caught one for sailfish. But the one about sailfish was a sad story. We were on our way to fish for permit about thirty-five miles south of our dock on Miami Beach. So, it's a good long run. We got about half way down and Heather complained that she was feeling queasy. She asked if we could please stop where we were and perhaps fish for a little while, and if she didn't feel any better, we would have to call it a day. At any rate, we gave it a shot hoping she would recover and we could stay out. (It's an interesting sidebar: people usually don't get seasick when they're running fast; they get seasick when the boat stops.)

We changed course, ran out to 200 feet of water and put out some live baits. In very short order a sailfish ate one of our baits. Heather grabbed the spinning rod and started fighting the sailfish.

Every time it jumped, my mate, Steve Huddleston, or I would comment on how huge this sailfish was. Heather was always pursuing records, and junior record fish for kids sixteen and under do not have to be killed. We can weight the fish at sea, let it go, and turn in the record application. The fish would still have to be weighed on certified scales, so if we caught an eighty-pound fish, but only had a sixty-pound scale, the only way to weigh it would be to use two scales, typically one on the head and one on the tail. We just lift the fish straight up and get its weight.

Eventually Heather wore down the sailfish to where Steve could get a hold of the bill. We set up two ropes in loops so we could wrap them around the bill and the tail, and slipped our scales into a loop in the rope. Steve picked up the bill of the fish, and I picked up the tail. The combined weights were ninety-four pounds. We put the fish back in the water and towed it around a little bit to revive it, and then we picked it up again. Ninety-four pounds. We put it back in the water, revived it again and picked it up again. Ninety-four pounds. We did not put it in the boat; we kept it over the water. We put it back down, removed the tail rope, and tagged it with a Billfish Foundation tag. We had all our photographs; we measured the length and girth, and made sure it was swimming real well, and sent it on its way. We were thrilled. We had a potential junior world record Atlantic sailfish: ninety-four pounds. The existing junior female world record sailfish was sixty-seven pounds, so we beat it by just shy of thirty pounds.

We continued fishing and caught a big blackfin tuna, not quite big enough for a record. We stopped and tried for a tarpon on the way in, but had no action there. Still we called it a very successful day. And by the way, once we stopped and started fishing, Heather felt fine and got through the rest of the day with no problems.

Since then she has caught many permit, and I must say that by the time she reached eighteen years of age and graduated from high school, she had 100 IGFA world records. We caught numerous world record horse eyed jacks, and she caught world record groupers, and all different kinds of fish.

104

But there was one bitter note to all this. This beautiful sailfish was disqualified as a world record because, by federal law, you cannot remove a billfish from the water if you do not intend to harvest it. We never brought the fish into the boat, but we did lift it out of the water, and that broke a federal law. To Heather's credit, her response to that was, "I have enough world records for a lifetime. I'd rather have that fish alive to catch another day than to kill it for a piece of paper."

That was very honorable on Heather's part, but a heartbreaker for all of us at the time. But the law is the law. And that law is a very good one because it discourages people from removing billfish from the water to take a picture and then throw them back overboard. Scientific proof now shows that by removing a billfish from the water for any reason, whether it's for scientific research or photographs, no matter how gently, there's a good chance that it will not survive. We want to preserve as much population as we can. There is an organization called Keeping Them Wet that encourages people to not harm fish by taking them out of the water unless they intend to harvest them.

Birthday Sailfish

John Watson came from England. Over there he was a Pike guy. They call it course fishing; dead baiting for Pike. He would get groups of Englishmen together and bring them to Miami to go fishing for a week or two. His format was to bring a total of seven guys, himself included. He would have two flats boats with two men on each, and me taking three guys offshore. They would switch around; some would go offshore, and some would fish for bonefish and tarpon on the inside.

It was April 29th, my birthday, and I took the three Englishmen out. It was the first time in my career that we caught ten sailfish. On top of the ten sailfish we also had yellowfin tuna, big dolphins, big kings, and blackfin tunas. It was a phenomenal day of fishing. We got back to the dock and those crazy Englishmen said, "Hey that was really good, but we don't want to catch any sailfish tomorrow. We want to do something different."

I was floored. We caught ten sailfish and they didn't want to do it again. As sometimes happens in nature, the next day the wind quit, and the water got dirty. We went shark fishing and caught a bunch of hammerhead sharks. So they were thrilled. But what a birthday that was catching my first ten sailfish.

Another time on my birthday it was flat calm and we were fishing off Key Biscayne, using live herring. We might have had the kite up, but I can't be sure. At any rate we caught six sailfish. We didn't get a tag into one of them, but we tagged the other five. What was really neat was that two of the five fish we tagged already had tags in them. One of the tags was from Trinidad, which is way down in the windward islands of the Caribbean. The other sailfish had been tagged in Islamorada, and still had the hook in his mouth with the wire from where the ballyhoo was tied on. The Caribbean tag was less than a year old, and the Islamorada tag was several years old. So here was this hook that still had the wire and a little piece of the mono, and it had been a couple of years.

That was a couple of interesting birthday sailfish events. I always look forward to fishing on my birthday because I never know what's going to happen next.

My Worst Days

Terry J. Smith

February 3, 1982 was probably one of the greatest days in my life. At about 3:30 in the afternoon my wife, Ruth, gave birth to my beautiful son, Terry Jean Smith. He started in life with a few physical challenges, nothing major, just typical kids stuff. Early in life he had an interest in doing everything Daddy did. He wanted to fish.

Terry was very creative as a young boy. When he was five years old he went into the garage and found some scraps of wood. He made an image of a sailfish that still hangs on my wall today. It was a challenge at times because I wanted him to love to fish, and there may have been times when I pushed too hard. I might ask something like, "Hey, Rob and Ben are going fishing today, do you want to go?"

And what I got as a reply might be, "No I don't feel like fishing today."

I'd ask again, "Are you sure you don't want to go fishing with us?"

Then when I'd come home he'd tell tales of spending all day trying to catch bass on his own in the canal behind our house. He liked doing things on his own. He loved to dig in the back yard and work with his GI Joes, and his Legos, and Lincoln Logs. And like all little boys he had bugs, and all kinds of creatures he thought were pets. He had chameleons on leashes several times as he was growing up. He went through a few dogs. His favorite dog was Dreyfus, and we had a cat named Caz.

An interesting challenge with him happened one day when we were out with a charter. We were with Steve Waters and Doug Olander. They were trying to get pictures for an article on surface lures for bonitos. I had five or six spinning rods set up and a plug rod, all with surface plugs. We finally found a school of bonitos and everybody started grabbing rods. In short order the only rod left was the plug rod, and the only person left without a rod was Terry. I started to say, "You can't use that." But my words turned into, "Well here, let me show you how it works." His casts that day were five feet and ten feet with a few backlashes. But from that day forth, I couldn't get a spinning rod in his hand. He wanted to fish with that plug casting reel all the time, and he got really good with it.

Then he moved on to a fly rod, and he got good with that too. The South Florida Fishing Club had an award for the most accomplished angler catching fish on fly rods, plug rods, spinning rods, and bait. Terry would qualify with fly rod, and plug rod, and bait with no problem, but he wouldn't use the spinning rod. He thought it was too easy. Everybody else used it, so to be the independent soul, he had to use the fly rod and plug rod.

His interest in fishing drifted away, as his interest in dinosaurs exploded. He grew up in the days of Jurassic Park, and in high school he got involved in the Graves Museum in Dania Beach. There he met Bobby DePalma, and they became the processors of all the dinosaur bones coming in from Wyoming. They would clean and stabilize the bones, and patch the damage to the bones to be put on display in the Museum.

When he got into high school, Terry was selected to go out to a prehistoric riverbed in Lusk, Wyoming, in the southeast corner of the state, to dig for dinosaur bones. They would just sit down and work bones out of the dirt all day long. It was tedious work, but very rewarding. They recovered thousands of dinosaur bones, mostly myosaurus, better known as the mother dinosaur. He became addicted to the Rocky Mountains and dinosaurs.

I felt very fortunate when our summer vacations became trips to the Rocky Mountains. We went to Colorado and Wyoming, Idaho and Utah, Alberta Canada, and eastern British Columbia. It was such a treat to see all this beauty and these ancient mountains. We drove from site to site where there were footprints at Dinosaur National Monument. We would stop on the side of the road and Terry would go walking off. He would come back with what looked like a rock and say, "This is a dinosaur bone. I can tell because it sticks to my tongue." He progressed over the years to where he found a half of a T-Rex tooth, in Drum Heller, Alberta, Canada.

He was on all these dig sites and made a really nice life for himself. He climbed the back of Mt. Rushmore, and he trudged through the jungles of Costa Rica. He and his buddy, Bobby, dreamed of the island where Jurassic Park was, and how it could become a reality one day.

Their most significant find happened in South Dakota. Bobby was negotiating with the rancher to be able to work his cattle ranch to look for dinosaur bones, which could only be harvested from private land. It was forbidden to take them from federal lands. While Bobby was negotiating with the rancher, Terry was kicking around a watering hole when he noticed a piece of a triceratops. That's the dinosaur with the frill around the back on their head and the three big horns. By the time the summer was over, they had recovered sixty percent of the bones from this watering hole triceratops. They had all of the head, all of the spine and the ribs, and two legs from one side of the dinosaur, but did not find the other side. They processed these bones, and stabilized and repaired them. They painted a backboard and made a metal frame, and set each bone in place. The display had a triceratops skeleton with the flora and fauna of sixty-five million years ago in the background, and the two painted legs looked like they still had skin on them. It was quite the creation. It was shown in museums all over the country. It was something for them to be very proud of.

He came home for Christmas vacation from Bozeman, Montana, where he was going to college. He had to show those kids back at school what a real fish looked like. They would come back after the weekends and brag about their twelve and fourteen inch trout. He wanted to catch a big tarpon to shut them all up. We went out by Haulover on a rather chilly night, and he caught about a 120-pound tarpon. We got a good picture of it that he laminated and took back to school. So every time these guys started talking about their big fourteen-inch trout, he would pull out the picture of the tarpon and say, "Are you talking about bait, or are you talking about fish?" It didn't necessarily make him popular with all these kids from Montana, but it certainly showed them what real fish looked like, and he had a lot of fun with it. He stayed at the University of Montana, Bozeman for one year, and then he went to Broward Community College after that. He found that Bozeman was too far from home cooked meals.

Terry and I took several trips up into Yellowstone National Park where we saw all the big game animals from moose to elk, to mule deer, to white tail deer, grizzly bears, black bears, coyotes, and buffalo. Yellowstone Park was such a beautiful place to spend time. It left me with some very fond memories.

Terry's last year, he left Miami about the first of June and drove out to South Dakota. He and Bobby went up to the cattle ranch. It was quite the site they had there. They had a sleeping tent, and a common area tent, like the cooking area, and a place to relax when it was raining, or when the sun was too hot. And they had a lab tent. They would get up in the morning, make breakfast, and on their walk down to where they were digging and working on their bones, they would pass rabbits and a burrowing owl. At night they slept under the stars most of the time. Once in a while they would have a rainstorm, which they considered a blessing because when it rained, it would uncover new dinosaur bones along the gulleys where there would be flash floods. They were always finding new dinosaur bones here or there. It was a productive summer.

On July 24th Terry called home and told his mom that they were going to get a U-Haul trailer, and start loading up their stuff. They planned to be home in about two weeks. An hour later Bobby

DePalma called my wife and informed her that our son had passed away. It turns out that he had misrouted blood vessels in his chest, and one of these blood vessels had kinked and shut off the blood supply to his heart. He had passed away walking out of the U-Haul rental place after renting a trailer. His good friend, Bobby, went to the hospital with him, and took care of all the arrangements out there. A week later Terry's ashes arrived in Miami. We had a beautiful memorial at the Miami Beach Rod and Reel Club. Hundreds and hundreds of friends showed up to give us support. I miss Terry dearly.

9/11

One thing we all remember is where we were on 9/11. What a tragic day in American history. I was in the Bimini Big Game Club with Scott Segal and a friend of his named Tom. We fueled up and left the dock about eight in the morning. We ran down south toward Beach Cay, which is about twenty-five miles away. We were anchored up fishing for yellowtails, and using yellowtails for bait targeting some barracudas, and sharks, and groupers, and the regular cast of characters from that area.

Scott had a satellite phone, and at about ten o'clock he called his office to check in with his people. The first thing we heard was, "Oh no, that can't be true. You've got to be kidding," and on and on. He was on the phone for about fifteen or twenty minutes, and he finally got off and told us about what had happened. Here we were in a foreign country fifty miles from home. What should we do? All of our families had to be in a panic. We were thinking we should probably get home, but we might not be able to. Maybe we should stay where we were for now.

We called everybody on the satellite phone to let them know we were OK. I got a hold of the dive boats over there on the radio and told them what happened. They were in disbelief, but unfortunately it was true.

We kicked it around, and I said I had to get home to my family. So we packed up our stuff and headed back to Miami. Scott and Tom

111

took a beating on the deal because now they were back in Miami, no longer fishing. All the airlines were grounded and it was hard to find a rental car. They were really in a pickle. Scott was a little upset that I didn't stay in Bimini with him, but by the same token, my wife and my son were grateful that I was back home with them.

It was such a tragic time in American history. We were in shock, but now we have gotten past it. We still live in the greatest country in the world and we have all these freedoms to travel wherever we want, whenever we want. We just have to take our shoes off at he airport now. But I'll never forget those who perished on that tragic day.

That's where we were on 9/11. I apologize to Scott and Tom, but I know I did the right thing by going home that day.

Trouble at the Pier

Ben-or was a really good client from Israel. He was a lot of fun, and a very intelligent man. He was an arms dealer for Israel to the Central American countries. He spoke fluent English and Spanish among others. He had a thirty-one foot Ocean Master that he kept up in Golden Isles, north of Haulover Inlet. We took it to the Bahamas many times, and fished off Miami plenty of times as well.

We were going out to Newport Pier at five o'clock in the morning to catch bait and then go offshore. We anchored up about 200 feet straight east of the pier and put a chum bag out. We were hoping to attract pilchards that we knew would probably show up just before dawn. There was another boat anchored about fifty feet northeast of the pier, and another on the north side of the pier.

We had the chum bag out, waiting with sabiki rigs and the cast net. Then some guy swam out to the boat, and into our chum line. We asked him to move on because he was scaring our bait away, so he continued swimming out toward the east. There started to be a ruckus on the pier, shouting that the guy was drowning, and we should rescue him. We knew the guy was OK, but they kept hollering on the pier. I asked Ben-or to shine the spotlight on the pier to see who was making all that noise. At about the time he was getting out the spotlight,

112

somebody jumped off the end of the pier. When Ben-or shined the spotlight up onto the pier the first thing we saw was a police officer's badge reflecting the light.

I got on the radio and called the boat on the north side of the pier and said, "That cop on the pier is concerned about these guys in the water. We better go get them. I'll get the one out here by me, and you go get the guy who just jumped off the pier."

We both pulled our anchors. I idled up to the guy who had been swimming around our boat and told him he had to get in the boat. He didn't respond very well, so Ben-or told him to come around the back where we had a boarding ladder. With that, the guy grabbed the side of the boat and did a pull up and climbed in the side of the boat, no strain, no pain.

The other boat picked up the other swimmer and pulled up to the beach and dropped him off. Our boat was bigger and the water was too shallow for us pull up to the beach. We had to stop because we were touching the bottom. I told the guy he had to swim the rest of the way into the beach. He climbed up onto the covering board and did a perfect dive, and swam into the beach.

Everything was done. The people were rescued, so I pulled around to the north side of the pier and anchored up again so we could start chumming again for our bait. The other boat came over and anchored up next to us.

By now it was 6:30 and I was on the phone, getting ready to go on the air with WIOD with the morning fishing report. The policeman came out. I said, "Give me just a minute. I'm doing a live radio show." I don't know what he said, if he even said anything.

At any rate I did the radio show at which point the policeman said, "Who is in charge of the boat?"

I said, "I am. It's not my boat, but I'm running it for the owner. The owner is right here."

He replied, "Consider yourself under arrest, and go to the Haulover fuel dock."

I said, "The Haulover fuel dock is very crowded on a Saturday morning. How about if I go to the boat ramp."

He said, "That's where I wanted to go anyway. Go over to the boat ramp."

So we pulled the anchor and headed for the boat ramp. The other boat that helped rescue people was also under arrest, so he pulled his anchor and headed for the boat ramp too. Just before we got to the inlet, the Florida Marine Patrol caught up with us. I stopped and told them I was going to the boat ramp.

They said, "OK, we'll follow you in."

So we idled into the ramp. When we got there they handcuffed us, told us again we were under arrest, and put us in the back of a squad car. We were taken to the North Dade County Metro Police substation. We were there for a couple of hours and then taken by squad car to the Dade County jail down by Jackson Memorial Hospital. There we were placed in a cell. Then later I was moved to another cell. About four o'clock in the afternoon a corrections officer came by and said, "Bouncer, is that you?"

I said, "Yeah."

He asked, "What are you in here for?"

I said, "My charges are resisting arrest without violence and failure to assist a police officer. "

He said, "Well, I'll get you out of here."

Five minutes later I was out of jail. The other guy had already gotten out. My sister was there waiting to get me out, and we went home.

The next morning I was scheduled to take twenty-five boats to Bimini, which I did. I was in Bimini for two days and my sister called and said, "You've got to get home right now. You're not allowed out of the country on account of these charges." So I packed up my family, my son and my wife, and I ran back to Miami.

A lawyer friend of ours met me at the dock and explained to me what was going on. He gave me the name of a friend who was a lawyer

114

for me to call. So I met with this other lawyer and he said, "The first thing you have to do is pay me seven grand."

I was scared. I had done nothing wrong. The swimmer was not drowning or in distress. When I learned that the officer wanted him picked up, I picked him up. I brought him as close to the beach as I could, and went back to fishing. The officer walked up when I was doing a scheduled radio show, and then I addressed the officer and he arrested me. At any rate, I ended up paying this guy seven thousand dollars.

There was a woman reporter for the Miami Herald who I had stopped to assist months before. She had been anchored right outside Haulover Inlet, and said I had to tow her in. I told her I could not tow her in because I had passengers on a charter, and it is against the insurance rules for me to tow anybody who is not in distress. I saw she was out of gas, but she was not in distress. I offered to call her a towboat if she did not have a radio. She told me that she didn't need anybody to call a towboat, but that I would regret this some day.

She got wind of this arrest and called Ralph Brown, the owner of Dusky and an important supporter and sponsor of mine. She made a big stink about how he was supporting me, and I was this criminal who was letting people drown in the ocean. He got mad at her for slandering me. He contacted her boss and she got suspended – rightfully so.

When I told my other lawyer friends about this lawyer charging me seven thousand dollars, they all had a fit and contacted him. He was done as my lawyer. I ended up doing some educational program for three or four nights. The other captain and I had to go to a class where they taught that I was a bad boy, and I shouldn't disrespect the law. We were never tried or prosecuted, or had charges filed for failure to assist an officer or resisting arrest without violence. How could we resist from the pier to the boat, or the boat to the pier? We did everything the officer said.

But anyway, it was really ugly, all these accusations of ignoring a guy who was drowning. Obviously he wasn't drowning. And there was no incident of resisting arrest. Nor did we fail to assist an officer; we did exactly as he asked.

It was quite an experience. It really traumatized my son, and my wife, and me, and I lost quite a few really good customers. But fortunately I had the backing of people like Ralph Brown and radio station WIOD, who defended me to the max. We got through it all and what is done is done. It was a stumbling time in my life. It was mentioned periodically for years, but fortunately I don't hear much about it anymore.

Everybody always wanted to know what happened. Well, that's what happened. There was no truth told in the charges, or in the newspaper, and that's the final word on it.

An interesting sidebar, while the other captain was in the prosecuting attorney's office, he overheard the prosecuting attorney encouraging the Florida Marine Patrol to say that I was running to escape when they stopped me on my way to Haulover. They said there was no way they were going to do it, because it wasn't evident in any way, shape, or form. So obviously there were some people who were out to get me.

But I really want to thank Ralph Brown and the people from WIOD. And I'm thankful it's behind me and that I survived another challenge in life. That's the story of the pier.

Tragedies in Bimini

Since 1968 I have been enjoying the beautiful destination of Bimini in the Bahamas Islands. And even though it is one of my favorite places to go, two of my worst days in boating, fishing, and guiding took place there.

I was running a twenty-eight foot Bertram at the time, and had a rancher from south Broward County charter me. He had been in the hospital with stage four cancer and was still in bad shape. He had real ugly tumors on the bottoms of his feet. Just to keep baby food down in his stomach his girlfriend had to inject medicine into his stomach

116

before he ate. And that was all he could eat. We would go to dinner and he would sit there sipping a glass of water while we ate.

He took himself out of the hospital and chartered me to take him and his girlfriend to Bimini, to fish and stay at the Compleat Angler for three days. Toward the end of the third day they were fishing and snorkeling, and we went back to Bimini to pick up our gear to head back to Miami. He said, "Bouncer, I want to stay two more days. Here's the cash to cover it." I didn't have anything else booked, so I called Miami and told them we were staying two more days.

First we went out fishing, and then he suggested we go snorkeling up toward Atlantis. Atlantis is a famous, mythical, underwater rock formation off North Bimini. I moved slowly into about twenty feet of water and got us into some nice coral bottom. He said, "Let's snorkel here." I would drift and he would snorkel and hold on to a rope on the back of the boat. He could dive down and look at stuff and come back up. He pulled out his gear bag, but the strap on his girlfriend's mask was broken. So we were down to one mask. He said to his girlfriend, "Well I'm going to go snorkel. Do you mind if I go alone for a while?"

She said, "Whatever you want. We're here for you to have some fun." So he put on the mask and fins and jumped into the water. He swam around and dove down and swam around some more. He acted like he had something in his hands, and he was kicking real hard right behind the boat. He grabbed the rope and was holding on and still kicking his fins. But it appeared that he had something heavy under his arm.

I said, "What have you got there? Hand it to me and I'll put it on the boat for you."

He exhaled and let go of the rope and sank feet first out of sight, and didn't come back up. I waited a minute and a half or two minutes and swung around to where I thought he had gone down. I grabbed the mask with the broken strap and jumped overboard to look for him. His girlfriend got on the radio and called 'mayday'. I couldn't find him, and as I climbed back in the boat here came a boat full of divers. I told them he went down right on that ledge. They went in and he was right straight under their boat. They brought him back up and took off for North Bimini. We followed them in as the doctors on the boat worked on him. They pronounced him dead.

His ranch manager chartered a plane and flew by air ambulance and picked up the body and his girlfriend. They had to take him to Nassau for an autopsy. While they were there the girlfriend and ranch manager were placed on house arrest in their hotel until the autopsy was completed and the officials cleared them of any responsibility in his death. But I know deep down inside my heart, and I know the girlfriend felt the same way, that he was dying in the hospital, and he chose to die on the beautiful reefs in the Bahamas. It's an event I'll never forget, but that's how life goes along sometimes.

I had another tragedy in Bimini. I was over there with George Poveromo doing a Saltwater Sportsman/George Poveromo Fleet Outing. Among those in the fleet was Sue Cocking from the Miami Herald and a guy named Paul from Evinrude up in Wisconsin. Paul was my guest for the day, as was Sue Cocking. We went and caught live pilchards, and while we did that Paul was telling us how he had a history of minor strokes, getting blood clots in his legs. He had medication and had not had a problem for a while.

We went to a sunken airplane and chummed a little with live pilchards. The mangrove snappers came up and Sue was catching them on DOA Terrorize, and Paul was catching them on live pilchards. We caught some nice mangroves and decided after a while to go on looking for bigger things. So we anchored up on a place called the barge, a sunken barge ten miles east of the North Bimini Rock. I started chumming and we caught a barracuda. Paul, who had never caught much of anything except these mangrove snappers, now graduated to a shark and caught one big one.

We left there and went to Hens and Chickens, which is a reef southwest of Great Isaacs Light. Our goal was to catch an amberjack for Paul, and for Sue to catch an amberjack on fly. We chummed up a bunch of yellowtails and put them in the live well. We kept catching yellowtails, and I knew that soon enough the amberjacks would show up. So we would put a yellowtail on a fifty-pound outfit. Paul would put the yellowtail out and let it go behind the boat a bit, and the amberjacks would come after it. He caught two or three amberjacks, while Sue tried and tried to get an amberjack on fly. They were just boiling on the yellowtail, but she could not get the fly in the right place at the right time.

There was to be a cocktail party back at the hotel, and it was Evinrude's turn to host the party. I had to be there for the party too, so we decided we had to wrap it up and head back to Bimini. I picked up the fly rod and threw that popping plug as far back as the line was stripped off, and I gave it a good hard chug and started to wind the line in. I gave it another good hard chug and an amberjack came up and engulfed it. It started burning off to the west, so I pulled the anchor and turned the boat around and headed west. Paul and I went up to the bow.

We glided over a beautiful reef. There wasn't a cloud in the sky or a breath of a breeze. The water was gin clear, and Paul and I were admiring this reef. The sea fans, and the coral, and the beautiful fish were simply amazing. It was just the most beautiful day. We were talking about how lucky we were to get to come down to Bimini. Paul was talking about how he wanted to bring his two sons to Bimini so they could experience all this.

We weren't making enough progress on the amberjack so I told Paul to crank up the boat so we could finish him off and run back to Bimini. Paul went back and bumped the boat up a couple of times. I got the amberjack up to the surface and began walking down the side to lift him into the boat. I wanted to get to the back of the boat. The configuration was such that there was a narrow passage to get past the helm. As I tried to pass, Paul had rolled around, still holding the steering wheel, but blocking my way. I said, "Paul, I have to get by." No response. "Come on, Paul. Let me get by and get this fish in the boat so we can get on our way." Then I realized he had literally fallen into my arms.

So I had the fly rod, the amberjack, and Paul. I called Sue for help. Sue took the rod and I took Paul to the back of the boat. He had fallen unconscious. We laid him down on the deck, propped his feet up, put a pillow under his head, and put some water on his shirt to cool him down.

I started back toward Bimini and was calling on the radio for help. Alan Wenchel, who is a paramedic, came back on the radio and gave us advice like give him a drink with sugar in it, keep him cool, try to get him to respond in any way. Paul gurgled and mumbled a couple of times, but he didn't really say anything. We ran as fast as we could to Bimini, and when we got to the Big Game Club, Alan Wenchel and an emergency room doctor jumped on the boat. They started working on Paul. Somebody called the Coast Guard and was told that because we were already on an island it was not a Coast Guard responsibility. We knew we needed medical help right away. The emergency room doctor worked at Mercy Hospital in Miami. He called them and they sent over an air ambulance that took Paul back to Mercy for two weeks. Then they flew him to Wisconsin for two weeks, and then he passed. He never regained consciousness. It was such a bummer because here was a nice young man with a couple of sons, over in Bimini, experiencing a beautiful day, and in the middle of all that he passed away.

I think it happens with all charter boats at one time or another that they lose a client, but I can tell you from my own experience it's not something I would wish on anybody to have to deal with.

Bob and Judy Lewis / Kite Fishing

Back in the early 1950s, Bob Lewis was trolling down to the Ocean Reef Club, or the Key Largo Anglers' Club, I'm not sure which, for a week of fishing. He trolled down the reef, and when he got down close to Key Largo he put out live blue runners on the outriggers to fish for sailfish. To the south he could see Tommy Gifford with some red contraption in the air. Every time he turned around, Tommy had a sailfish on. Bob kept his bow pointed at Tommy Gifford so his people wouldn't see that Tommy was catching sailfish one right after another, while Bob and his party were not having that much luck.

At the end of the day Bob went into Key Largo to spend the night, and he looked up Tommy Gifford. He asked what in the world was he doing with that red thing in the air, and how do you catch so many sailfish. Tommy told him that if he suspended live pinfish from a kite, the live bait splashed around at the surface and attracted the sailfish.

Tommy was building kites out of scarfs with sticks from the five and dime store. He was making kites, and he would take them out and test them. One would fly, but one wouldn't, and he would have to go back and rebuild it or reengineer it. Then he would get one that would fly. As a matter of fact, that night Tommy Gifford gave a kite to Bob Lewis.

A couple of years later, Bob Lewis' father had a heart attack and needed something to do at home in the leisure of the garage, as opposed to going to work everyday. Bob had been experimenting and had figured out a way to make collapsible, dependable fishing kites out

121

of fishing rod blanks and certain fabric materials. He was making kites that could be disassembled, rolled up, and put away. They would consistently fly quite dependably. Bob would sell these kites to all the tackle shops and the charter boats, and his father would build them in the garage. This became the Bob Lewis Fishing Kite Company, with permission from Tommy Gifford to merchandise the kites.

Bob Lewis became 'Mr. Kite'. As time passed he developed heart trouble and had to have a transplant. His care nurse all during his transplant and recuperation was a young lady named Judy. After Bob had recuperated, he married Judy. After his father passed away, Bob sold the rights to the Bob Lewis Fishing Kites Company to Pompanette for a set number of years.

When Bob left the hospital he was looking for something to make an income. Pompanette's exclusivity rights for the kites had run out, and they were not keeping up quality control. So Bob went into competition with them and in short order Pompanette quit making the kites. It was back to Bob Lewis Fishing Kites being the premier fishing kites all over the east coast of the United States. Most kites were flown in Dade and Broward Counties, but there were some flown up in the Carolinas, and even some up into Canada for bluefin tuna fishing.

When Bob married Judy, in his vows he promised that he would catch her a bonefish, a sailfish, and a tarpon. On their honeymoon Judy caught a bonefish. So that was off the list. Now Judy was due a sailfish and a tarpon. But they were so busy making kites that they never had time for themselves. I kept egging them on, "Come on, let's go catch Judy a sailfish." But they kept making excuses. So, I guess I tricked them. I called them up and said I was really in a bind. My son wanted to catch his first sailfish. There was no school on the following Monday, and I wanted to take my son and his buddy out to try to catch a sailfish, but I needed somebody to help me out. Was there any way that Bob and Judy could go with me?

Bob said, "Sure, we'll come with you and see if we can help." Long story short, we tried to put the kite up, but the wind quit and it was slick glass calm. Helium, which can be used in balloons to simulate a kite, wasn't around yet to speak of. I think it was on the backburner of the most innovative kite fishermen. The bottom line was, we fished flat lines with live herring. Terry caught his first sailfish, and then Judy caught her first sailfish. And then the sailfish quit biting. So Terry and Judy caught their first sailfish, and they were thrilled. But neither one of them was caught on a kite. Here I was with the man for kites, Bob Lewis, and both my son's and Judy's first sailfish were caught on flat line herring.

Now Judy still needed to catch a tarpon. We went back to the same game. "Come on Bob and Judy. The tarpon are biting let's go catch one."

"No, we're too busy. I wish we could make it. No we can't make it." So, I tricked them again. I called up Bob and told him I was really in a bind and that I had to have a story out on catching tarpon by the first of the week, and I didn't have the photographs, and can't sell the story without photographs. I said I was not busy on Monday night, and asked if he and Judy could go out and help catch a tarpon and get some photographs for this magazine article I wrote. Bob and Judy relented and said they would come with me.

Bob, Judy, and I headed out tarpon fishing at five o'clock in the afternoon. We ran from Haulover Inlet down to Government Cut. We put out a couple of live mullets that we slow trolled. There were two or three boats there, but nobody was getting any bites. There were plenty of tarpon rolling, but they weren't biting. So, after a little while with no bites, Bob said, "Hey, did you ever use a kite for tarpon?"

I said, "Yeah, I've used a kite on occasion for tarpon. I don't do it all the time, but every once in a while I'll pull it out." So we went back to trolling around with our live mullet. The tarpon continued to roll, but not bite.

Bob asked, "Hey, Bouncer. Do you have your kites on board?"

I replied, "Of course, Bob. I always have my kites on board." We trolled around some more with our flat line mullets, but we didn't get any bites.

123

It was not too much later when Bob said, "You know, Bouncer. I think there's enough wind that a kite would fly tonight."

I said, "Yeah, Bob, You're probably right. There's probably enough southeast breeze to get the kite to fly, I imagine." We trolled around some more. The other boats were trolling around, and still nobody was getting any bites. I said, "Hey Bob, how about we put the kites up?"

He said, "Doggone, I thought you'd never ask!" We launched the kite. We put the line in the kite clip and ran it out, and no sooner got the mullet out there on the kite and Bam! We caught a tarpon on the kite. After we caught that nice seventy-five or eighty pound tarpon, Judy Lewis' first tarpon ever, we put the kite up again, and Pow! We got another tarpon, and got it up to the boat and released it, and we called it a night. All the other boats out there fishing had not had a bite yet.

There was a lot of proof that the kite had a lot to do with it, but I always get a kick out of the fact that Bob Lewis promised Judy a bonefish, a tarpon, and a sailfish in their wedding vows. Everybody catches sailfish on a kite, but Judy and my son both caught theirs on a flat line. And everybody flat lines for tarpon, and Judy caught her first two tarpons on a kite. It just goes to show that you're never too old to learn new tricks to catch more fish.

Put the Camera Strap Around Your Neck

A fellow called me from Orlando and booked me for a full day on a Saturday. He and his buddy showed up in the morning and loaded their equipment on board and we took off. The fellow who booked me made it a point that his friend was doing him a solid, and he wanted to make him the primary angler.

We started out targeting tarpon and set up on the south side of Government Cut. In short order we hooked a really nice tarpon. So the guest of honor had been fighting the tarpon for a while and after it had jumped a few times he asked the host if he would grab his 35-millimeter camera to see if he could get some pictures. So the host grabbed the camera, wrapped the strap around his hand four or five times, and tried to get some shots of the tarpon jumping or rolling, or the angler fighting the fish. The angler said, "Please put the strap around your neck."

The host said that he had everything under control, that he would not drop the camera. The guest again asked, "Please put the strap around your neck."

Again the host assured him that he had everything under control and not to worry about a thing, everything was in good shape. This banter kept going back and forth, the guest insisting that he put the strap around his neck, while the host continued to insist that the camera strap was firmly wrapped around his hand and nothing could happen.

The conversation became more heated with the guest becoming more insistent that his host put the camera strap around his neck, and

125

the host being equally obstinate that he had a firm grip on the camera and would not drop it. He said, "I've got the strap wrapped around my hand four times, it ain't going nowhere. Quit giving me a hard time and fight your fish."

The fight with the fish went on and on, as did the argument between the two guys. The fight with the tarpon took an hour. It was a really nice tarpon. We got a leader on it and brought it up close enough so they could see it. The fighting with the fish was beautiful, but the argument about the camera never ended, and was becoming annoying. From the time he got the camera out of the bag, until we released the tarpon, all they did was argue. Once we released the tarpon guest said, "That's enough. Take me home. I've had enough of this BS about my camera."

I said, "Are you sure you want to go home? We've got hours left to fish."

He said, "No! Take me home."

So the host said, "Ok, let's go home. I don't want to upset him anymore."

I ran back to the dock. It was a very short run, less than a mile. As soon as I backed into my slip, the angler/guest grabbed his couple of items and headed out to the parking lot. The host settled up for the trip and said, "Boy, I don't know why he's so upset. He's so volatile. He was getting pretty crazy about putting the camera strap around my neck." Then kind of regretfully he added, "But what would it have hurt to do what he asked?"

The host paid me and headed off to the parking lot. A couple of minutes later he came back and said, "I can't believe he drove off and left me here."

So I asked, "Oh, wow. How are you going to get back to Miami Lakes?"

He said, "Miami Lakes ain't nothing. This is a total tragedy."

I asked, "What's the problem?"

He said, "Well, my mother lives in Miami Lakes here in Dade County, but she's moving to Orlando a couple of hundred miles away.

126

I didn't have any way to move all her stuff, so I got my friend here to drive down from Orlando. We rented a trailer to hook up to the back of his car. We were going to go out this afternoon and pick up the trailer, then tomorrow morning we would load up and head to Orlando. Now he has gotten in his car and left. I'm stuck in Miami with no way to get to my mom's house, no way to tow the trailer, and no way to get to Orlando. What in the world am I going to do?"

That's the last I ever heard from those guys. But I guarantee if I ever fish with them again I'm putting that strap around his neck myself.

White Marlin on Orange Skirted Ballyhoo

Jack Plachter is a very well known private boat captain, very involved in the billfish trail all over the Bahamas. He won the Bahamas Billfish Championship, and he also fished out of Costa Rica and Panama. He's an all around great fisherman, great chef, and a great host on any boat he's on with his owners or his guests. Jack was mating for me on Jim Atrey's boat, the *Jennifer Lynn*, a forty-three foot Hatteras.

Years ago the Pompano Rodeo was a kill tournament: a point a pound. Being held in the middle of May, I thought we should go way offshore looking for a blue marlin, because if we caught one, it would be hard for anyone to beat us. One fish could be three or four hundred points. And if we didn't catch a blue marlin, that time of year we would still have a good chance at a big dolphin, maybe a white marlin or sailfish, at least a chance to catch some quality fish.

Jerry Webb, Terry Guthrie, and Mike Marino were fishing on a small boat. We had worked together through the Miami Billfish Tournament, the Ft. Lauderdale Billfish Tournament, and now the Pompano Rodeo, sharing bait, information, tackle or whatever we needed. We were in our last tournament of the series. They were live baiting, targeting kingfish and sailfish, and we were going offshore.

It was the first day. We had caught some big dolphin; they had caught some kingfish and sailfish. We were trolling with orange-skirted ballyhoo on the left long outrigger the whole time. That was a go-to bait for me; I never trolled without that bait in the water.

I was sitting up on the bridge at about 1:30 in the afternoon. Things were slow and I was daydreaming about this white marlin

128

coming up and eating my orange-skirted ballyhoo. Meanwhile Jack was down in the cockpit. He spent about a half an hour engineering this beautiful bait. He cut the dorsal fin off a schoolie dolphin and rigged it like a strip bait with a skirt in front of it. He would hold it in the water to make sure it was swimming real well. Then he'd bring it in the boat and fine tune it, and put it back in the water and make sure it was swimming better. He finally got it dialed right in where it was a beautiful bait and, lo and behold, he wound in the orange skirted ballyhoo.

Now I was certain that a white marlin was going to eat the orange-skirted ballyhoo any minute. But Jack wound it in and put it in the bait box and put his dorsal fin bait on the left outrigger. He cleaned up the cockpit and came up and sat at the top of the ladder.

I said, "Jack, you're not going to like this, but you've got to put that orange skirted ballyhoo back on the left rigger. You can put your bait on any other line but that left outrigger. A white marlin is going to eat that one."

Jack was livid. He stormed down off the ladder and pulled in his dorsal bait, and put the orange-skirted ballyhoo back on and ran it out, locked it up and turned to walk away. At that moment the line came out of the outrigger, and it was a tournament record white marlin. What a thrill it was!

(On the third and final day of the Rodeo Jerry, Terry, and Mike were in first place, and we were behind them by thirty-nine points. They got skunked that day and we caught a nice wahoo, but only 38 ½ pounds. They won and we came in second.)

And believe it or not, it wasn't my first successful premonition. When I was fishing out of Bud and Mary's in Islamorada, I had a dream where I was anchored up where a flat came in from our right, and there was a creek straight off the transom. We were looking for bonefish and this permit came along that bank and went up into that creek. I wound in a bait and cast it right over the permit's shoulder. The bait and the permit both sank out of sight, and that was the end of the dream. In the morning I told Sonny Eslinger about the dream and how vivid it was. That afternoon I went fun fishing with Big D up at Whale Harbor. I anchored the boat where this beautiful white sand was on the edge of a flat that ran for almost a mile. Where I anchored there was a creek running right up under the flats where the sand turned to grass. I was sitting there with a live shrimp on the bottom looking for bonefish. I looked over and here came this permit along the edge of the grass. I hurried up and wound in my line and put on a crab, and the permit turned and went up this side creek. So I threw the crab out and it sank out of sight, and the permit sank out of sight, and thump. I wound up and got him on. He took off east out into deeper water. We pulled the stake and took off after him and chased him down. I caught a thirty-pound permit on eight-pound test. Its mount is hanging on my wall even today.

That was another premonition that came true when that permit came down the bank, turned up the channel and I cast the bait, he sank out of sight, and I caught him. Don't ever disregard those premonitions, they may come true.

Clients

The Arosteguis

One of my favorite and most loyal clients is Dr. Marty Arostegui, who comes complete with his wife Roberta, son Martini, oldest daughter Alia, and Daniela the youngest. They live in Coral Gables. Marty and I have fished together since the beginning of time. He has a thirty-five foot Cabo, the *Timely Sale* that has twin diesels and a marlin tower. Some of my fondest memories are of his son and daughter, Martini and Daniela, when they were very young. They took gymnastics classes and brought their skill onto the boat. They would swing from support to support like a couple of monkeys. First they were into gymnastics, and then they were into wrestling, then chess, then just about everything else. Now they've been through college, and they're great young adults.

The family does some serious, hard-core fishing and has somewhat cornered the market on IGFA world records. Marty, who has already been inducted into the prestigious IGFA Hall of Fame, has 432 world records; Martini has 202, Roberta 196, and Daniela 17. Even Marty's brother, Gonzalo, has seven. I'm proud to say that I have been present when many of those records were made.

I've had great memories of fishing with the Arostegui family. One of those was from a day of slow trolling live speedos off Miami Beach. Up came a sailfish, and I believe it was Daniela who caught it. It put up a great fight and it was her first sailfish ever, and she did it all herself. The family were sticklers for IGFA rules. So, a half hour later here came another sailfish, and Martini caught his first sailfish ever. Then they looked up at me on the bridge and called up, "We're having a big argument down here in the cockpit – whose sailfish was the biggest?"

I said, "From up here in the tower, I can tell you for sure they were both exactly the same size." Talk about a diplomat, I was hitting them out of the park that day.

Another great time with Martini was when we were fishing off Key Biscayne on some shallow wrecks. Martini caught what I believed at the time was a junior world record, or peewee world record permit on a light spinning outfit. Anyone who has never caught a permit cannot appreciate what great fighters they are. Martini fought that fish forever. He was nearly ready to give up the ghost, but persevered. The fight took well over an hour, and in the end this brave young boy prevailed.

On one of our first trips with Martini when he was only about six years old, we were fishing off Key Biscayne, an easy run from their home Coral Gables. We were anchored on a wreck, fishing the bottom with a twenty-pound conventional outfit, and he got a strike. Marty aroused and yelled, "Martini, get it!"

And I was thinking, "Oh boy, this fish is getting away." So I ran over and pointed at the drag lever, and said, "Martini, pull this lever down to right here. Don't go any further." He backed the drag lever off until there was just a couple of pounds of drag. I said, "Pick up the rod and reel, and climb in the fighting chair with it." He did as I instructed. Then I said, "Now push the lever up and go to work on it." I'll be doggone if that kid didn't catch a twenty-pound mutton snapper. He was six years old with a twenty-pound outfit, and he caught it completely IGFA legal. What an event for any kid to have.

Another time when Martini was about eight years old we were fishing in the first Miami Swordfish Tournament in this century. We were on Marty's boat and it was some mighty rough seas. On board was my mate Ron Jon Cook, Marty and Martini Arostegui, and Daryl Keith from Atlanta, Georgia, the owner of Hydro-Glow fishing lights.

We headed out in eight-foot seas. The only way we could keep the line straight up and down was to back into the waves. We had two rods out with jugs on them, and two lines straight up and down. When the waves approached, the jugs would completely disappear up into the sky behind the boat. Then a wave would break against the back of the boat and the dive platform and throw spray all the way into the inside of the windshield about twenty-five feet from the stern. We all got soaked, but we hung in there. At the end of the night we had tagged and released two swordfish, which put Martini in first place.

Every boat that entered into the tournament got a bucket of Kentucky fried chicken, a case of water, and a case of beer. Nobody was drinking much beer, but we were drinking the water and eating the fried chicken. Well, Daryl Keith got seasick, and was losing his dinner over the side repeatedly. At the end of the night his new nickname was Chicken Chum One.

We were in first place. The wind the next morning was blowing even harder, and all the captains were calling each other on the radio: "You're not going out in this mess, are you?" "No way! I'm not going out there." I must have talked to fifteen different captains who weren't going to go out. But in the afternoon we all had to show up at the dock with our anglers to discuss what was going to happen. Maybe the tournament was over and we had won it. Who knows? But I'll be doggone if the charter boat *L & H* didn't come up to the dock, get their chicken, their beer and water, and take off fishing. Marty said that if they were going, we were going. We had the lead, and we had to defend our position.

That night thirteen boats went out. Daryl stayed at my sister's house, and my brother-in-law, Joe Singer, went with us as our backup mate. Again we were eating the fried chicken and drinking the water, but not having any of the beer. Before long Joe was seasick and chumming recycled chicken over the side. Well, guess what his nickname became – Chicken Chum Two. So, we had Chicken Chum One and Chicken Chum Two.

We got a bite and Martini ran down in the cockpit from up in the salon to fight the fish. He wound tight on the fish but it came off, and then a wave came roaring in behind the boat. He looked up at that

133

wave and ran into the salon and said, "If we get another bite, somebody else is catching it. I'm not going out there any more."

We fished for a couple more hours but didn't get any more bites. Joe started to feel tingly, which Marty diagnosed as low electrolytes, a dangerous situation. We ran back to the dock and got back in time to hear the crowd at Monty's, the restaurant behind the boat, when the Florida Marlins won the World Series that night. We went from winning the swordfish tournament to hearing about the Marlins winning the World Series. What a great evening that was!

Of the thirteen boats that went out that night, only two stayed out, and they didn't catch a fish. The end result was that we were the number one boat with two releases. Martini Arostegui, the only junior angler in the tournament, was the top angler. We won a pile of fishing tackle in that tournament, and a few dollars too. It was a hard fought tournament, but a lot of good memories too.

I talk about Marty everywhere I go. Marty allowed me to be witness to, in my opinion, the greatest angling feat of all time. Years before this incident, around 1999 or 2000, Martini said, "My grandpa caught swordfish in Cuba, and I want to go catch a swordfish." Marty relayed that to me, so we went out sword fishing and caught a hammerhead shark and a swordfish.

After Marty saw how we fished at night he said, "You know, I think we could catch one of those fish on fly." So, a couple of months later Marty called and said, "Martini is busy, he can't go, but my brother would like to go out, and we'd like to try to catch a swordfish on fly, and maybe catch some swordfish on bait."

We often fished off Key Biscayne in a place we called the Triple Lumps. But the area had stopped producing real well, so I was looking for a new place to try. On an earlier occasion we were four miles south of Haulover at 25"50'.000 north, and 79"51'.000 west, and the bottom looked really good. We had to name the waypoint to make it easy to work in Marty's GPS, so I named it the Haul O Swords for Haulover and all the zeros in the coordinates.

We went out this night with Marty with his brother, Gonzalo. We ran down off Key Biscayne, but didn't get any bites, so I decided we would try something else. I ran up north and got about a mile south of the Haul O Swords and started putting the baits out. Marty was setting up by the electronics and I asked, "Marty, how are we doing on the Haul O Swords?"

He said, "We're lined right up with it. Looking real good."

A few more minutes and we got four baits out and I asked again, "How we doing on the Haul O Swords?"

"Oh, we're looking real good. We're coming right up on it. We're doing great."

A few more minutes, again, "How we looking?"

"Oh, we're doing real great." All of a sudden, zing! And Marty said, "We're right at the Haul O Swords."

We hooked a swordfish and caught it. Gonzalo caught his first swordfish ever right at the Haul O Swords. We ran back to the south and put the baits out again. We went through the same rigmarole, "How we coming on the Haul O Swords?"

"We're going to be really close, just a hair outside. And we're going to be really close. We're almost there." And then, "Now we're right on the Haul O Swords." And zing!! We got another swordfish on. We caught that swordfish and we went home. We never did try the fly rod that night.

But then, the next time Marty said we were going to go he said emphatically, "We are going to fish the fly rod." So, Marty, Martini, and I headed out to Key Biscayne on *Timely Sale*. And here's something that makes this feat so amazing: Marty ties his own flies. He ties up his own leaders, which in fly-fishing is very complicated with tapers, and a bunch of knots, and everything else. Fly-fishing is one guy casting and retrieving the fly, and then when he hooks the fish, he fights the fish, and catches it. That's the principal of fly-fishing to the very max: when the angler ties his own fly, and rigs his own leader, and does the whole nine yards. This is what Marty did.

I made one tiny addition to his program: I brought some little, tiny, baby cyalume chemical light sticks. They were about an inch and a quarter long, and an eighth of an inch in diameter. Marty rigged a double fly, and we tied the light sticks between the two hooks. That gave the fly a little bit of glow.

So, we went to the spot. We put out a dead bait, and a live bait on floats far away from the boat and hung the Hydro Glow light in the water. Marty started making casts, and letting his fly sink to the 120-foot mark on his reel. The rules of IGFA say that that 120-foot mark has to be on the reel for IGFA legal fly-casting. He'd let it out, and he'd strip in forty or fifty feet, and he'd let it sink, and he'd strip in thirty, or forty, or fifty feet. And he'd keep doing that all the way back to the boat. He kept going through this routine. We had only been fishing for about thirty or forty minutes, and low and behold, Marty hooked a fish. The fish was violently jerking the rod. And I was thinking, 'It couldn't possibly be a swordfish, not in the first half hour of trying to catch a swordfish on fly.' And just about the time all that processed through my mind, the fish came off. So, Marty pulled up the fly, and seeing there was no damage to it, he went back to fishing.

He cast and retrieved for another hour and Bango! He's on again. I ran up to the controls to chase the fish. The fish was running north, and before I could put the boat in gear, Marty said, "Never mind, he's coming back this way." I stood up there ready to go on a moment's notice. The fish was getting closer and closer. Marty was having no trouble with it running around, or under the boat, or up to the bow. I came back and stood with Marty as he fought the fish. After an hour long fight, I guarantee they heard me all the way in Jacksonville while I hollered, "It's got a bill!" We pulled that swordfish into the boat. He had a forty-six inches lower jaw fork length. But he had to be forty-seven inches to keep him. We took a couple of quick photographs and let him go. All the time that Marty was fighting him, I was trying to wake up Martini, but he wouldn't wake up. After we released the fish, I finally roused Martini out of his sleep. And he actually caught a swordfish on the rigged squid that night.

That was in my opinion the most amazing catch in fishing history. He rigged his own fly, rigged his own fly leader, and cast and retrieved his own fly. He hooked his swordfish and then landed it from a dead boat.

I still fish with the Arosteguis. They're phenomenal anglers. They fish all kinds of fish, all over the world. Whenever we get together to sit around and talk about fishing, sooner or later it comes around to that swordfish.

We came in second in another swordfish tournament up in Pompano. We caught oodles of world records, and Marty was awarded the prestigious title of Met Master Angler. It has been a wonderful time fishing with the Arostegui family from Coral Gables.

King of Sweden

A couple of years ago we took out Martin and another gentleman from Sweden. They were writers and video producers. They had been to Cabo San Lucas and done a marlin story, and thanks to our good friend Dr. Russell Nelson, may he rest in peace, we got hooked up to take Martin and his partner to do a piece on broadbill swordfishing out of Miami. Dan Kipnis joined us in this, as he was a real good friend of Russell Nelson as well.

Martin had planned for four days of fishing. The first day we went swordfishing it was super rough and we didn't get any bites. The second day it was rough again, and we didn't get any bites. On the third day Russell couldn't join us. We headed out and it was still rough, and I turned back to the dock. I told the guys that the weather forecast for the next day was calm, and they could plan on four days of fishing. I told them that if the weatherman was right, we would fish all the next day and all night too, as long as it took until we caught some swordfish to make their story.

When we were getting ready to go, a good friend of ours, Cory Wayne Leonard, from Kansas, was helping us set up the tackle for the trip. He threaded the line through the guides on one of our night rods. Everybody knows that the line comes off the top of the reel, between the two rollers on the first guide, and then over all the other rollers and out the tip. Then we tie on the rig. He strung the guides and I tied on the Bimini Twist. I put on the wind-on leader and wound it onto the reel and put it aside. We didn't look at it all day long.

Sure enough, the next day was calm. We went out and started daytime swordfishing, but we weren't getting any bites. Martin came over to me and said, "Captain, the first day was really rough, and you said that was why we weren't catching anything. The second day was rough, and you told us the same thing. Now it's flat calm, so what's your excuse for not catching any swordfish?"

I said to Martin, "I checked the solunar table today and the moon will be on the other side of the earth at almost 2:00 p.m., and the swordfish will bite just about that time."

This is a major feeding time for fish and wildlife, and we have been following this lunar phenomenon as far back as the early 1970s. Captain John Callan, who owned two charter boats, the *Helen C* and the *Helen C II*, would come on the radio and say, "We're coming into a major feeding period, make sure your baits are good." Or, "We're coming into a minor feeding period, which is when the moon is at the horizon. Make sure your lines are in the water, because these are fine feeding times." John was staying home taking care of his wife, Helen, because she was real sick, so he broadcast on the radio from his condo on Miami Beach to update us on when these solunar periods were.

So, getting back to the story about Martin, I told him that at ten minutes till two the fish would bite. And it happened, at ten minutes till two, we hooked and landed a swordfish. It was only about ninety or a hundred pounds, but we had caught one, and they were thrilled. On the next two drops we had bites, but we didn't get tight on them. We fished out the rest of the afternoon with no action. At about six o'clock thirteen other boats showed up to fish a swordfish tournament. But nobody got any bites.

Martin came over and said, "OK, Captain. You called it really good this afternoon. What time are the swordfish going to bite next?"

I said, "They are going to bite about nine o'clock."

Sure enough, at about nine the radio came on, "Committee boat, we're hooked up. Committee boat, we're hooked up." Five boats hooked up on sharks or swordfish between quarter to nine and nine o'clock.

We didn't get a bite and I was starting to sweat bullets. Then at nine ten we hooked up and got a good swordfish on. We were fighting the fish and Martin said, "There's something wrong. This line is not feeling right coming through the guides."

I said, "No there can't be anything wrong. The line is brand new and in really good shape." But he insisted that there was something wrong.

I turned on the spotlight, and found that Cory had gone between the two rollers on the first guide and then up underneath all the other rollers except for the tip. The line was chewed to pieces. We quickly grabbed another rod and pulled the wind on leader off and cut it back. We pulled a hundred feet of line off the reel we had the fish on, and lowered it into the water. I was hand line fighting the swordfish with 100 feet of backup line, just in case. We tied the line that was on the rod with the bad guides to the rod where our line that went through the rollers the right way. We caught that 200-pound swordfish, and called it a night.

The rest of the night those other boats never got any more action. I had called the shot when the moon was directly underneath the earth, and I called it at moonrise. Just as the solunar prime time of the moon overhead was approaching the tournament hours ended.

It turns out that Martin was a good friend of the King of Sweden. He told the King that if he was coming to Miami to fish, that he should fish with me. Sure enough, I got a call from Martin that the King was coming to Miami and looking to go fishing, and I should expect a call from the King's Aide de Camp. The man called me and said something to the effect that they wanted to fish on a Wednesday and Friday.

We had to give them our names, addresses, and social security numbers in advance so they could do security checks on Abie and me.

139

So, we set up this trip. We went over to Fisher Island, tied up the boat at the prescribed time, seven thirty in the morning. The U.S. Secret Service guy, and the rescue diver came aboard. They opened up every hatch and decided they didn't have to dive under the boat. He had originally told us he would be diving under the boat to check the hull, but he decided against that because they were running a little late.

The Aide de Camp said they were going to the deli and would then be down to the boat. A short while later here came the Aide de Camp, and the Swedish Secret Service, and the King. The King and his Aide de Camp got on the boat. The U.S. Secret Service and the Swedish Secret Service got on a second boat. We left that marina and ran down to Key Biscayne to a house. We tied up there and the King's son came on board with a buddy of his, and we went out fishing with our secret service escort.

The Prince came to me and asked for a pen and paper. I gave it to him and he wrote one, two, three, four on four little pieces of paper and folded them up. He shook them up in his two hands. He held them up and he, and the King, and his friend, and the Aid de Camp each took a piece of paper. They all opened them up. Number one was the guest. Number two was the King; number three was the Aid de Camp, and number four was the Prince. And that was the rotation for the day. Everybody had an equal opportunity.

I took us to the *Ultra Freeze* and held the boat in position, and we started fishing a couple of flat lines and a bottom rod. We had really good fishing. We caught snappers, and amberjacks, and barracudas, and kingfish. A big silky shark showed up. The King had him on for a few minutes. He was obviously pretty good with a rod and reel, but the shark came off. Then we were fishing some more and the shark came back. But this time the guest was in rotation and he caught the big shark.

At one in the afternoon everybody was getting hungry. Abie and I had our lunch and we had already eaten, but no one else said anything about eating. Now everyone was ready to eat, but where was the bag of sandwiches? Nobody had it. Abie said nobody gave it to him. They searched the boat, and there were no sandwiches. So we called the other boat and asked if they had the bag of sandwiches. The bag had gotten on the Secret Service boat, and by the time we called they had eaten all the sandwiches. So our people didn't have anything to eat.

In the afternoon we caught a couple of sailfish, and a couple more sharks and called it a day. We had a very good day of fishing. We cleaned up some fish for them to have for dinner and dropped everyone off at the house on Key Biscayne, and Abie and I went on our way alone.

The second day we had a little more wind, so we targeted sailfish more aggressively. The Aide de Camp and the King each caught. The King had showed good form when he had that shark on the previous day, but on twenty-pound test he was pumping that rod so fast that he was just peeling line off. I didn't want to call across the boat about how to pump and wind, so I told Abie to go over and tell him how to do it. So Abie went over, and was about to say, "If you would . . ."

Abruptly the King said, "No! I've got it."

Abie backed away and said to me, kind of joking, "You set me up one that one, didn't you."

The King had a good idea of the principles. He had obviously been taught by someone how to fight fish, but there were some flaws in the training. At his level, with the respect he was due, it was hard to approach the subject of improving his style. The important thing was the King successfully caught a sailfish.

He was a very fine gentleman. Everybody was treated absolutely equal on the boat. There was no 'I am the King'. It was a trip I will always remember that we were honored to fish with the King of Sweden, and everybody had a great time.

Don and Sandra Blake

Sandra Blake, what a sweetheart! Don Blake was a member of the Miami Beach Rod and Reel Club who fished with me for years. He went up to Cape Cod and brought back a wonderful young lady named

Sandra. She had extensive fishing experience, but no fishing knowledge. That means that she had gone fishing many times and probably caught many fish, but she had no knowledge of plug casting, or working artificial lures, or fly casting, or anything like that. She was now a member of the Miami Beach Rod and Reel Club. This club strived to create well-rounded anglers. So she had to learn all this different tackle. Don was an avid member of the club, and it was very important to him that she became versed in all the different kinds of tackle.

She would go out there and backlash her plug reel, or hook somebody in the ear with her fly. At first her plugs looked like they were dying, not attractive to fish. But she persevered and got better and better, and over time she was a major competitor in the International Women's Fishing Association, also known as the IWFA. To compete with these anglers she was up against some of the best women anglers in the world. They strive for really high catch counts.

Sandy would come fishing with Don, and my mate, and me. We would anchor off a shallow wreck and set out two flat line rods, and two rods on the bottom. Whenever a rod bent over Sandy had to run over and grab it. We would be yelling, "Bottom line on the right, top line on the left, top line on the right." Back and forth, just a mad scramble running from rod to rod. She would catch Spanish mackerel, small amberjacks that were five to fifteen pounds; she'd catch fifteen pound bonitos, or she'd have a thirty pound king mackerel, or a one or three pound yellowtail snapper. She would run around the boat, back and forth. And when she used up all the fish from one location, we would change to another spot and try to catch another kind of fish. In between we would have her fly casting, and spin casting, then plug casting – bluefish, tarpon, jack crevalles, dolphin, tunas; you name it, we beat this lady to pieces.

She was adamant about being great at what she did. She became a phenomenal angler in all aspects of the sport. They fished with us, and with Alan Sherman in the bay. They fished with Gill Torre down in south Biscayne Bay. They fished the canals behind their house for peacock bass, and before long Sandra Blake was one of the top award winners in the IWFA.

Whenever Sandra called me up the day after a fishing trip she would describe it only one way: how many Advil it took for her to get through the day. She had two Advil days, six Advil days, ten Advil days. But if anyone wanted to have a great time, Sandra Blake was the one to do it with.

Not to sell Don short, he had gone through times in his life when his COPD, or related illnesses, were so bad that he could not possibly wind in a decent fish. When this occurred Sandra would take care of him and whip him into shape, and before you knew it Don was catching sailfish and tarpon again. Then he would get an infection and take a turn for the worst, and would be back to just keeping score of whatever Sandra caught. Sandra would work on him again, taking him to the doctors and whatever else he needed. She would get him back in shape so he could get back in the action.

They had a funny thing they did. They lived in Homestead where there's a gas station down there that sells fried chicken. No matter what time they showed up in the morning or afternoon to go fishing, they always had a box of chicken for me, and homemade sandwiches for Abie and Don. The only exception was one night when they had won a prize where they got a big order of stone crabs from Joe's Stone Crabs. We went out tarpon fishing at night with Abie Raymond and his wife, Yudith, my sister Sue, and Don and Sandra, and more stone crabs and Key Lime pie than all of us could eat put together. And we even caught some tarpon that night too.

They retired and moved to Alabama, and there is nothing that brings more thrill to me than reading a Facebook post, or getting a note from them, because they were some of the greatest clients I ever had on the boat.

Mikey Falk– Four Species

Another interesting client I had was Michael Falk. When he was about eleven or twelve years old Michael and his grandfather went out with me. We took the girls out, but it was too rough so we brought them back to the dock. We went fishing for the morning and caught one small shark, but the fishing was actually very slow. We went back and picked up the girls, and went into Biscayne Bay. They caught blue fish, ladyfish, and sea trout, and had a lot of laughs, and a lot of fun.

Michael called me several times and always wanted to know about catching another specie of fish. After months of going back and forth on the telephone, he finally decided what he wanted. He wanted a ten-hour day, and he wanted to catch a swordfish, a blackfin tuna, a grouper, and a large tarpon. I told him that was a pretty tough menu, but we'll see what we can do.

We set a date for this trip in early June with Michael and his dad. We ran offshore and made a drop for swordfish. We didn't get a bite for an hour or so, so we wound it up. The rig had gotten tangled, so we reset and we made another drop. Almost as soon as we hit the bottom we hooked a swordfish. With the help of the Hooker electric reel, Michael brought the swordfish in. We put it in the boat and Michael said, "Now, let's go catch a tuna."

So, from about eighteen miles offshore, we headed back toward the beach. In the ten to twelve mile offshore distance, everybody in the whole fleet was catching dolphin hand over fist. It was red-hot dolphin fishing. One of the boats a couple of hundred yards away called and said, "Why don't you catch a few dolphins off this school?"

I turned toward his boat and Michael jumped up off his seat and asked, "Where you going?"

I said, "They're doing really good on dolphin right here. I was going to stop and let you catch a few."

He said, "We don't need any dolphin. We need a tuna fish. Let's go catch that tuna."

So we ran into an area that's normally good for blackfin tunas. The conditions were terrible. The water was dirty and green. There was no current, and no wind. It was the middle of the morning. I was thinking, 'This ain't going to work.' But, oh well, I decided we would put out a couple of tuna baits and see what happens. We put out twenty pound spinning rods with fifty-pound fluorocarbon leaders and 6/0 VMC circle hooks, and baited them with big live pilchards. We bump drifted with these pilchards out. We also put one down on the bottom, because we also needed to catch a grouper. So, we were waiting for something to happen, and I'll be a son of a gun if we didn't get a bite on one of the flat lines. Michael jumped on the rod, and the bottom rod went off. So his father jumped on that rod. The father came up with a little mutton snapper. But Michael came up with a thirty-pound blackfin tuna. The worst possible conditions, but he caught his blackfin tuna.

Now he had his swordfish and his blackfin tuna, so we wound up our lines and ran to another wreck to try for a grouper. We dropped down and caught half of a mutton snapper. So we ran to another wreck, and Michael came up and said, "You know, we're having so much success, we've already got two fish, and it's not even eleven o'clock. I want to add another fish to the list."

I said, "Boy, you really don't want much out of life do you."

He said, "No, I just need to catch a snook too."

I said, "I'll see what we can do, but you're sure asking for a lot."

The next place we stopped, we dropped down and immediately caught a gag grouper. It wasn't big enough to keep, but Michael was happy, and we released it. Next we headed back to the dock to pick up our tarpon bait. As we were going in the inlet, the conditions looked perfect for snook. It was an outgoing tide, so we tied up the boat, and my mate, Billy Springer, was getting the crabs out of the crab bucket. While he was doing that, I tied a couple of snook rigs on spinning rods.

On our way out of the inlet to go catch a tarpon, we stopped with the snook rods. We put the baits out and caught a couple of jack crevalles. Then we made another pass, and darned if we didn't catch a twenty-eight or twenty-nine inch snook. We took a couple of pictures, but it was out of season so we let it go. Now we had four out of a potential five species that Mikey had asked to catch in the course of the day, one of which he didn't even ask for until eleven o'clock in the morning.

We went out on the south side of Government Cut. We put out live crabs and made a drift. The tarpon were showing about 100 feet north of us, so we wound in the lines and started another drift. Then we hooked a big tarpon. We chased it down and got the leader. It was about 120 pounds. A few more minutes after we got the leader, it spit the hook. Then Michael said, "Now we've got to catch one for my dad." We made two more drifts, but didn't get any more bites.

Dad said, "We've had a phenomenal day. Let's go home." Michael Falk asked for four kinds of fish, added a fifth fish after eleven o'clock in the morning, and caught all five species of fish in nine hours. He caught a swordfish, a big blackfin tuna, a gag grouper, a nice snook, and a big tarpon in nine hours. What a crazy day of fishing that was.

Hoffa

In the late 1960s I was working out of the Castaways charter boat docks, which were owned by the Teamster's Union. The Teamsters had a boat there, but at this particular time it was in the boatyard, and Jimmy Hoffa wanted to go fishing. We knew that he liked to fish with chicken rigs for yellow eye and vermillion snappers. The weather was perfect for that, flat calm, with little or no current in the wintertime.

We rigged up our rods with double hooked bottom rigs with a sinker on the bottom and a couple of 3/0 hooks spaced out above that about eighteen inches apart. We baited them with squid. So Jimmy Hoffa came down to the boat with his entourage and said, "Oh, we're going chicken fishing. That'll be great, but I like five hooks on each rod."

I replied, "Well, Mr. Hoffa, we'll catch plenty of fish on two hooks."

He said, "No, we've got to have five hooks on each rod."

So I told him, "Well, on the way out the mate will make up all new rigs. We'll be ready to go when we get out there."

On the way out my mate made up new rigs for everybody, with five hooks on each, and baited them up with squid. We got out to 240 feet of water on a ledge and I said, "OK, we're ready to drop."

Mr. Hoffa said, "Well, I need a coffee can." So, we found him a coffee can and he put fifty cents or a dollar in the can and said, "All right guys, ante up." Everybody put fifty cents or a dollar in the coffee can, and asked me if they were ready to drop.

I said, "Yes, Sir."

They all dropped their lines down to the bottom. They were all hootin' and hollerin' about the bites they were getting, and pretty soon somebody said, "OK, wind them up."

So they wound up all the lines and one guy hollered, "OK, I got a pair."

Next guy said, "Oh that ain't nothing. I got three of a kind."

Next guy, "Oh you think you're a hotshot, but I've got a full house." And the next guy said, "Well, I got four of a kind."

It was the craziest thing ever. Jimmy Hoffa and his entourage played poker with their fishing rods all day long. They ended up with a great poker game and a box full of snappers at the end of the day. It was really a fun way to spend the day.

Della Monica

Joe Della Monica used to come to fish with me with his two sons, Joseph and Jay. Joseph lived in Chicago, and Joe and Jay lived in New York. They owned seventeen Burger Kings in New York and also had a condo in North Miami. They were a treat to fish with.

Usually Joe and Jay would fish with me in the morning, and then Joseph would fly in from Chicago and we would pick him up and go out in the afternoon. Then we would fish a couple of more days while they were here. They did this nearly every month during the winter season.

This one time we heard that the sailfish were biting twenty miles south of Government Cut. It was pretty good weather, so when Joe and Jay got on the boat we ran the twenty miles to fish for sailfish. But we didn't get a single bite. Then we ran back up to Government Cut to pick up Joseph. On this particular day Joe said to me, "Bouncer, I'm in my eighties, and I'm getting too old for that run. I just can't take those long runs. So this afternoon I want you to go one mile to the north and three miles out, and I want to fish right there."

I agreed. When we got to the destination the water wasn't very clean and the wind had quit. Not the best conditions, so I figured we should start out on a wreck. Among other things, Joe always wanted to fish for dinner. We dropped down a live bait and got a good hook up. We had a vertical jig on the other side of the boat but didn't catch anything with that. But on the live bait, up came a beautiful twelve-pound red snapper. We continued to drop down and time after time we hooked up. After all was said and done we had caught ten and a half - ten to twelve pound red snappers using live bait. We didn't catch a single one of them on the vertical jig.

It was a memorable outing on the wreck, and I named the spot Monica in honor of the Della Monica name. We returned to the spot the following day to prove it wasn't a fluke, and we caught six or seven more. That happened in March, and in the course of that summer, almost every time we went to that wreck we could catch a red snapper. We would only stay long enough to catch one or two in the interest of not wiping out the school. It remained a very consistent producer of red snappers all the way up to twenty pounds.

Red snappers are beautiful and quite protected. Any to be harvested have to be caught within three miles of the shore. This spot was 2.8 miles off Government Cut so we were still legal. We caught some beautiful fish and had some great meals. And I'll never forget about Joe Della Monica picking this spot. He chose the location and it paid off really well. I miss you Joe and I hope you're catching a lot of fish in that fishing hole in the sky.

Kingfish

My Biggest Kingfish

I was fishing with Bruce Jackaback, whom I called B.J., when I was still in high school. We would make runs down to Islamorada, and go to Estes Boat Rentals in Whale Harbor. One day we went out into Hawk's Channel and found a red-hot school of Spanish mackerel. We were catching them on bait, on jigs, and on flies. We didn't have a gaff on the boat so every time we got a small one, we would flip him into the boat. Every time we got a big one we would grab him by the tail and lift him into the boat.

We had been catching them for an hour or two; it was really chaotic, red hot fishing. And it was fabulous. One of us had a Spanish mackerel on near the boat. A giant kingfish skyrocketed out of the water and came down and landed literally right on top of the outboard motor with his mouth wide open. He cut grooves in the top of the motor cowling and fell back into Hawk's Channel and sank away. After that, reaching into the water to grab Spanish mackerel was not a popular chore.

We had a box full of Spanish mackerels and it was getting close to the end of the day, so we headed back to Estes Fish Camp. The following weekend we came down again on Sunday and rented a boat and headed out to the same general area. This time we were smart enough to borrow a gaff from Estes.

And sure enough, the mackerel were there. We were casting salt water sinking Rapalas. I was using a plug-casting reel with twelve-pound Ande line. It was a Pflueger Supreme, with no drag. Correction, my thumb was the drag! That was my reel of choice growing up. And boy, did I get fast at licking my thumbs or dipping the reel in the water, because they would sure get hot.

At any rate, I hooked this big kingfish and fought it and fought it, and it came into sight. My fishing buddy for the day was J.B. Garwood. He grabbed the gaff and hooked the fish. When he went to pull it into the boat, the kingfish was struggling and the gaff straightened out. It looked like a straight pin. So, while I was nursing the fish, J.B. figured out some way to bend the gaff back into a hook.

I said to J.B., "Try to get him in the boat this time. It's a miracle I've had him on this long." J.B. gaffed him again, and the gaff straightened out again. Then he bent the hook in a tighter radius and sure enough, he hit the fish with the gaff a third time and we got it into the boat.

It turned out to be my biggest kingfish ever: thirty-nine pounds on a Pflueger Supreme direct drive reel, a six-foot Uslan custom-built plug rod, and twelve-pound monofilament line. What a great thrill on that salt water sinking Rapala, and boy did we have fun catching those Spanish mackerel.

Limit Your Take

But those were also perilous times in Florida for the Spanish mackerel fishery. More than once, and this was one of those times, we were lucky because we were fishing in Islamorada on Sunday, and that was the night the net boats came in from Marathon. They would set their nets on that school of mackerel and literally wipe it out. By the end of the week the mackerel would settle back into the area, but the net boats would come back again, and by sunset would wipe them out again.

There was a school of Spanish mackerels off Miami Beach back in the 80s that was so popular that the tackle suppliers were running out of jigs, and spoons, and swivels, and wire. It was just phenomenal. We'd go out there everyday. One hundred or more boats fishing for Spanish mackerel having a ball, all recreational fishermen. In the Port Salerno/Stewart Inlet area the commercial mackerel boats heard about this big school of mackerel and invaded our area. They were catching so many mackerel their boats were nearly sinking. They would take them up the Miami River to the fish houses. The fish were in very poor shape from being overloaded on the boats. The fish markets were overwhelmed and couldn't take anymore Spanish mackerel, and they just shoveled them into the river. A total waste. They couldn't take them to market, because they caught too many. They wiped out the school and shut down the mackerel industry that was supplying the fuel docks, the tackle shops, and the sandwich shops.

Everybody had been having a field day, enjoying this giant run of Spanish mackerel. Then one day of commercial fishing with high rolling netting wiped out this fantastic run. It's a lesson to be learned about 'limit your take, not take your limit.'

Recipe for Kingfish

For years I was single, living the bachelor life, and I would put in a full day on the water, and sometimes an evening as well. I'd get home and have to make up some dinner after a long day on the water. Well, kingfish were perfect for making up a quick dinner. I would put a package of sealed-in-plastic peas in the microwave and nuke them for about five minutes. Then I would take a microwave-proof bowl and start with twelve ounces of king mackerel. I would add a third to a half cup of orange juice, and a good healthy dash of garlic salt. I'd put a lid on it and microwave it for about three or four minutes. Then I would stir it around and microwave it for another three or four minutes. It would take eight minutes altogether, and when it was all done I would stir it all up and it would make a nice chowder of kingfish. I would have that and a package of peas, and that would be my dinner.

It's very important to use boneless, skinless filets. If you don't take the skin off the kingfish, it's got a strong, oily, fishy taste. All the undesirable flavor is in the skin. The bottom line is, I would take home one medium sized kingfish, and it would give me kingfish for dinner three or four days in a row. And believe me, it didn't bother me at all eating it three or four days in a row. I would eat it straight out of the pot. I would have it with rice; I would dip bread in it. Whatever I wanted to do to mix it up, but I found it delicious and I absolutely loved it.

I got into making the same thing for guests who came onto my boat. We would go to a park after a fishing trip. I would take an eighteen-inch by eighteen-inch piece of tin foil and put twelve ounces of kingfish in the middle of the foil. I'd put a pad of butter, a slice of orange, and a healthy dash of garlic salt. Then I would roll down the top of the tin foil and roll up both ends of the foil to seal the ends. We would have a nice fire on the grill and lay the tin foil right on the charcoal, or as close to the gas burners as we could. I would cook it for four or five minutes then turn it over for four or five minutes, and then lay the tin foil on a paper plate. It was absolutely delicious.

A little sidebar of how I came to discover this recipe: I was working as a mate on a fifty-five foot sportfishing boat out of Miami, and we were taking the owner's shop manager up to West Palm Beach to go sail fishing for a couple of days. We got up there and put the baits out. On the first afternoon the only thing we caught was a fifteen-pound kingfish. The guest on the boat said, "That's going to be our dinner. Great!"

The captain and I visualized going out to dinner, but now we were having kingfish for dinner. So, at the end of fishing on the way back to the dock, the captain told me that if I cleaned the fish and made dinner, he would wash and chamois the whole boat. What a deal that was for me, because as much as I love fishing and being on boats, I hate washing and chamoising them. But now I had to figure out what I was going to do with that kingfish. The first thing I had to do was clean it. So I took it to the cleaning table at the Sailfish Marina and fileted it. I decided to take the skin off which was a struggle because it's pretty tough trying to skin a kingfish. But I found out that by going out from the centerline out to the bottom, and the centerline out to the top, it's much easier than going from the tail to the head. Abie Raymond cuts the filet into eight-inch sections and skins it that way. It makes really short work out of skinning kingfish.

So now I had all this boneless, skinless meat in a Ziploc bag, and I went into the galley looking for ingredients. We had a spice rack, and there was some garlic salt. I always like garlic so I used that. We also had some oranges and some butter. And we had a French baguette. I put the fish in a microwave proof bowl. I figured I wanted to keep it moist, so I squeezed some orange juice in there, and added a pat of butter. The only problem was that I didn't know how to cook kingfish in a microwave oven. So I cooked it for two minutes.

When I took it out, the edges were cooked, but the center was raw. So I stirred it all around and put it back in the microwave for two more minutes. When I took it out some was cooked and some was still raw, so I stirred it up some more. By the time I was done cooking it for eight minutes, this two and a half pounds of kingfish was all broken up from the juice, and the butter. So what am I to do? I sliced up the baguette and served everybody a bowl of fish soup and a piece of baguette. By the end of the night we had eaten all of the kingfish and all of the baguette.

Kingfish, with orange juice, garlic salt, butter, and a baguette became a mainstay of my diet through the years.

Snook

Snook are an elongated fish that we target in places like jetties and shorelines. Looking at a snook's profile we see they are designed to sit on the bottom in a strong current. The bottom of their body is flat, all the way out to the tip of their nose. From the tip of their nose to their forehead is sloped so water will flow right over them. One of the distinguishing features of snook is the jet-black line along each side called the lateral line. The lateral line picks up sound waves, or any kind of shock waves that come through the water. It works against fishermen because the pressure waves of the boat going through the water reach the snook way ahead of the boat. So a snook is aware that something has entered his territory and he goes on alert. He doesn't know whether that pressure wave is coming from a big shark, or a porpoise, or a boat. And all three are a threat to a snook.

Four Snook in Government Cut

In the summer of 1967 I was working on the *Seabreeze*, a head boat out of Pier Five in downtown Miami. My captain and the daytime mate had bought a damaged boat from Hurricane Betsy and rebuilt it for use as a commercial fishing boat. We used it all during the winter of 1966-67. Now we were into the early summer, and we decided to go snook fishing one night.

Red was the cleanup guy on the *Seabreeze* at night, and he was our designated captain for this trip. J.B. Garwood and I were the anglers. We had been told by one of our *Seabreeze* customers that we should use Parrothead jigs with black eel pork rinds, and troll back and forth along the jetties.

We found the Parrothead jigs, but we couldn't find any pork rind black eels, so we used long Uncle Josh's pork rind strips. We were using conventional rods with Jigmaster 500s. We used a four-ounce egg sinker with a four-foot leader, and then the jig with the pork rind on it. We trolled along the jetties as slow as the boat would go, which was still too fast. As we trolled out Government Cut along the north jetty on the first pass, I was the one up against the rocks, and I caught a snook that was about eleven pounds. We turned around to go back in the channel and J.B. was up against the rocks, but I was the one to catch a sixteen-pound snook. J.B. didn't get a bite.

We turned around again and J.B. and I switched sides of the boat, so he was up against the rocks. As we trolled out the inlet I caught a seven-pound snook. We turned around to troll back in again. I got a slamming strike, and I caught a thirty-pound, eight-ounce snook on the fourth pass. On four passes I caught four snook.

We were yipping, and hollering, and carrying on, celebrating this catch. Red looked up, and we were about to take a channel buoy broadside right in the middle of the side of this old wooden lap strake boat. It probably would have sunk us if we had hit it as hard as the current was running. Red jumped up and gunned the boat ahead and we just missed the buoy.

All was good when we were done. We had four beautiful snook, seven, eleven, seventeen, and thirty and a half pounds on four passes along the jetty. J.B. was disgusted, "I don't want to fish anymore."

I said, "I got my limit. I can't fish anymore." Back then we were allowed four snook per person, so we went home.

I fished Government Cut for the rest of my life but I never trolled Parrotheads again after all that success. I've caught a lot of snook in the Cut many different ways: live bait, artificial lures, trolling plugs, casting plugs, bucktails, shrimp, mullet, herring, pilchards, sardines, but never another snook on a Parrothead jig.

Buck Fever at Point East

B.J., Wayne Conn, and I, and sometimes Randy White, would fight over positions on the tip of Point East which was off Biscayne Boulevard at about 180th Street. The east wall in Eastern Shores was one of the top places to plug cast for snook. First thing in the morning was the best time. I went to Point East one time in the middle of the day. Back then there was no development yet on Point East. It was later to become condominiums. The land was filled and there were a bunch of boulders right off the point. We could hopscotch from boulder to boulder and not even get wet. I'd get out on the biggest boulder at the end of the point. From there I could cast plugs, or fly-cast for snook or jack crevalles, and every once in a while someone would catch a tarpon or a fluke.

This particular day I was throwing a creek chub diver. It's a plug about five or six inches long. It was bright yellow with red and black polka dots. I called them clown plugs the first time I ever saw one. As I worked the creek chump darter it would jerk and stop and jerk and stop, and it would dart in opposite directions staying just below the surface. I would work this lure back to my feet. Right at my feet the water was deep enough for a snook.

Just two feet from the rod tip a monster snook ate my plug. I was using a Pflueger Supreme direct drive reel. The spool and handle on the reel turned simultaneously, and I used my thumb for a drag. This big snook ate my plug and I was so in shock that I panicked. I clamped down on the reel handles and reared back on the rod, and broke the fish off. How dumb could I be? The snook of a lifetime could have easily been close to fifty pounds, and I broke it off.

I hop scotched back across the rocks to my car and got a new creek chub diver, and walked back onto the rocks again and resumed casting. I can't imagine it was the same snook, but it could have been its twin. The biggest snook I ever saw in my life just five or six casts later! Right at the end of the rod he sucked in my plug. I got buck fever again and clamped down; and I broke him off again. I can't believe the two biggest snook I ever saw, maybe ten minutes apart, and I broke them both off with buck fever. What a fool I was!

But that area gave us so much great fishing. I can remember standing on that same rock with an eight-weight fly rod catching twenty-seven snook on fly in one session. Again, mid morning using little red and white flies, floating fly line, catching one small snook after another.

Death by Fright

Years later we were catching a lot of snook right across the canal from where I would stand on the rocks. Back then it was a mangrove shoreline; now it's a developed shoreline with a seawall - it was developed as Williams Island. The tide coming out of Maule Lake would push against that seawall, and it held a lot of snook. We'd been doing real well on the snook in that location.

I had a charter customer who wanted to catch a big snook to have mounted. I took him over there in my flats boat and had him climb up and walk along the seawall, and work plugs along the way. He was using a sinking Rapala at the time. All of a sudden he started going ape, "There's this big snook coming down the seawall!"

I said, "Ok, well cast in front of him." But the snook wouldn't eat. I could see it pushing water as it came down the seawall. The last two feet of my skiff stuck out beyond the end of the seawall, and this snook was going to eventually swim right into the side of my skiff.

I'll be doggone if he didn't swim right up to my skiff and roll over and die. I put a stringer through his lower lip and towed him around. I couldn't do anything to revive him - he was just stone cold dead. We didn't see any more snook that morning.

My client got in the boat and we went back to Keystone Point Marina. We put the boat away and took the snook to Fred Lou Bait and Tackle in North Miami and weighed it. It weighed twenty-five pounds. We arranged for the client to get him mounted because, what could be a crazier story than having a snook swim by and have it die of a heart attack?

157

But before mounting it, we arranged for the snook to go to the Rosenstiel School at the University of Miami to see if we could find out why it died. The school determined it had died from lack of oxygen, which made no logical sense to me. There were plenty of other fish living there that didn't seem to have a problem with oxygen in the water.

I took the client back the next day and he caught a big snook. Not quite as big, but almost. He used a Rapala casting on the same shoreline, and we released it because we already had the big one to mount. He ended up with a trophy story and a trophy snook. It was a great event at the mouth of Maule Lake. We had some great days fishing in Maule Lake over the years.

Organizations

The Billfish Foundation (TBF) was founded several decades ago by the likes of Winthrop Rockefeller III, Tim Choate, Dr. Eric Prince, and a group of fifty founding members. When it first started I was a little slow to jump in. I sat back and watched. It was made up of all heavy hitters in the sportfishing industry, and I didn't feel like I qualified for that group. I let them get settled in, and finally decided they were doing good work and for a good cause, so I became involved. I'm proud to say that I've been a member and strong supporter for quite a while, and I'm always encouraging people to join.

TBF has had some great staff. They have had a number of people there doing the hard work of advocacy, planning events, creating marketing materials, promoting their tagging program, and covering boat shows. They have also had some great scientists such as Peter Chaibongsai, Dr. Russell Nelson, Elliott Stark, and many others.

They have all done great work, one after another. But there's one firecracker who always keeps the ball rolling. That's Ellen Peel. She's simply a dynamo. She was a lawyer before taking over as President of TBF. She has been their key lobbyist and has done a great job of keeping TBF in front of our congressmen up in Washington, the National Marine Fishery Services, NOAA Fisheries, and ICAAT, and the list goes on. If there ever was a person to represent billfish and recreational fishermen, it's Ellen Peel. I recommend that anybody who has a few extra dollars, perhaps didn't have to buy fuel this week or something like that, write a check to The Billfish Foundation. Ellen and the Foundation will take ten dollars or hundred dollars and turn it into many more dollars worth of good work saving our billfish for the future.

Another group that I have been involved with for years is the International Game Fish Association, or IGFA. Since I have been involved with the IGFA, they have had three presidents, Mike Leach, Rob Kramer, and now Nehl Horton. All of those guys have had different approaches, but all three have been highly focused on the future of game fishing, keeping good records of what has been caught, and establishing standards and rules for tournament fishing. When a person has had an application for a world record accepted by the IGFA, it means he has crossed all the T's and dotted all the I's. These guys are meticulous in making sure the rules are followed, that everything was done by the book, and it was a good, legitimate catch.

They have a great staff to back up each of these presidents. Today we have Nehl Horton. Nehl has been a heavy hitter in business for years. He grabbed IGFA by the horns, and he's rattling cages, making moves that are making the IGFA that much better. Each man has added a little bit of new blood and new ideas. Again, IGFA relies on contributions and memberships, so anyone who can send them a few extra dollars in the form of a contribution can be assured that it will be put to good use.

Then there's another group that touches on everybody who fishes. These two groups, TBF and IGFA are centered on the game fish aspect of fishing. But there's another group, the CCA of Florida. It has done a phenomenal job of touching on every subject imaginable including sea trout, redfish, pilchards, sardines, tarpon, long lining, or swordfish, all connected issues across the board.

I remember when CCA (Coastal Conservation Association) first came around. They were going shoulder to shoulder with Karl Wickstrom from Florida Sportsman Magazine. Together they fought for the Florida net ban. These two organizations pushed through a vote by the citizens of Florida that cast 72% in favor of the ban. That prohibited all gill nets for three miles offshore, and all nets over 300 square feet, from operating in Florida waters altogether. No seines or anything, and I cannot imagine what South Florida fishing would be like without that effort, but I'm certain it would not be pretty. It helped bring back our snook population, and protects our pilchard and thread herring populations. With a healthy baitfish population we are assured of a better game fish population too. CCA and Florida Sportsman were early advocates for making redfish a game fish. Day after day this organization has hammered home the importance of our fisheries.

Talk about lobbyists. Ellen Peel is an amazing advocate and lobbyist for billfish. The IGFA has had numerous people advocating for them, such as Jason Schratwieser who has been their primary lobbyist, and has done a phenomenal job. When it comes to CCA, it was Ted Forestgren who professionally covered everything of importance for recreational fishermen in the State of Florida.

Contributions to any of these organizations, TBF, IGFA, and CCA are appreciated, and help keep alive the hope for excellent recreational fishing not only in Florida, but across the globe.

Trips

Sturgeon in Oregon

Something I always wanted to do was to see the Pacific Northwest coast. I'd been to the Rocky Mountains and New England. I'd gone by car from Miami all the way to California, along the southern border through Arizona and New Mexico, Texas and all that. I'd been to Louisiana and the mid Atlantic states. The Pacific Northwest really had a draw for me. My sister, Sue, always wanted to catch a sturgeon, and the Pacific Northwest was a good place for that. So, we both wanted to go.

One of my clients named Steve told me about a guide called the Sturgeon General from just east of Portland, Oregon. So I called and booked two days of fishing with him, and planned a five-day trip to the Pacific Northwest. My nephew Keith agreed to join us. Sue and Keith and I flew out to Portland and rented a car. We drove about an hour to the east, and checked into a hotel. The next morning we met Charlie, the Sturgeon General, at the boat ramp on the Columbia River. I had been thinking that if we caught one sturgeon within a couple of days, it would be a miracle. But the General told me that we would get tired of catching them if we targeted small ones. So that was what we chose to do; we went for the small ones. And the Sturgeon General knew his business. Not only did he know the right place to anchor, but he was also right about being able to catch too many sturgeons. In seven hours we caught forty-five sturgeons from ten to thirty-five pounds.

It was a hoot and we had a great time. So, after catching all these sturgeons, we booked again for two days later. The Sturgeon

162

General asked if we wanted to go after sturgeon or salmon. Salmon season had just opened. We kicked it around for a few minutes, but the fact of the matter was, we came to Oregon to catch sturgeon, so we chose to go in that direction. We might catch fewer, but they would be bigger.

The following day, our day off from fishing, we drove up to Mount Hood. We stopped at a produce stand and bought wonderful produce. We found acres of lavender, and fruit trees, and produce. We saw mountains, and desert, and power dams. It was just a great day driving around.

The next morning we met with the Sturgeon General at a different boat ramp. We launched the boat and took off sturgeon fishing again. The first day we used squid and sardines for bait. The second day we were using big dead shad for bait on a much different part of the river. He anchored the boat and put out two rods. Here was the deal: Sue was up first, and then me, and then Keith in that rotation. That was our respective order. There was no "Oh this is a big one, you take it" kind of discussion. In short order Sue caught one about sixty-five or seventy pounds, and we were very impressed. Then I caught one over 100 pounds. We were thrilled. The next one was Keith's turn. He's a healthy, strapping young man, and he caught one estimated at 400 pounds. It jumped and put up a great fight, and we were on cloud nine. We had each caught the size fish we respectively thought we could handle. And Keith caught the biggest one, which is the way we wanted it to happen.

As the rotations went on, by the end of the day I had a couple of them that were 200 pounds, and a couple of others that were between 100 and 200 pounds. Sue had four or five fish and they were sixty-five to 120 pounds. Keith had two 400 pounders, two 200 pounders, and a couple of twenty-five pounders. We caught seventeen sturgeons on the day we went for quality instead of quantity, and they were nice big fish.

The following day we got up early in the morning and drove to Astoria to the mouth of the Columbia River. In Astoria we met Steve who had given me the General's name in the beginning. Then we drove down the Oregon coast for two days. The first day was just like I wanted to see the Pacific Northwest: real strong winds, sometimes thirty or forty miles an hour, crashing waves, and occasional rain. It was an inspiring power of nature day.

As we drove along the coast, whenever we came across a picturesque spot we would stop. That meant it was stop, go a quarter of a mile. Stop, go 100 yards, and stop again. There was so much beautiful coast, and Sue and Keith would often get out of the car and hike down to the beach, which was often a long downhill and uphill climb. Every time they came back up the hill they would bring me a handful of wild blackberries right off the bushes. The coastline was lined with blackberries, rocky shorelines with little sand beaches, and pounding waves. We would stop in little seaports to look at the fishing boats and scenery.

We spent the night in a hotel, and when we got up in the morning it was not like the previous day. The coast was still magnificent although the southern half of the Oregon coast has more beach and less rocks. It was slick glass calm, not a cloud in the sky. No wind, no rain – just a gorgeous day. One of the highlights of our trip was when we were driving over a bridge, and there was a derelict boat down on the side. We turned around and went back to take pictures. The boat had been a freighter and commercial boat in Alaska. It had a huge history. It was in its last days, but it was really neat to check it out.

Then we went into the gift shop and the coffee shop, and there was a dog that played fetch with a thirty-pound rock. It was unbelievable. I'd throw the rock across the parking lot and he'd go get it and push it back to me.

What a great trip. We ended up with forty-five sturgeon one day, seventeen the next day, and saw the Oregon coast of the Pacific Northwest. It looked exactly as it was supposed to be.

Halibut

Paul Leader and I grew up fishing on Sunny Isles Pier at the end of 163rd Street at Collins Avenue. We slammed the Spanish mackerels, and bonitos, and kingfish, and cobias. Just great fishing back then in the good old days on the pier. We stayed friends all through the ages, and Paul ended up being my sister's personal and business accountant, my personal and business accountant, and the accountant for a lot of my friends. He was a good CPA, and a great guy too.

He went to Kodiak, Alaska, in 1987 with several local businessmen where they fished for sockeye salmon on the west side of Kodiak Island. Then they went over to the town of Kodiak to go out on a boat called *Ten Bears* to fish for halibut. Back then the halibut were all fished on eighty-pound tackle, big heavy rods and reels, with big sinkers and big chunks of meat. Paul had polio when he was a kid and had braces on both legs, so he couldn't use real heavy tackle. He went aboard the boat with a South Florida deep jigging plug rod and reel, a hand full of three-ounce deep jigs, and a bag of glow-in-the-dark worms.

Captain Eric said, "What are you going to do with that stuff?"

Paul said, "Well, I can't use heavy tackle, so I'll play around with this while the guys are catching halibut on the heavy tackle." By the end of the trip Paul had schooled Eric because he had caught all kinds of halibut on fifteen-pound line with a plug rod and reel, and bucktails with rubber worms. Eric was so impressed he tried to talk Paul into selling him everything he had with him. Paul gave him the jigs and the worms, but he wouldn't give up his favorite deep jigging rod, or his plug reel. But he certainly got Eric started.

From 1987 to about 2010 Paul and his group fished for halibut every year with Eric on the *Ten Bears*. They would go out for three days and live on the boat. Then they would go back to town and rent a car for the day and go out on their own to fish the river system for salmon. Then they would come back and fish with Eric for three more days. Then back to town and fish the river system for another day. They would fly back to Miami with coolers full of packaged and processed halibut, rockfish, lingcod, and salmon. They also caught a lot of king salmon out in the ocean.

Finally, in 1999, Paul talked my sister and brother-in-law into going up to Alaska with him. It turned out they were one person short for the trip, so my sister and brother-in-law brought me along as their guest. We all flew to Anchorage and spent a couple of nights there. We drove around and saw the sights of Seward.

After Paul caught up with us, we got on an airplane and flew down to Kodiak Island. It was quite a landing because it's a very small runway that ends at the base of a mountain. When we were up a few thousand feet we could see through the patchwork clouds. The plane would fly over and check out the runway. Looking straight down, the clouds had holes in them, but when we got down to make an approach, the clouds would block out the view of the runway. So we went around six times without landing. My brother-in-law, Joe, hates to fly. He was chewing his fingernails off and crushing the arms of his seat – and I think he crushed my sister's arms while he was at it. But at any rate, on the seventh approach, the trail from behind the plane had cleared out the clouds enough so we could see the runway, and we finally landed safe and sound.

We went to the *Ten Bears* and hooked up with Eric, and loaded up all our fishing gear. We headed out for three days of halibut and salmon fishing. We went rock fishing that afternoon and caught some yellow eye rockfish and some black rockfish. I happened to catch a world record yellow eye rockfish weighing twelve pounds on eight-pound test. Then we went over and anchored for the night off Strawberry Island. Sally, the assistant and cook on the boat, made us a nice dinner. Then we went out on the back deck catching halibut, and losing halibut, and catching a few Pacific cod. My sister came out and said, "Aren't you guys ever coming to bed?"

Her husband said, "It's still early. It isn't even dark yet."

She said, "Yeah, well it's eleven thirty. This is the land of the Midnight Sun. You better get in here and go to bed or you won't be able to fish tomorrow."

We all went to bed and got a pretty good night's sleep, although we were all tossing and turning, thinking about what tomorrow would bring. We headed out the next day to fly fish for halibut. Eric said, "You know, with this crew on board, we could catch the first one hundred pound halibut on fly." Paul Leader held all of the world's records for halibut on light tackle and on fly-casting tackle. We had another person with us from the Keys who was an experienced fly fisherman. Paul had all kinds of tackle; Sue primarily fished with bait, as did one of the other anglers on the boat. I chose to fly fish too, so we had three fly fishermen on the stern and the other three people fished along the side. The fishing was pretty good.

Paul hooked a big halibut on fly. He had it all the way up to the surface. The way they gaff these fish is, once they get them to the surface, the mate and the captain would have long handled gaffs. The captain would say, "Go." And the mate would say, "Go." Together they would gaff the halibut in the head and quickly pull it up over the side before it could flop off of the gaffs. Then everybody would run because it would beat a tattoo on the deck for several minutes.

This fish was a potential world record. The captain and the mate lowered their gaffs into the water. In positioning the gaffs, the fly line got wrapped around the back end of the handle of the mate's gaff. The captain said, "Go."

The mate said, "No." Which was misunderstood for 'go'. The captain hit the fish with the gaff. The mate did not. The fish jumped off the gaff and broke the tippet, and got away. That was very possibly a halibut of over 100 pounds on fly. It would have been the first one ever.

We fished for salmon for a day, and came back to *Ten Bears* and fished for three more days. Some days we couldn't fly fish because the current was too strong. Some days were rough, and some were calm. On the last day it was flat calm, the current was light, and everybody was having great luck except for me. My brother-in-law caught a beautiful king salmon on real light tackle. Paul caught several king salmon and several halibut. One of the other guys on the boat caught a halibut of about 120 pounds on six-pound test. Everybody was on cloud nine, but I was snake bit. I couldn't get a bite.

Finally, after lunch I told Paul that I was going to steal one of his flies because mine weren't working. I put on one of his flies and finally caught a halibut weighing about thirty pounds. Now, mind you, we had caught lots of halibut on fly by this point, but on that particular day I couldn't get one to eat the fly. Paul made two casts after lunch and caught two halibut over sixty pounds.

At about two o'clock Eric came over and said, "Paul, we gotta head for the barn at three o'clock. I've got another charter tomorrow, and we have to get your fish to the processors, and we have to get everything unloaded and cleaned up for the next charter."

Paul said, "Remember, we had a couple of rough days. And today is really beautiful, so give us as long as you can." That being said, at 3:10 in the afternoon, ten minutes after we were supposed to head home, I got a solid bite on the fly. I set the hook. The fish raced around the transom of the boat, up the port side, all the way up to the bow, and under the anchor chain. I had to pass my line from one hand to the other under the pulpit and the railings to get my fly rod out on the other side. Eric started up the boat and followed the fish till he was straight up and down on the anchor. When I was almost out of line on my fly reel, the fish stopped. I started to gain a little line and Paul hollered from the back of the boat that he was hooked up.

The captain stepped out of the wheelhouse and said, "What am I supposed to do now? I have a fish running off the bow and another one running off the stern. I can't perform miracles." Paul clamped down on his line and broke his fish off. What an honorable thing to do.

When questioned about it later he said, "Hey, Bouncer hooked his fish first. First guy has the right of way." I was disappointed that he didn't hang in there and see if he could turn his fish, but actually I could never thank him enough; first of all for putting the trip together, and second of all for inviting us and then breaking off his fish.

168

Well, after an hour of fighting, my fish finally came to the surface. It dove all the way back down to the bottom. But we had seen it, and we were in a panic. I got it back up, and they hit it with both gaffs and hauled it in the boat. It was the first halibut ever caught on fly in the Pacific Ocean over 100 pounds. It was 111 pounds. It was the twenty-pound tippet world's record for several years. And what a thrill! The best angling accomplishment of my life, and it was all because of the generosity of my sister, and my brother-in-law, Joe, and the planning and the arrangements made by Paul Leader. I can't thank them all enough.

Alaska Events

On our trip to Alaska we were sleeping six people in the v-berths in triple bunk beds – three bunks on one side and three on the other. On a boat, these bunks are generally wider toward the aft end and narrower, coming to a point at the bow of the boat. So we sleep with our heads facing aft and our feet toward the bow.

It was about two in the morning and I was sleeping on the bottom bunk on the port side. Something woke me up and I reached to my right and hit solid wood. And I reached to my left, and it too was solid wood. I reached up and it was only inches to solid wood, and the cushion I was sleeping on was also on solid wood. I woke up in a panic that I was in a coffin. The poor guy in the bunk opposite me on the starboard side – I kicked the hell out of him trying to find my way out of this coffin. It turned out I was way up in the corner of the bunk bed, but boy did he take a beating.

Another thing about Alaska was how nice and warm it was (I'm being facetious). I was wearing seven layers of clothing and full foul weather gear from 7:00 a.m. to 11:00 p.m. every day we were on the boat. It was unbearably cold! I walked around looking like the Pillsbury Dough Boy.

We were on a fifty-five foot steel body walk around party boat. It had a nice salon galley in the middle, and fish boxes in the aft section. The helm was above the galley, and below were the v-berths.

On the first or second day we were anchored and the captain decided to move to another spot. So we went into the cabin, just sitting around having something to eat or drink while he pulled the anchor. Pretty soon the mate came down all in a huff. And the captain came down also in a huff. I asked what the problem was.

"We've got a great big boulder on the anchor, and we have to figure out how to get it off."

This boulder was so big that they had to run the cable from the winch they used to pick up their dinghy to the anchor rope, and hook them up. They were able to wench the boulder over to the side. It was so heavy that the boat was heeling over fifteen or twenty degrees just from the weight of the boulder. We sat just inside the window, and the boulder was hanging just outside the window. We decided that wasn't a very smart move so we relocated.

There were two firefighters and three captains, and my brother in law who was an engineer, on board. We kicked the problem around and decided that the best way to get rid of the boulder was to tie the bottom of the anchor to the end of the winch, and when we lowered the top of the anchor it would tip upside down and the boulder would fall out. And it did fall out, and the boat went whipping the other way. But the boulder problem was over.

What a fantastic trip that was. Whales surfacing and breeching and landing with their tails way up in the air. There were sea otters lying around on their backs with clams on their bellies, gnawing away. We saw beautiful forests and mountains. Near Seward, Alaska, we walked up and examined at arms length a glacier with blue ice. It's just the most spectacular place to see.

Cayman Islands

In about 2007 Clarence Flowers, better known as "King," from the Cayman Islands, was in Captain Harry's Fishing Supply and asked about swordfishing. Somebody there gave King my phone number, and he contacted me about going out on the Fourth of July. This was back in the days when we were doing a lot of nighttime swordfishing.

So we headed out just before dark, and set up four lines. We had a free line of rigged squid on a twenty-five foot wind-on leader, and then a five-foot bait leader; so we had a total of thirty feet of leader. At the top of that we had an electralume light. We fastened a two-liter bottle with a cyalume light stick taped to the top of it, and then ran off three hundred feet of line.

We ran away from that for a ways and deployed a tinker mackerel, a blue runner, or a small bonito. Again, we used a five-foot bait leader and a twenty-three foot wind on leader. On this electralume we tie wrapped a one-pound lead, then fastened it with long line clips to the top of the wind-on leader. We measured out 200 feet of line on the downrigger and fastened a two-liter bottle, there again with a cyalume stick. We put that about 100 feet off the side of the boat.

Then we deployed a bait straight off the rod tip with a one-pound lead with an electralume light and a rigged squid, and sent it straight down 100 feet off the bow of the boat. We had another rod in the stern of the boat with a two-pound lead under the electralume light, and the same leader combination with the rigged squid. This bait we fished 300 to 500 feet below the surface. Those two rigs that were straight off the rod tips were key to getting bites, in that we would wind them up a ways then let them down. With those two baits it seemed the more we moved them around, the more bites we got. We moved our tip rods a lot while our jug rods were pretty much stuck in place.

On this holiday the fireworks had just started going off out on the western horizon. Then we got a good strike. We caught a nice swordfish about 125 pounds. We took pictures of the fish, and King said that was enough and let's call it a night. So we headed back to shore.

King had a five star restaurant in Grand Cayman, so we cut the head and the tail off his fish and gutted it. We packed it in ice and shipped it back to the Cayman Islands for his restaurant.

All the time we were out there, King was talking about evidence of swordfish in the Cayman Islands, but no directed or developed fishery for swordfish. He thought that if he held a tournament, he could get up enough interest that people would start to fish for swordfish in the islands. That was the end of the discussion for the time.

A couple of months later he called me up and said he was coming up with Buster McLain, and they wanted to go out swordfishing again. We went out, and in the course of the evening I asked him what had happened to the swordfish tournament. He said, "Oh, we're going to get on that right away. Let's get it done. We'll get seven or eight Miami captains to come down and do a seminar on how to catch swordfish. We'll have a couple of local fishermen there to talk about where they've seen swordfish. We'll have a hands-on rigging program, and then we'll go swordfishing for the night. It'll be really helpful to the people of the island."

Sure enough, in just a few days we were on our way to the Cayman Islands. It was my mate, six other crewmembers, and me going down. When we got down there we gave a round table discussion about how we fish for swordfish in Miami. The Caymanian natives discussed where they had seen swordfish. It was a very productive evening.

We got a good night's sleep because we going to be up all night the next night. We went to a marina where there was a big grass lot with a giant tent they had put up. They had rigging tables, and rod holders, and downriggers to measure line, and buckets of water for rinsing our hands after rigging baits. There were flats of squid, and some small bonitos, goggle eyes, and tinker mackerels for bait.

We spent all day marking lines; 100 feet was one mark, 200 feet was two marks, and so on. We discussed all kinds of rigging, line to line connections, setting the drag, installing the electralume lights onto the line. We rigged hundreds of baits, and late in the afternoon we packed it all up, and took off and went fishing.

It was not a very productive night for swordfishing. There was one swordfish caught by Charles Ebank in his canoe with an outboard motor. He caught a fish I think about 175 pounds; but it proved that it could be done.

Now here we are, twelve years later, and almost every week we get a report where there has been another nice swordfish caught in the Cayman Islands. They hold the Cayman Islands Swordfish Challenge every year. We played around with having it in October, and in the summer, and the spring. We settled on early spring on the March full moon as being the best time to hold it.

In the Cayman Islands we've fished out of Southwest Point, and Seven Mile Beach, and the East Point, and there are also boats fishing out of Cayman Brac. They run forty miles to a seamount where they have had the most consistent activity so far. It's really a successful fishery, and it's all because of the efforts of Clarence Flowers.

To give an idea of what it is like to go there, I usually fly down on a Wednesday or Thursday, and my sister goes with me. I do a radio show promoting the upcoming event. We each get private rooms. My mate, Abie, comes down with his wife and they get a room. On that one occasion we had six other crew members come down, and each had his own private room. They put us up first class and treat us like royalty. We fly on Cayman Airlines and go to King's five star restaurant for lunch the day we arrive; we do the radio show, and then get all our tackle ready to go.

Abie and I switch off being the emcee. Abie does a wonderful job of showing how to rig baits, and what we do with the baits after we rig them. I talk about the latest things, like how we went from only nighttime fishing to daytime fishing, and now fishing part of the day and part of the night. We have scientists down there talking about tagging swordfish and where the tagged swordfish travel. We have some science, and some technology, some techniques, some bait rigging, and good camaraderie.

We fish for a couple of days and brag about our catches. On Monday night we have the awards dinner, and frequently they have a drawing for fishing tackle. We give accolades for all the great fish that were caught and there's a slide show. We just really have a good time.

173

I thank the Cayman Islands Ministry Of Tourism, and the Tourism Board, and Cayman Airlines, and the Flowers Group, and the Cayman Islands Challenge Board of Directors for putting on a spectacular tournament, and for treating us so well. On top of all that, for anyone who hasn't ever been there, it's the cleanest island I've ever been to, and it's a treat to visit any of the Cayman Islands.

Cozumel

In 1975 I was working on a charter boat out of the A Dock at Bahia Mar in Ft. Lauderdale. The boat was a forty-seven foot Pacemaker called the *Doctor's Orders*. A fellow named John Wilson from the Ft. Lauderdale Sun Sentinel, who was heavily involved in the Ft. Lauderdale publicity scene, brought a Mexican gentleman by the name of Eugenio Colado to the dock to talk about chartering me to take the *Doctor's Orders* to Cozumel, Mexico. There we would fish for a month, and then bring the boat back. There would be two Mexicans fishing on the boat, my mate, and me. John would go down on the boat with us.

I agreed to do it, which among other things, meant I had to do a lot of research, particularly about plotting the course. My good friend Jack Plachter had been a quartermaster in the Coast Guard, and he helped me plot my course. We plotted out the whole trip accounting for the speed of the boat, and available chart information for currents we would encounter along the way. We made arrangements to buy a bladder tank so we could carry more fuel.

This trip would take us first from Ft. Lauderdale to Key West. From Key West we would run to the northwestern most edge of Cuba, staying far enough offshore not to be stopped by the Cuban Navy, because Cuba at the time was hostile to America. When we got to the very western tip of Cuba, we would take off through open water and head for Cozumel.

We consulted with Cliff North. He had made the trip numerous times with a whole fleet of Strikers. He looked at all of our calculations and said we didn't allow enough for the currents in the Yucatan Channel. We would have to up our current allotments for the trip

174

across. So we re-plotted the course from Cuba to Cozumel, and got the boat all loaded up and ready to go. Dennis was my mate; John was going along to help out. We would be meeting Eugenio in Cozumel for a month of phenomenal sail fishing off the Yucatan Channel. We had all our ducks in a row.

We left Ft. Lauderdale and ran to Key West. There we filled the bladder tank, changed all the filters, and left at about four in the afternoon. The weather was good and we had nice sailing. Everybody took turns running the boat. When we had been running for about thirty-six hours, we thought we should be approaching Cozumel; but we must have miscalculated because we didn't find it.

We continued straight ahead. I figured that if we were too far north, our depth finder that went to 600 feet would pick up the bottom. East of Mexico the water was deeper so we wouldn't have seen the bottom. But if we missed all of the Yucatan Peninsula, we would be able to read the bottom north of Yucatan. So I figured that if we couldn't read the bottom, we were either too far west, or too far south.

We were four hours overdue to find land, and the depth finder still couldn't reach the bottom. I said that we were too far south. I re-plotted our course based upon the fact that we had used Cliff North's information about currents, when we really should have used our own current calculation. I came up on the bridge and said, "Guys, I figured out where we are."

They said, "Oh, thank goodness. Where are we?"

I said, "We're in the compass rose." The compass rose is on all paper charts, and the one on this chart was way straight south of Cozumel. I said, "Just head due west and let's see if we can find the coast." We headed due west for several more hours, calling on the AM radio (we didn't have VHF back then). The good news about AM is that it will reach hundreds of miles. I started making regular radio calls, trying to find anybody who was out fishing out of Cozumel to come back to us. Finally Tiny Brown replied to my radio call.

He said, "I've got you on my RDF and you are straight south of me. I'm fishing west of Cozumel, so come straight north, find me and I'll help you get back across the straights of Cozumel, which is about twelve miles off the mainland of Yucatan. Sure enough, thanks to Tiny Brown, we turned due north, found him, and found Cozumel. We got there with about thirty gallons of fuel left.

We started off trolling four baits and practice fished. What I learned next has effected my life ever since. I would holler, "Sailfish on the left long rigger." Or, "There's seaweed on the short rigger; or a sailfish on the short left rigger." Eugenio spoke very good English, but he wasn't used to our terminology. The other Mexican spoke almost no English at all, and my mate spoke no Spanish whatsoever.

Eugenio came up and said, "We're having a communication problem. Let's solve this real quick." We were only allowed to fish four lines at any time while we were down there, so he suggested, "That's number one, that's number two, and that's number three. If you'll tell us which line it's on, we'll figure out what's on it. So, one, two, three, four. Everybody will know what you're talking about. We don't have to do uno, dos, tres, quatro. Just one, two, three, four from left to right around the cockpit, and that's how we'll identify the rods."

I agreed, and now every rod holder on my boat is numbered, and it came from that moment.

We caught a lot of sailfish. We came in second in the General Tackle Sailfish Tournament. We came in second along with everybody else in the two-day marlin tournament, because only one boat caught a marlin. And we came in second in the twelve-pound sailfish tournament because, when we hooked a stubborn fish and lost an engine, another boat caught up and passed us in the last hour. The bottom line is we fished three tournaments and came in second.

By the twelve pound tournament there were so many huge dolphin that we could hardly troll. What we would have to do in order to not have giant dolphins on twelve pound test all the time, was just put out a daisy chain of squid and a Boone teaser. We would drag those teasers, and when a sailfish would come up we would pitch him a ballyhoo. If we put ballyhoos in the outriggers we'd have five or six, twenty to fifty pound dolphins come charging in and eat all the ballyhoo. We started to just tease up a sailfish, pitch him a bait, and catch him. The dolphins would come in, beat up on the teasers, and leave and then come back and do it again. We didn't take that many dolphins because every night when we came in we would throw dolphin up on the dock and the residents would go crazy and take them all away. We might keep one for dinner and give the rest away. There was no way to do anything with that much fish and we didn't want to waste it.

Bill Wells, of Wells Shrimp Company, said he was going to go up to Isla Mujeres and check on his shrimp boats. He told us the fishing was even better up there. Isla Mujeres and Cancun were unheard of at the time, but he came back with tales of twice as many sails as we had in Cozumel. That would be pretty hard to imagine. He also brought back huge buckets of shrimp for everybody on the dock. We all had giant shrimp to eat for the rest of out trip.

Finally, after a month down there, it was time to go home. My mate and I got everything prepared to go. We got up in the morning and took off out of Cozumel. The way to leave Cozumel is to run north along Cozumel to the tip of the island, and then head off toward the tip of Cuba. Then, just when we could see Cuba, we would run along north of the coast, and then cut over to Key West. We were almost to the end of Cozumel when there was a huge shuttering and shaking of the boat. I turned around just in time to see our big bronze propeller blade skipping off to the west for as far as we could see. Now we were down to running on one engine. The only thing we could do was to turn around and head back to Cozumel. After I turned around I looked down into the cockpit. My mate was shot gunning beers, shaking like a leaf, and crying. He had a complete nervous breakdown when we lost the propeller.

When we got back to Cozumel, Tiny Brown again came to my rescue. He helped me get my mate on an airplane, and off the island and back to Miami. I arranged for my brother, Flip, to fly down to help

177

bring the boat back. We got the propeller changed, and we were back in business. Flip came in on the airplane and we had dinner together. We were going to leave at first light. Tiny Brown came down and asked, "What are you doing sitting here?"

I told him we were going to leave first thing in the morning. He said, "No, you can't leave in the morning. You've got to leave tonight."

I said, "Why is that?"

He said, "You're only going to do ten or twelve knots over to Key West. The *CATV* is going to leave at first light and he'll be gone. If you leave now he'll be coming up behind you almost all the way to Cuba. So, whatever happens to you guys, there will be a boat coming up behind you if you have problem. If you wait until the morning, you'll be on your own and there won't be anybody to help you."

Flip had been drinking with all the guys on the dock, and was now drunk. He had been thinking he'd be able to sleep it off and get up in the morning and go. At any rate, we loaded up and took off. All we had to do was throw the lines off, unplug the shore cord, and we were on our way.

When we took off it was blowing like crazy. I ran the boat up the coast, and headed across from the edge of Cozumel to the tip of Cuba. It was so rough I had to pull the throttles back about every third or fourth wave. I'd been up since six in the morning, so by about three or four in the morning I hallucinated, thinking I saw a pelican sitting on the bow rail.

I was running the boat through these big waves and the spray. The rocking and rolling, and pitching and yawing was epic. It was a horrible crossing, but down below my drunken brother slept through the whole thing.

When sunlight came up in the morning I was still dealing with these big waves and I told my brother, "You've got to take the wheel."

He said, "I can't drive the boat in these big waves. I'm not a seaman. I don't know anything about this. I'm a welder."

I said, "Ok, but when we get into the calm water in Cuba you're going to run the boat."

He said, "Yeah, when we get to Cuba I'll run the boat."

Finally we got close to Cuba and it was flat calm. I told him he had to make sure to stay in the blue water. If we see a brown bottom in the water, that's the Coronados Reef, and it'll tear the bottom right out of the boat.

We slowed down to an idle and I went below to check the oil and everything else. We were having fuel problems so I changed the fuel filters. My brother idled along in the blue water. I came back up and said, "OK I'm going to lay down and go to sleep. You can run along the coast here."

He said, "Oh, no. I can't run along the coast. It's too dangerous. I don't want to tear the bottom out of the boat. I don't know what you're talking about, this brown water and blue water. You've got to run the boat."

So by now I'd been up for thirty hours, and was going to have to run the boat along the coast of Cuba. "I'm telling you right now, when we leave Cuba you're running the boat, no if, ands, or buts about it."

It was so rough coming across the Yucatan Channel that *CATV* did not catch us. Just as we were leaving the coast of Cuba headed for Key West I could hear from the *CATV* and they were just approaching the coast of Cuba. So I lay down on the bridge and went to sleep. After I slept for about two hours my brother woke me up. "You gotta wake up! You gotta wake up!"

Half asleep I asked him, "What do you want now?"

He said, "I just heard mayday on the radio. Somebody was hollering they were out on the reef and breaking up."

I tried to get *CATV* on the radio but I couldn't reach them. It was now getting dark; we had no radar, or navigational equipment to speak of. All I had to navigate by was a compass and a depth finder, so I couldn't turn back and look for them. We chugged on toward Key West.

As if things weren't crazy enough already, when the sun came up in the morning, and we were in the middle of the Gulf Stream, my brother said he wanted to fish. I said, "You can't fish. We've got to get to Key West. We're going to be running on fumes when we get there. We've got to keep running."

He said, "Well, can I put the teaser out?" So he put the Boone teaser out, and sure enough a blue marlin came up and ate it. After five or six times of hitting the teaser, my brother tried to drop back to try to get the teaser caught in the fish's throat, which did not work. But it was a pretty little blue marlin that added excitement to the trip.

Now we were navigating by a Radio Direction Finder and I screwed up. I thought the RDF end was pointed in the direction of our destination, but it was really at the middle of the side. Therefore I was headed for the Dry Tortugas instead of Key West. When we were still overdue to reach Key West I figured out what I had done wrong and changed course. Finally we got into Key West.

When we cleared customs and I asked the Customs Officer if he had cleared in the *CATV* boat, because they should have been in there way ahead of us. The agent said, "No I haven't cleared in anybody from Mexico."

I asked again, "Nothing at all?"

Finally he called the Coast Guard and it turned out the *CATV* had started to run up the coast of Cuba in the dark. The Captain went down and got a Loran fix and hollered up to the bridge to turn left because they were getting close to the reef. They were actually inside the reef, and when they turned they plowed right up on top of it. They tore the bottom out of the boat, which was only a few months old. They sunk the boat right there on top of the reef.

The Cubans put them all under house arrest. It cost the owner of the boat $10,000 a man to get them released, plus all the expenses of having them flown from Cuba to the Cayman Islands, and from Cayman back to the states, plus the cost of the brand new boat. It was a real tragedy for the *CATV* boat. I felt bad that we hadn't been able to execute a rescue.

180

At any rate, we got home and it was a memorable trip to be down in Cozumel, Mexico, catching sailfish, and fighting off giant dolphin for days on end.

St. Thomas

In 1979 I was asked if I could get away to go to St. Thomas with Stu Loveland, to blue marlin fish with Winthrop Rockefeller III. I said that I would love to go. Stu and I were going to bring a forty-five foot Chris Craft down. We were going to fish with Mr. Rockefeller for a week or two, and then bring the boat back to Allied Yachts in Miami. At that time Mr. Rockefeller owned Allied Yachts.

When we were getting ready to go, Stu and I went to the grocery store to buy provisions for the trip. While there, we came upon the cookie department. At this point the shopping cart was empty. He looked around and found the oatmeal cookies (without raisins) and started loading them in the cart. When we had fifteen boxes, the shelf was empty, but we still did not have enough. The store manager helped us with some more cookies out of storage, and we ended up with twenty-five packages of oatmeal cookies without raisins. I asked, "What are you doing Stu? We couldn't possibly use twenty-five packages of these cookies."

Stu said quite emphatically, "We do not want to run out of oatmeal cookies!"

It seems that on Winthrop Rockefeller's boat there had to be oatmeal cookies without raisins at all times. And in his airplane there must be Oreo cookies at all times. Stu said he had been on Rockefeller's jet one day when it ran out of Oreo cookies. He witnessed Mr. Rockefeller go ballistic when there were no Oreos on the jet. So we were not going to run out of oatmeal cookies on the boat.

We readied the tackle, loaded up the boat, and took off for St. Thomas. We ran to Nassau and tied up there. We ran into another boat in the marina that was going to Venezuela. Their route took them to Clarencetown, Long Island, through Puerto Rico, and then southeast from there. That was the route taken in those days so the boats could be assured of having the fuel they needed to make the trip. We were in a forty-five foot sport fish, and they were in a fifty-five foot Hatteras. We were both going the same way, and probably about the same speed, so we decided to run together the rest of the way.

We left Nassau the following day and headed across the Bahamas Bank. It's tricky navigation because of the shallow water and coral heads. We ran down into the Exuma Sound and it started to really blow. The waves were going all over the tops of the boats with solid spray. Fortunately we were taking everything on the beam, so we beat our way down to Clarencetown. There we found out that there were a number of tropical depressions coming through. Next we left Clarencetown, headed east-southeast to the very southeastern Bahamas, to end up in West Caicos.

We ran in a horrific head sea with everybody wearing life jackets. Always two men on the bridge and one man down below, and never traveling back and forth to or from the salon to the bridge without everyone knowing we were on the move. If all else failed, the ditch kit was right inside the door. It was a miserable crossing, but we finally finished that run.

Then we got to run south in flat calm water for fifty or sixty miles and turned east again. Our next run took us right into West Caicos; and boy was it rough there. The boat was going straight up, crashed down, straight up, and crashed down. And we were following the bigger boat that was knocking the waves down for us a little bit. These were huge vertical waves, like when the wind blows against the tide in an inlet. This went on all day long as we beat our way into West Caicos.

Then we ran from West Caicos down to the Turks and anchored up at a lighthouse. It was a beautiful calm evening. We watched TV and videos. We left there the following morning and chugged to Samana Bay in the Dominican Republic. This was really scary for me. All the military officials came down and took whatever they wanted off the boat. We were giving them bags of clothes for the

182

children. From the DR we headed to Puerto Rico, and I'll be doggone if we didn't get horrific weather again. We were still following that Hatteras, up one wave and crashing down the other side.

The sea was so bad it ripped the radar off, causing leaks into the salon and water running right down into the circuit panel. This caused all kinds of electrical shorts. Finally we got into Ponce on the south side of Puerto Rico where we learned that we had been running through a tropical depression. Then the weather straightened out and we put the boat back together, and ran on to St. Thomas.

We arrived in St. Thomas just in time for the Boy Scout Blue Marlin Tournament. Now it was Jimmy and Stuart Loveland from St. Thomas, and me running the boat. Stuart and I were working the cockpit. We ran up past North Rock to fish, and we were going past the last island before entering the open ocean when chaos broke out. We rung off a drive shaft right at the coupling at the back of the engine. We had to limp back to St. Thomas, put the boat in the yard, and get a shaft from somewhere. Then we had to sand it down until it would fit into the coupling.

The format for the tournament was to have the host, that was Winthrop Rockefeller III, and a guest host, someone who was not providing the boat but would be on the boat everyday. Then every boat had a rotating guest everyday, and that's how we worked out the observers. We used observers because this was a release tournament.

We fished with three lines and rotated them every hour. Our guest on the boat for the second day of the tournament was a woman. Before she joined us she had caught a very big blue marlin. Actually the crew hooked it, and she wound it in; but she got the credit for it. That was her only angling feat. When she was on our boat, every blue marlin that came up came up on her bait. She would be sitting in the cabin and we'd have to call her. She would come walking out leisurely, and the fish would be gone. Then we'd set everything up again and a blue marlin would come up, and she wouldn't do anything right. We never did catch a blue marlin that day. We caught all our blue marlin on the lay day in between the tournament days.

183

The next fiasco happened because there was the bank audit of the boat yard in Miami while we were away in St. Thomas. The auditors were asking, "Where is this forty-five foot Chris Craft that's on your inventory?"

"It's in St. Thomas."

"Is there a Chris Craft crew on board?"

"No, two professional captains."

"Well, they have to work for Chris Craft. We're not accepting liability for this boat. Chris Craft will only accept liability if their captains are on the boat."

"Well, it's Winthrop Rockefeller III."

"OK, Mr. Rockefeller can use the boat until he's done. But when he gets off the boat, the Chris Craft captains have to get on the boat and take over running it. And they have to bring it back to the states." That was so frustrating. Someone else had to run the boat back to Miami. But we had a wonderful time and Winthrop Rockefeller III was just the nicest guy in the world.

Traveling with Mr. Rockefeller was his bodyguard named Rich. Mr. Rockefeller didn't want anybody to recognize him, so when we would go out to dinner he did a thing where Rich became Mr. Rich, and his bodyguard became Winthrop Rockefeller. Win would be running around getting drinks for Rich, and Rich would be giving Win orders on what to do, and we'd all have a good laugh out of it. And Win was also no slouch when we were done fishing for the day. He would grab a scrub brush or chamois mop. He was always right there doing everything with the guys, cleaning the boat and rigging baits.

We cruised down to Anegada, and to the Bitter End, and down to the eastern end of the Virgin Islands. Jimmy and Stu Loveland stayed in St. Thomas when we were done fishing and cruising. Mr. Rockefeller and I flew back to Miami on Rockefeller's private jet.

Then a fortunate thing happened. We arrived in Miami at about nine at night, and I took a cab home. When I got home my wife was badly under the weather, and said she had been in the emergency room all day. She worked in the hospital, but this time she had been in the emergency room as a patient. At the time they couldn't figure out what was wrong with her and they sent her home. At five in the morning she woke me up and we rushed to the hospital. She had a severe internal dysfunction. She was bleeding profusely, but fortunately I was there to take her to the hospital and it probably saved her life.

All's well that ends well. I had a great trip, met some wonderful people, and got home in time to save my wife, which made me a hero.

Italy

Massimo Canali is a very nice Italian lawyer with a condo in Rome, and a home on the southern tip of Italy. He came to Florida to learn how to catch swordfish. After a couple of trips here he asked if we could come to Italy and teach swordfishing. He invited Abie and me to go to the seaside village of Ventotene, but we had some charters during the time he needed us. So I convinced Abie to stay and run the boat while I went to Rome and on to Ventotene. They asked me how much it would cost. I said I wasn't too worried about the finances, but I had to go first class all the way.

So, I flew first class on Alitalia Airlines to Rome. When I got to Rome, I was picked up by a thirty-one year old Italian girl named Margherita who was my guide and translator. We got into a black Audi touring car with a chauffeur, and he drove us around Rome and took me to my hotel. For two days we saw all the sights in Rome. I had my own personal guide explain every event. We saw everything at great length whether it was the Vatican or the Coliseum.

One of the funny things we did happened at the Trevi Fountain. Next to the Fountain they had torn up part of the cobblestone street for repairs. There were four armed guards standing around these cobblestones. I joked to Margherita that my sister collects rocks from all over the world, and when I visit some place she doesn't want me to bring some trinket that was made in Asia; she wants an authentic stone from wherever I go. One of these cobblestones would be perfect to bring to her. I asked my guide if she thought these four armed guards would mind if I picked one up and took it back to my hotel? We laughed about it and went on our way.

We had a great time in Rome. I ate wonderful things I never get a chance to eat anywhere else, like some kind of cheese with figs; and I drank wine at dinner every night. From there they took me down to the mouth of the Tiber River that runs through Rome and down to the seaport at Ostia. I got on a boat with Massimo Canali and his good doctor friend, Domenico Scopelliti, and we made the eighty-mile run down the coast to Ventotene.

Ventotene is about ten miles north of the Isle of Capri. It had been a prison island at one time. They dug the harbor out of the rock of the island, and on the other side of the harbor there was a prison on an island completely surrounded by water. At one time the island we were on was just a guard's quarters for this prison. Now it's a beautiful resort with live volcanic rock, and it's just amazing. I could look down over the harbor and see all the boats. The food was terrific, and I had my first exposure to genuine Italian ice. I wish I could have it everyday. It was a mixed berry Italian ice, and it was exceptional.

I was there to teach people how to swordfish, so the second day I was on the island I got all my gear together in the cockpit of the doctor's boat and started to rig the baits and rods. There were a hundred people circled on the dock behind us with professional television cameras, and video cameras, and still cameras. Everybody was listening and taking videotape of everything I did. I went all the way through rigging the baits, and rigging the rods, and getting everything ready. Then about twenty guys got onto this thirty-five foot boat and we ran up to the north toward Ponza. There we did a couple of day drops for swordfish. We saw one jump, but we didn't get any bites.

We didn't have a whole lot of time to fish. We went back to town for a beautiful dinner, and got up in the morning and did the whole performance again. We had a nice lunch and then went into a meeting room where an Italian scientist talked about the history and habits of swordfish in the Mediterranean Sea. Then I did a talk on

186

daytime and nighttime swordfishing, as the scientist translated what I said. That night we got on a bigger Hatteras and went out again.

There was no current and we saw a million moon jellies in the water. We fished a couple of different spots and they decided we needed to wrap it up because the regular tournament started the next day. About midnight we started to wind in the lines. Lo and behold, the farthest rod from the boat had a bite on, and we caught a sixty-pound swordfish. Those people were sure excited about that. We had caught a swordfish in Italy using the American style.

Then we fished a two-day tournament. In their tournaments they troll in the daytime and quite often get bites, and even catch a swordfish now and then. They also catch tuna and spearfish, and an occasional dolphin or bonito. What's really interesting is that all of their trolling lures like our Billy baits, or any of our mold craft lures, are homemade out of different materials for the heads, and then rubber skirts applied. Or they troll Rapalas. Every place I looked there were rows and rows of Rapalas.

They caught a lot of nice fish. I saw a lot of nice fish on the dock, and we did catch one long fin albacore. We also saw another big swordfish jumping while we were out there. It was a very exciting trip. When we were done I got on a ferry back to the mainland. My chauffeur and Margherita picked me up and drove me back to Rome, and put me back on Alitalia for the first class flight back home. The memories are unforgettable about my great trip to Italy. I can't thank Massimo Canali enough for putting it together.

Abie Goes to Italy

A year after my trip to Italy they asked me to come back to teach them kite fishing. I told them thank you very much, but since Abie had stayed home the year before, he should be the one to go. So Abie took his then fiancé, now wife Yudith, and they went to Italy to teach kite fishing. They flew to Rome where they were put up in Massimo's condominium. They had two or three days in Rome to walk the streets, and drink wine and see the sites, and then they went to Ponza and attempted to show the guys how to swordfish and to kite fish.

It was kind of funny. Abie managed to find schools of tinker mackerel down deep in the water column, and they filled the live well. All the Italians could talk about was eating the bait. They didn't want to hear about using it to catch any other kind of fish. They just thought the bait was for eating.

Abie showed them how to kite fish with helium balloons. They did some more swordfishing, but unfortunately all they managed to catch was mackerel. But he and Yudith had a great time in Ponza, and I'm so glad he got to go as well. He certainly deserved a trip to Italy after being invited the first time and staying home to watch the office.

Wahoo

Wahoo are long and slender with a nose that comes to a slow taper, and a mouth full of razor sharp teeth. They are dark blue along the top of the back and then turn lighter blue and then, from right behind the head all the way to the tail, there are lightning stripes of gray bars that run up and down their sides. They are beautiful; and they are also fast and powerful.

Ninety-nine Pound Wahoo

Back about 1973 I decided to try my hand at private boat work. I worked a lot at Ryder Boat Sales, a Hatteras dealer in Miami. They had several different boats I worked on, a thirty-six foot Hatteras called the *Sly Mongoose* captained by John Graves, and fifty-three foot sport fish. This particular day Captain Neil Orange and I were splitting the duties on the fifty-three footer.

We ran down the bay and spent the night a little north of Ocean Reef. We went offshore from Caesar's Creek but didn't catch much, if anything at all. In the afternoon we headed north and caught a couple of live bonitos at the Miami Sea Buoy. We put them out for bait, one on the left outrigger, and one on the right and we slow trolled around.

If live bonitos can be deployed successfully, they are deadly baits. So we dragged them around at two or three miles an hour to keep them breathing. After a little while the bonito on the left outrigger was starting to die. He was just barely able to swim, and was staying right on top of the water. The bonito on the right outrigger was still swimming pretty well, and he was staying down a little deeper. So we made a pass, west to east, just south of the sea buoy. When I say just south, I mean the weaker bait on the right rigger passed within fifty feet of the buoy. As we were passing the buoy, this torpedo left the buoy and came racing across the surface throwing a rooster tail. It nailed that half dead bonito and took off screaming.

We got this big fish on and locked up the reel. We fought it for quite a while and finally got it up to the boat. It was one of the most beautiful wahoos I'd ever seen. We got it up close and gaffed it. What a thrill it was to catch this ninety-nine pound wahoo at the Miami Sea Buoy. I'll always remember that one.

Segal Wahoo Releases

Scott Segal and I did a lot of fishing together for a long, long time. Back in the early days, when I still had my boat up at Keystone Point Marina, Scott brought his new wife, Meredith, fishing with me. In the course of our running, we ended up at the Miami Sea Buoy. While we were there, we pulled up to the buoy and put the chum bag into the water. On light line, with small split shots, we baited real small hooks with tiny pieces of fish. We proceeded to catch about a dozen speedos and put them in the live well.

We fired out a couple of live baits on flat lines, and one on the outrigger. It didn't take long for us to get a really good strike. In a relatively short time we had a fifty-pound wahoo up to the boat. I gaffed it and brought it in. We took some pictures, put it in the cooler and threw ice on top of it. We still had two speedos out, and we continued fishing by the buoy.

Soon enough we got slammed again with a good strike. This fish fought the same as that fifty-pound wahoo, and sure enough, here came another one about the same size. I turned to Scott and Meredith and said that we had all the fish we needed to eat. They were in complete agreement. I don't harvest fish we don't want to eat ourselves, and I don't sell any fish, so we turned that wahoo loose.

We went back to the buoy, and put those speedos out again and, lo and behold, caught a third fifty-pound wahoo. When I got back to the dock and was telling my buddies that I released fifty-pound wahoos, they wanted to rush me to the hospital; I had to be sick to be releasing wahoos like that that everybody loves so much.

Rigging for Wahoo

We were catching frigate bonitos, which is their proper name. Everybody in Miami and in the Keys call them speedos. Up in Palm Beach they call them fire tails, because they have a bright orange or red tail. They are long cylindrical fish much like a tinker mackerel, except the mouth is much smaller, and they don't have any stripes. They have a greenish back with a little bit darker stripe on their side. These are bait fish that average about sixteen to eighteen inches long. We have to swish them around in the live well, and we have to swim them around on the line, and move the boat with a little headway. If we stop moving them they will drown.

If we are targeting sailfish or dolphin only, we rig them up with a 9/0 VMC lightweight circle hook and a sixty-pound fluorocarbon leader about fifteen feet long. Then we normally fasten them to twenty-pound test.

These speedos really attract wahoos, barracudas, and big kings, so we often use number seven wire about three feet long. Then, if we're really serious about targeting the toothy critters, we run another ten or twelve inches of number seven wire to a 6/0 or 7/0 j-hook; Mustad 9174 is ideal for this. We just tag that underneath the skin wherever it reaches, and bridle the bait with a bridle band through the nostrils or through the eye sockets to hold that 9/0 circle hook in place. So we've got a circle hook on the nose, and a j-hook about three quarters of the way back on the bait. The trick is to combine them. Thus, if a sailfish or dolphin eats that speedo, and we give him just a few second of drop back, he'll get the that circle hook in his mouth, but he may very well still have that j-hook outside of his mouth. That gives us a good chance of hooking the sailfish with the circle hook and not harming him with the j-hook. Then we can tag him and release him, which is what we always want to do.

191

Conversely, wahoo, and kingfish, and barracudas love to bite the bait about two thirds of the way back on the body, so the ideal position of that j-hook is just about the anal opening. That's where those teeth are going to close around both sides of that hook. So the j-hook will be inside the fish's mouth when he chomps down on the bait. The wire leader cannot be bitten through, so it will be a good hookup when he tries to bite the bait in half.

There's another trick when the water is real clear and the fish are spooky, but we want to catch those kings, wahoo, barracudas, and sharks. We use fluorocarbon for fifteen feet from our main twenty-pound line to the circle hook. Then we just use the wire from the circle hook to the j-hook. When they bite the tail off, those ten inches of wire is all we'll need to hook the fish, but we still have the stealth of the fluorocarbon running thorough the water to the bait.

Cooking Wahoo

While on the subject of wahoo, there are a lot of different ways it can be prepared. Never overcook it, because it can overcook very fast. The way we like to do it is we filet the fish and then skin it. It is very hard to skin from the tail to the head, and it's not a fish we would want to peel. So we skin it from the centerline out to the top, or out to the bottom of the filet, the exact same way we skin kingfish. We cut the fish up into eight-inch sections and then go down next to the centerline and out to the dorsal, and then down to the centerline and out to the belly. We do that with each section and end up with these beautiful eight-inch long filets of snow-white wahoo meat.

Do not get the wahoo chunks wet. We roll each chunk in a paper towel and then put it in a dry Ziploc bag and refrigerate it, or bury it in ice. The bottom line is: wrap it in paper towels, in a Ziploc bag, kept dry, and keep it cold for two days. Then it can be dipped in sesame oil and rolled in sesame seeds. Sear each side, then put it on a plate and cut it thin and serve it with a bowl of soy sauce and some wasabi on a plate.

For anyone who does not like raw fish, the wahoo can be cut into about half inch thick medallions then dipped in soy sauce, then pressed in the sesame seeds, and then into a hot skillet, a couple of minutes on each side. Flip it over, put it on the plate and serve it with the soy sauce and a little wasabi. Either way, that wahoo will be a treat to eat.

South Pass, Louisiana

Van Avery from Jackson, Mississippi, hired me in June of 1971 to come to Gulfport, Mississippi, to fish the Gulfport Rodeo Tournament, an all around big game fishing tournament. We left out of Biloxi, Mississippi, and ran down to South Pass, which is called Port Eads, at the mouth of the Mississippi River. We pulled up to a lighthouse where we were able to purchase fuel and ice. Then we pulled around into a swamp where there were about ten slips where we could tie up and live on our boat.

Down the dock was a double decker houseboat with rooms on the second level. On the bottom level was a restaurant where it was family style eating and there was no menu. They served whatever they were having, steaks, hamburgers, spaghetti, or just whatever. That was complicated for me because everyone knows I am the world's pickiest eater. When we were walking from the houseboat back to the boat we could hear giant alligator gar slashing in the water between the houseboat and the sportfishing boats.

They chartered a forty-one Hatteras out of Mobile, Alabama, that came with a captain who had no blue water fishing experience. All he had ever fished for was kingfish, so they hired me to come up from Miami and be the cruise director and the mate. We got up in the morning and headed out. I had rigged some baits, and on the way out I rigged some more. As we ran offshore it began to get light and the water was just coffee brown with really heavy cream. It was the ugliest brown water in the world.

After about an hour of running, one of the anglers came off the bridge to tell me we were coming up on a beautiful rip, and get ready to put the lines out. We went through a weed line and the water went from coffee brown to split soup green, a real pale muddy green water. They were hollering for me to put the baits out because there were tunas busting off the bow. I started putting the baits out thinking, 'We're fishing in this, trying to catch a blue marlin? This is insane.' They were claiming to see tunas but I was wondering if it was just some bonitos busting. Anyhow, we didn't get any bites, so I talked the clients to running further offshore to find some cleaner water.

We ran to about sixty miles offshore and the water was better, a pale bluish green, not bad, at least OK for sailfish. We spent the day trolling in that and we caught a sailfish and a couple of wahoo, and that was about it. Running in we were discussing the plans for the next day. I told them we had to find some bluer water. We needed to leave earlier in the morning and head offshore.

The following morning we took off early and chugged along until the sun came up because there is a lot of floating debris out there. When we got 100 miles offshore we came to a weed line that was so thick the captain was afraid to go through it. It was probably a good idea because there was so much grass he could have easily stalled out an engine. We found a thinner spot and cut through, and started trolling down this weed line. It was chaos. There were giant dolphin, twenty-five to fifty pounds, an occasional wahoo, and yellowfin tuna.

My line with the mackerel was covered over with Sargasso weed. My habit was to pull the outrigger down and pull on the line to get the weed off. I would pull on the line, let it out, pull on it some more, and let it out again until I got rid of most of the weeds, then I would pull the line all the way in and take the rest of the weeds off and then let the line back out.

That's what I was doing, and I pulled the line half way up and the seaweed would keep digging and it would jerk like crazy. I would jerk back on it trying to shake it loose. It kept going back and forth like this. I would get the line half way back up the rigger and it would jerk again. Finally when I looked back there, it wasn't just the weeds, it was a blue marlin trying to eat the bait and the seaweed and everything. When I saw what was happening I let go of the line and the blue marlin ate the mackerel. It was a 255-pound blue, the first blue marlin caught in this Gulfport Rodeo in six years. That was quite a thrill and, of course, it won the blue marlin category of the tournament.

It was a kind of a bummer. After our first day of fishing we had a load of dolphin, tuna, and wahoo. We put them all in the freezer at Port Eads and they called the tournament director to make sure we were eligible for the Grand Angler. Normally what they did was to keep all the fish in Port Eads, take the four winning fish, like the four biggest dolphin or tuna, or billfish, and take them back to the Gulfport weigh in. The rest of the fish would be left in Port Eads and a truck would come down and take the rest of them to some charity in New Orleans. From Port Eads they called up to Gulfport to ask about this and were told not to send ours because we were eligible for the Grand Angler, an award that goes to the boat that weight is the most fish total.

So they kept all the fish there and we went offshore the next day and caught so much fish we were out of bait and all our lures were shredded, and they had no skirts left on them. We took a bed sheet and tore up strips and tied them to skirts to make out homemade lures. And believe me, the dolphin could care less, they ate them like they were candy.

On the way back in the second day we hit a log and bent a prop. Then we went a few more miles and blew an engine. So now we were on one engine (fortunately that one had a good propeller). We got into Port Eads in the middle of the night. Because we were eligible for Grand Angler we piled all our fish in the cockpit of the boat and put some ice on them, and pulled out and headed for tournament headquarters in Gulfport. When we got to Gulfport we off-loaded all the fish. They hung the fish on a chain link fence that stretched for 150 feet or so. It was strange, all these fish hanging on the fence, all the dolphin, and a 255-pound marlin, and wahoos, and tuna.

196

When it came to giving out the awards we had the four biggest dolphins, which was first place, and the four biggest wahoos, and two of the four biggest tuna, a sailfish, and the only blue marlin. It was just crazy with all these fish up on the fence. We won a bunch of trophies, but the fact was they decided we were not eligible for Grand Angler because we didn't come back and weigh our fish every night, which they had already told us we did not have to do. We had two anglers, and they had three times as many fish as anybody else, so it was hands down a tournament we had to win.

The bottom line was we did not get the Grand Angler award, but we sure filled the table with trophies. That was a great trip to South Pass, Louisiana, and really great fishing.

Grouper

Andrew's Grouper

Andrew was the son of a long time friend of mine named Baron. Baron always wanted to catch a cobia, and Andrew wanted to catch a big grouper. We were over in the Bahamas for the weekend for the Dusky Owners' Bimini Bash. We started off hitting artificial reefs on the Bahamas Bank. We ran thirty miles to the east to a sunken boat where we frequently caught cobia. We had also caught some groupers in this area in the past, but this time when we got there the fish we were looking for weren't there. So we fished for some sharks, and yellowtail snappers, and porgies, and threw a few fish in the live well for later on.

We moved on to another wreck, a sunken boat, twenty-seven miles south from the first wreck. In the past we had caught loads of cobia in this spot, but again there were none this day. We caught some more yellowtails for bait, and a few that were big enough to eat. We caught a lot of barracudas and small sharks, but no cobia, and no grouper.

We moved on to another wreck where we have consistently caught cobia. This was a DC-3 that crashed during the days when marijuana smuggling was common throughout the Caribbean and Florida. The area had been notorious for its marijuana smuggling, and this DC-3 had crashed during those days. In the past this wreck had produced some beautiful mangrove snappers, blue runners, yellow jacks, sharks, barracudas, and Spanish mackerel, but again, no cobia and no grouper.

By now we had traveled seventy-five miles, and were a good thirty miles from the Island of Bimini where we were spending the week. So by the time we ran back to Bimini we had clocked more than 100 miles searching for cobia and grouper. I decided to make a couple of drops on wrecks right in front of Bimini. There were two boats anchored on the first wreck, so we decided to go to a second wreck. But there was a ferry ship that was used to service Bimini and the other islands anchored on top of that wreck. So I said, "Oh the heck with it. There's this spot right on the dropoff. We catch some nice grouper there sometimes." So, after running a hundred miles, and giving up on two spots because they were inaccessible, I just stopped on the dropoff a mile from our home for the week.

It wasn't five minutes and Andrew got a big bite on the bait on the bottom. He was fighting and fighting, and my mate Abie Raymond said, "Oh it's definitely a shark."

I said, "I don't think it's a shark. I think it got hung up on the rocks for a minute." Just then Ralph Brown, the owner of Dusky Boats, and the host for the week's event, pulled up to say hello. His eyes grew wide as Andrew's seventy pound black grouper popped up. After running over a hundred miles in search of a cobia or grouper, we found the grouper a mile from homeport. That was Andrew's big grouper and a lifetime dream fulfilled for a seventeen year old boy.

Vertical Jig

There's a group of four guys from the west coast of Florida who come over and fish with me every spring. They predominately target sailfish. Several years ago one of the guys came with a vertical jigging spinning outfit with fifty-pound braid on a short, light spinning rod. He brought with him a whole satchel full of vertical jigs of all shapes and sizes.

We went out in the morning, but the fishing was slow. I took us over to a wreck in a couple of hundred feet of water and said, "Let's drop a pinfish down and see if we can catch a grouper. And we can set you up with a vertical jig at the same time."

There was one fellow on the boat who was dying to catch an amberjack. It was on his bucket list for his fishing club up north.

Jack, the gentleman who arranged the charter, said, "I'm not going to drop that rig down to the bottom. All we're going to do is catch an amberjack."

So the fellow who wanted the amberjack got on the rod with the live pinfish. While he dropped that down on the starboard side of the boat, the other fellow, the one with the vertical jig, dropped on the portside. They both got down to the bottom. We drifted for a few seconds and they both got bites. The guy with the vertical jig started fighting his fish, but it cut him off on the bottom. The guy using the pinfish for bait fought his fish to the boat, and it turned out to be a beautiful twenty-five pound gag grouper.

Jack then said, "Oh my gosh, you didn't tell me there were groupers here. I'm getting on the rod next." He jumped on the live bait rod.

My mate, Sherman, re-rigged the vertical jig. We pulled back up to the wreck and Jack dropped down a live pinfish. The guy who brought the vertical jig rod jumped on the jig rod. Soon enough they both hooked up, but the guy with the vertical jig got cut off at the bottom again. The guy with the pinfish, who definitely did not want to catch an amberjack, of course, caught a nice amberjack.

The guy who caught the grouper was still kind of jealous and said, "Man I wanted to catch an amberjack so bad. I hope I can get one before we go home today. We've got a lot of wrecks out here."

We went back to the wreck again and the third angler got on the live bait. The vertical jig guy got on his rig, and we pulled upstream of the wreck. (We always want to drop our baits upstream of the wreck, because the current is going to carry it back toward the wreck. Then we try to hold the boat just upstream of the wreck to present the baits to the grouper. Then, when we hook up, we pull the boat away from the wreck and fight the fish.)

The third man dropped his pinfish down. He didn't care what he caught. The guy with the vertical jig dropped down, and sure

200

enough he got cut off again. The guy with the live bait came up with an amberjack. Everybody was catching fish on the live bait. The guy with the vertical jig caught nothing. He stayed on the jig the whole time. They all said: "Come on, catch a fish, use the live bait. You can't keep losing jigs all day."

The vertical jig guy came over to the live bait rod and the one who was dying for an amberjack took the vertical jigging rod. Sherman rigged up the vertical jigging rod again with another brand new leader and new jig. We pulled up to the wreck. One angler dropped the pinfish down, and the amberjack hunter dropped down the vertical jig. He had never fished that kind of rig before and didn't know what to do. He just stood there with his right hand on the fore grip and his left hand on the butt. He slowly jerked the rod up in the air and let it go down, not seriously winding at all. He seemed to be disconnected from what he was doing.

As he spoke slowly, he jerked the rod. "What . . ." Jerk, "do..." Jerk, "I . . ." Jerk, "Do. . ." Jerk? And bam! He got a fish on. He composed himself and started cranking. I drove ahead with the boat while the angler jerked and yanked. Finally he had hooked his amberjack, or so he thought. Then, believe it or not, he came up with a fifty-seven pound Warsaw grouper, the biggest grouper that we've caught in the last twenty years in Miami.

The guy hadn't been doing any winding; he wasn't doing anything but jerking the rod up and down and letting his jig sink. He was dying to catch an amberjack and ended up catching a fifty-seven pound Warsaw grouper. The other guys just shook their heads, and we went back to sail fishing.

The good news is that the amberjack fisherman did catch a nice amberjack the following year, so all was well, and they had plenty of grouper filets to take home from that trip.

Abie's Goliath

One afternoon we had a trip with a real good client of ours, Cal Levy. Cal brought a guest on this trip. Cal was a mutton snapper and grouper guy. We were anchored on the *Ultra Freeze* and fishing was pretty slow. Finally we had a bite on a fifty-pound outfit on the bottom. We were using a fifty-pound mono leader and a 6/0 circle hook baited with a pilchard. Cal's guest started fighting the fish, but was worn out in short order. It was obviously a very big fish. Then Cal took over and fought it, and after a while he tired and gave it back to his guest. Again the guest fought it and, too tired to fight any longer, finally asked Abie to take it.

In the meantime, as a sidebar, I was sitting on the downwind side of the boat. There was no air movement where I sat, and it was stifling hot in the sun, and the humidity was high. Abie fought and fought with this fifty-pound outfit for over a half hour. I could not believe that none of the rigging failed. But finally, up from the depths here it came. It was a goliath grouper every bit of 200 pounds. A fifty-pound mono leader and a little light wire circle hook, and Abie, and Cal, and his guest managed to get it all the way to the surface. What a unique catch that was. Whether that goliath ate the pilchard or ate a snapper, we'll never know. When we got him up to the boat, we put a lot of effort into reviving him so we could send him back down. Some fish get the bends coming up, so we have to reduce the gas pressure and then get them headed back toward the bottom.

Eventually we did, but by this time I was absolutely drained. I was really a wreck. I started to get dizzy, and had a headache, and felt sick. I went and sat in the shade, and Abie brought me a couple of bottles of water. Eventually I felt better. It's a lesson to be learned even after fifty years. Fishermen have to be careful. Working in the outdoors everyday, I have to watch out for dehydration and heat problems in the direct sun with no breeze. The sun and heat can be bad news no matter how much experience a person has. I learned a valuable lesson from that goliath grouper, plus I had the thrill of seeing those guys beat that big fish.

John Mahoney

John Mahoney and Rick Aizpuru were two customers who fished together with me quite a bit. John, who we simply called Mahoney, was a very laid back fisherman. He was a tax evasion lawyer for the federal government who loved to sip on a few beers, and always wanted to catch a bigger snapper. We would run to Caesar's Creek down in South Miami where he often caught mutton snappers in the eight, ten, and occasionally twelve-pound range. He always enjoyed these outings, but he was obsessed with catching a giant mutton snapper.

This time we were on an all day fishing trip live baiting off Miami Beach. We were hitting the local wrecks trying to find him a mutton snapper. We dropped on a wreck in about 175 feet of water a little bit south of Government Cut. We had a good bite and Mahoney grabbed the rod, pulled the line tight, and started fighting the fish. I'll be doggone if he didn't catch the biggest mutton snapper that I've ever had anybody catch. It weighed twenty-four pounds. After he caught that fish he became a guru on targeting groupers.

Mahoney and Rich went with us to Bimini almost every summer for five or six days. Every time we went over there we had to try to get Mahoney a bigger grouper. The first time we went he caught a really nice twelve-pound yellowfin grouper. It had beautiful colors, reds on the back, and yellow on the fins, and a million polka dots. Just a beautiful fish. That was his first decent grouper.

The next year we went over, and after Mahoney stocked up on his favorite beer, Kalik Gold, we went deep dropping for queen snappers in a thousand feet of water. We got a big bite and his rig but it hung up on the bottom. He was working on it, and working on it, and finally got it loose, and came up with a thirty pound mystic grouper, a big old fat thing with stripes.

When these groupers come from very deep water, they fight and pull, and then the weight disappears. The line goes looser and looser because the gasses in the grouper are expanding as the atmospheric pressure around them is reduced in shallower water. This often causes the grouper to rise to the surface faster than we can wind, and pretty soon they come popping out of the water behind the boat. They're so full of air that when they come up they can actually bounce out of the water and land on the surface. Mahoney could have been heard all the way back in Miami when he came up with that mystic grouper. He was just thrilled with it.

We went to the Bahamas together one more time. We were down off Beach Cay catching yellow tail snappers. Whenever we caught yellow tails we would take some of the one pound snappers and drop them down as live bait. Typically we would catch sharks and some amberjacks, and every once in a while we'd catch a nice black grouper. This time Mahoney was fishing for his black grouper, trying to beat his mystic grouper record.

He used a live snapper on a great big seven and a half feet long solid glass rod, with a dual speed Penn International fifty. He could downshift into low gear where he could crank against anything, or up shift it and wind it up real fast. He was cranking with the rod in the rod holder. We would joke that he should use a football helmet or a hardhat when fishing with that rod. The solid glass rod bends from the butt end all the way to the tip end, and if he got a big fish on with 130 pound braid, the rod would be bent way over with a big curve. He'd have to back up to protect himself in case the line parted and the rod came flying back in his face. As this fish came up, the tension would let up a little and he'd take a few cranks. Then the fish would pull a little, and the rod would bend way over, and he'd have to back away to protect himself. Then it would come up a little and he'd wind on it. It was pure tension watching him.

Soon enough we found out that Mahoney had hooked a goliath grouper that was running for its life with three sharks hot on his tail. The fish had the bends, and was floating on top of the water. It was legal in the Bahamas to keep him so we put it to a vote. I figured if we let him go we were just going to feed those sharks. So we put him in the boat to take him back to Bimini and feed the natives. Anytime we had fish we didn't want, they'd love to have it. So, John Mahoney's last biggest 'groupa' as he would call it, was a 250-pound goliath.

Unfortunately his health has forced him to retire since then. We don't get to see him. We get email forwarded from him all the time with jokes and fishing blogs, and we talk to him on the phone once in a while. John's just a really great fisherman, and great company. He loved his beers, and everyday was a great day when John Mahoney was catching 'groupas' on the boat with us.

Floating Goliath

One day Abie and I were fishing way down south offshore of Caesar's Creek with Heidi Knute and her brother. When we were running down the coast we spotted something floating and went over to check it out. It was a goliath grouper, probably close to 300 pounds. The poor thing was floating on top of the water because it had the bends. It had a tear in the corner of its mouth like it had been caught but then got away. At any rate, it had been left floating in the ocean. Whoever caught it couldn't harvest it, and didn't have the sense to help it go down so it could be saved for the future.

Unfortunately, the only way I could save its life was to injure it at the same time. Abie held it with a lip gaff while I used about a half-inch knife blade so it wouldn't make too big of an incision. I slipped the blade under the scales and poked it into the area where the air bladder is located. Immediately the goliath was startled, but I'm sure it was also relieved. He kicked his tail in the air and almost knocked Abie out of the boat. He slipped the lip gaff and splashed water all over the four of us from one end of the boat to the other. But this saved his life and he went on about his business.

Grouper Fingers

Back when I fished by myself with my customers, this one particular day I had a customer who, after catching two or three sailfish, said, "Boy, I'd really like to have something for dinner."

I looked at where we were and said, "We're almost right on top of a good grouper spot." So I rigged up a bottom rod with a live pinfish. We dropped it down, and it just barely hit the bottom when we had a good fish on. It turned out to be a twenty-pound grouper. I figured that since we were there, and the current wasn't too strong, we could make another drop. I started setting up a new rig. The grouper was lying on the deck and the client started studying it. While I dropped another pinfish down, the guy looked all over the fish. He looked it up, down and around. Finally he rolled it over with his toe. He was perplexed.

He said, "I absolutely love grouper fingers. Where are the grouper's fingers?" That was a huge laugh. For anybody who doesn't know, the way we make grouper fingers is to cut the filets up into pieces maybe a half inch by a half inch by a couple of inches. Those are grouper fingers; it's not some protrusions sticking out of the grouper's side.

Cooking Grouper

I think the best grouper I ever ate was when I cut black grouper into two-inch square chunks, a half to three quarters inch thick. I made a beer batter with beer and flour and a little bit of sugar. Then I dipped the fish in the batter and dropped it into a deep fryer at about 325 degrees. I'd leave it in the deep fryer until the filets floated to the top. By encasing the fish in the beer batter, the batter would turn very crisp, but it would encapsulate the grouper so it would steam in its own liquids, and came out flakey and moist and delicious.

It's hard to go wrong with grouper. Take a saucepan with butter and a little garlic, and a little salt and pepper. Drop the grouper in that sizzling garlic and butter; fry one side, and flip it over and fry it on the other side. As soon as it flakes with a knife it's done. That should take about ten minutes.

Grouper is very good broiled as well. Use your favorite spices on it; put a pat of butter on it, and place it underneath the broiler and cook it that way. Cook it for five to ten minutes depending on how you like it. I prefer mine to be cooked more like ten minutes. No matter what you do it's very hard to beat a nice fresh grouper filet.

The best grouper in my opinion is scamp grouper; second best is black grouper, and then gag grouper. It doesn't sound very appealing but it is my favorite fish to eat – fried grouper in a beer batter.

Wire Leaders / Jerry and Jesse Webb

Back in 1978 or 79 I had moved my flats skiff from Islamorada back up into Miami to Keystone Point Marina. I would run trips down into the finger channels below Key Biscayne to go shark fishing. We would anchor on the edges of the channels, catch a barracuda and filet it, and hang the carcass off the back of the boat. Then we cut up big chunks, four inches by six inches by two inches thick, and put these on a 9/0 j-hook with a piece of number eight or nine wire. Then we would cast them out into the channel on a spinning rod or a light conventional, with twenty-pound test. Sharks would smell the barracuda carcass hanging out in the water, and would track it back to the boat. When they found the slabs of barracuda we would catch lemon, and spinner, and nurse, and black tips. It was always fun sport.

But often when we were fishing for sharks, we would catch beautiful ten and twelve-pound mutton snappers, and they would become the highlight of the day. At that time, Pflueger Marine Taxidermy was owned by Jerry Webb. He had hired his cousin Jesse Webb as his public relations officer. Whenever I'd go into their shop they would hear my tales about shark fishing and the mutton snappers, and they decided to see if they could catch some of those muttons.

We ran down to the finger channels, caught a couple barracudas, anchored up the boat, and put on monofilament leaders, because these guys had no interest in catching sharks. We put on sixty or eighty pound monofilament leaders on twenty-pound rods with the same 9/0 hooks, and threw our baits out in the channel; nothing bit. We caught a nurse shark, and that was all. Finally in the afternoon I said, "You know I want to try something." I put a wire leader on and threw it out, and sure enough, before long we caught a mutton snapper.

Scratching my head, I took a monofilament leader with a chunk of barracuda and a wire leader with a chunk of barracuda, and I threw them on the sandy bottom right behind the boat where I could watch them. After just a couple of minutes the wire leader would settle underneath the sand, so there would just be a chunk of barracuda laying on top of the sand. The mono leader didn't settle into the sand, but collected sediment, so the mono leader became more and more visible the longer it lay in the water. I decided that was what the problem was with catching these mutton snappers on the mono leaders. They could see the leaders, whereas the wire leader buried itself in the sand and they couldn't see it.

It's an interesting thing that leads to other observations. When I'm dead bait fishing for tarpon, even sometimes with live mullet, I will put my bait on a wire leader. The reason for this is because when a tarpon sucks the bait into his mouth, and I pull on a 100-pound monofilament leader, the roughness of the fish's lip begins too fray the line. So, the wire leader makes all the difference in the world.

Arlin Liebe, who fished out of Duck Key, used wire leaders for bonefish on two counts. The wire leader sank to the bottom almost like using a sinker, and when he had tourists from up north and the bonefish weren't biting, he could tell them to flip that shrimp over to that little shark or barracuda, and they'd catch them as well. So, thanks to Arlin Liebe, when I go sail fishing off Miami Beach, I almost always put nine or ten inches of number five wire leader above my circle hook. My clients might be targeting sailfish, but sometimes they catch sharks, barracudas, kingfish, or wahoo; and the sailfish don't care about the wire. Sometimes wire leaders are good, but one thing for sure, where Jerry and Jesse Webb fish for mutton snappers, wire leaders are the only way to go.

Cubera Snappers

First Cubera Snapper

A fish that I have been obsessed with my whole life is the cubera snapper. It took me a long time before I finally got to go for them. In about 1975 we had a young man named Bobby who fished with us when I was running the *Good Time IV* out of the Castaways. He chartered me to take him to Chub Cay to target cubera snappers. Cuberas are very similar to mangrove snappers, except that where mangroves reach a maximum of about fifteen or eighteen pounds, cubera snappers grow to over 100 pounds. And with their big broad tail they are very powerful.

We ran to Chub Cay and anchored right out in front of the Club. We had been told that was the spot. We were using cut bonito and yellowtail snappers for bait. But all we kept hooking was sharks. The sharks would be hooked and pull out a bunch of drag, and then they would go over the dropoff and cut us off. We couldn't land any of them. We finally hooked one, and instead of running over the dropoff, it ran higher up onto the reef. We were able to keep it on the line, and it fought like the dickens. We were only fishing in about sixty feet of water, where no self-respecting fish would ever get the bends. This guy really put up a heck of a fight. But what we thought at first was a shark was actually a fifty-pound cubera snapper, my first one ever.

We had a nice cooler full of muttons, and some beautiful yellow tails. But how many of those sharks were actually cubera snappers, we'll never know, because we didn't catch another one. But we caught that one, and it was the first of many in my life. A few were caught in the Bahamas, and a whole lot off Florida, including some up to 100 pounds.

18 ½ in One Day

Abie had an opportunity to go to St. Thomas to be an observer in the Boy Scout Blue Marlin Tournament. While he was gone I had a charter on the full moon in August to go for cubera snappers. And what a trip we had! I think we caught nine or ten cuberas. We used up twenty-four lobsters and were done before midnight. It was a great night. We caught a lot of nice sized fish, and this was after several years that the cubera snapper fishing had been slow.

When Abie came back, he said he had a great time at the Boy Scout Tournament, but he was bummed that he missed this red-hot cubera trip. I think we had a couple of trips, and we might have caught some world record cuberas when he wasn't there. At any rate, when he came back he talked to his uncle, Adam, and his uncle's best friend, Larry, about it. They booked me to go cubera fishing in September with Abie.

Where we fish for cubera snappers locally is about thirty-five miles from our dock. Down there, we get upstream of a wreck, and as we drift by the wreck, we keep the sinkers up off the bottom. In past times we used to fish with the sinkers about ten feet off the bottom. The last couple of years we've caught cubera snappers with sinkers as high as 100 feet off the bottom in 200 feet of water. It's amazing what we learn from studying the depth finder and trying different things, one of which was to use the longer leaders and fish way up off the bottom.

This particular trip there was hardly any current, and the cubera snappers were way off the wreck. One of the cuberas was bitten in half by a shark. There were years where the sharks were really bad there, but there were also years when there were no sharks. We caught eighteen and a half cubera snappers and used twenty-four lobsters, and we were done fishing before one in the morning. Most of these fish were thirty-five to sixty-five pounds, and I'm so glad Abie got to make up for lost time. It was just an unbelievable cubera snapper bite, and a thrilling trip.

One Hundred Pound Cubera

One of the most memorable cubera snapper trips in 2018 was with a young man who was going to diving school in Key West on a military scholarship. His father lived in the Florida panhandle and came down to fish with us. For this trip the young man was going to bring the bait, and his father was going to meet us. They showed up, but they had a shortage of bait. I don't know how we ended up getting enough bait to go fishing, but at any rate, we managed to get enough and headed out.

We use six-foot rods that are made for standing up and fighting big fish. They're fifty to eighty pound class rods. We use dual speed Penn Internationals, either fifties or thirties, filled with sixty-five pound braid. The braid cuts through the water real well, so we can use a smaller sinker. The standup rods are shorter, so the angler has the leverage advantage fighting the fish. The dual speed reels are such that if the angler is having trouble with the fish he can downshift to a lower gear. The low gear is one and a half to one. That means the angler does a lot of cranking and does not gain a lot of line. But, by the same token, it gives a whole lot of power to pull the fish to the surface.

The father had brought his own rod with him. His rod was seven-feet long and solid glass. That means it had no taper whatsoever. When it bends it does so from the butt to the tip; but in its defense, it's nearly unbreakable. He had a Penn Senator Nine O reel. It had a three and a half gear ratio, or maybe three to one, but not a variable speed, that's for sure. He had it filled up with brand new eighty-pound monofilament line. That meant it would be harder to feel what was going on down on the bottom. It had a lot of disadvantages. I said, "Well, we'll take it along, and if things go well we'll give it a try. But let's start out with my rods."

We ran down to Ocean Reef with the live lobsters, and the fishing was really good. I think we were up to seven or eight cubera snappers, so I told Abie to put a leader and sinker on Dad's rod to see if we can't catch him one on his own rod. Instead of the sixteen-ounce lead we were using on the braid, we used twenty-four ounce lead on the mono. We rigged the same long leader and double hooks, and live lobster. He dropped it down, and sure enough, before long he got hammered on his own rod and reel. He struggled and struggled while the fish put up an awesome fight. The son took over and fought it for a while. Then the father took it back and finished it off. But what a beast! Here we were, a father and son fishing trip, and good fishing all night. Beautiful weather, and pops comes up with a huge cubera snapper on his very own favorite grouper rod and reel. He was thrilled. And we were happy for him that he was able to catch this beautiful fish on his own rod and reel. And, what a beautiful fish! We took its measurements before we released it. Our best estimate was that it was right at 100 pounds.

There was a lot of buoyancy in that fish when it got to the surface. It took twenty-seven pounds of lead to get it to go back down into the depths with our seaQualizer. (This is a device that clamps to the lower jaw of the fish and pulls it down onto the depths on a hand line with a release clip. We set the release clip for 100 feet. When it got down to that depth, the release clip popped open and let the fish go.) We were able to release this beautiful cubera snapper healthy, and what a beautiful catch, and a great trip!

Father and Son Cubera
I was running cubera snapper trips out of the Ocean Reef Club in North Key Largo. Offshore in a couple of hundred feet of water is a wreck where we go to catch cubera snappers, a really great giant snapper catch and release spot. The way we fish is we have a standup outfit with a pound or two of lead, a couple of ten O hooks with live lobster for bait. We drop down to the bottom, hook up, wind the fish in, take his picture and do it all again.

I had done an article for Saltwater Sportsman Magazine on cubera snapper fishing and got a booking from a father and son team, an adult son. They came on the boat and the only outfits were fifty-pound standup rods, and kidney harnesses for each of them sitting on the back seat. There was a bucket of one and two pound leads in the corner. So they put their gear on the boat and we took off from the dock. I knew they contacted me from the magazine article I had written. We ran out to the wreck and stopped. I told them, "Here's the deal. You put this harness on, and you clip the rod in like so. I'm going to get into position and you're going to drop down a lobster. When you hit the bottom, wind it up four or five cranks and hold on. If something bites, you start fighting him. If you ever feel like you're losing control, just fall down inside the boat. Don't fall overboard."

They both chimed up, "We don't bottom fish. We never bottom fish."

I said, "Well, this is a bottom fishing operation. The whole article you read was about bottom fishing for the cubera snappers."

The father said, "Well, I just read that it was cubera snapper fishing in Miami, but we want to do like we did in Costa Rica."

I asked, "Well how did you fish in Costa Rica."

He said, "Well, we went to the concierge and told him we wanted to go fishing. He said be in the lobby at five thirty in the morning. So we went to the lobby and we were sitting there, and this guy walked in wearing a straw hat and no shoes, cut off pants and a plaid shirt, and he communicated to us in broken Spanish/English that he was our fishing guide. We went out and got into a rusty old pick up truck and drove down through town. He drove onto a beach to where there were a couple of other trucks parked and there were people fishing along the shoreline. He grabbed three buckets that contained some hand lines and a couple of dead fish, and carried them down to the mouth of a river. He showed us how to hook on a dead fish and we swung them around over our head and threw it out over the river. We waited a while and reeled them in to see if we still had bait, and threw it out again. We didn't catch anything and that was it."

I said, "And that's what you booked as a fishing charter, and that's what you got?"

He replied, "We didn't know anything about booking a fishing charter so we went to the concierge and that's what he set us up to do."

I asked, "You read this article, and that's how you thought we fished for cubera snappers? And you didn't see it was bottom fishing?"

"No," he said, "we didn't see that part. We just read the headline that it was cubera snapper fishing. We went to the man and he called you up to go fishing. And here we are."

It wasn't a half an hour and they were both seasick. We went back to the dock. I felt sorry taking their money, but hey, they had expected to be hand lining, when the whole article was about bottom fishing, and they showed up to go hand lining at the river mouth. I don't know what to say.

Rigging for Cuberas

When fishing for cuberas we take two-dozen live lobsters, so the cost for bait is around $250. We rig fifty-pound outfits with fifty to eighty pound braid, on Penn International fifty reels on standup rods with fighting belts. We rig a three-way swivel to a one-pound lead. We used to use an eight-foot leader to a pair of 10/0 hooks, but we have since gone to twenty-five foot leaders.

The way we hook the lobster is just at the base of the tail at the anal opening. We stab the lead hook through the tail of the lobster. The length between the two hooks is set so that the second hook, the hanging hook, would reach the base of the antenna of the lobster. Then we would tie wrap the hook to the base of the antenna. So, we have a hook at each end of the bait, and a good purchase on both ends.

215

Light Tackle

Eight-Hour Swordfish

Gary Carter is a world-renowned light tackle bill fisherman. He has set records for Atlantic and Pacific sailfish, blue marlin, striped marlin, white marlin, and black marlin on the lightest tackle, like two-pound, four-pound, and six-pound line. And not to be outdone, his wife has set a few light tackle records as well. He was in the process of building a new boat in Miami, so he needed a guide for this adventure. He arranged for me to take him out at night for swordfish with eight-pound test.

We went out to the swordfish grounds and, because we were using eight-pound line, we couldn't use big sinkers and Electralume lights. We had to use much smaller sinkers and hooks, and cyalume light sticks to help attract the swordfish to the baits. Hanging off the side of the boat was a Hydro Glow light, a two-foot long fluorescent light that glowed bright green. We have always found them to be very effective in attracting swordfish to the general vicinity of the boat. With their great night vision the fish would see this light, which would result in them noticing our bait rigs.

Sure enough, after a couple of hours of fishing we got a hook up. Gary is an absolute artist with the reel. If the fish was making a hot run, he would back the drag off to literally nothing, and just let him run until it got burned out of energy. Then he'd push the drag back up to a measured setting of about two pounds. If the fish was cooperative, but not coming too fast, he might push it up to three pounds, and then pull it back to two, then back to one pound. Whatever the fish was doing,

216

Gary was always in tune with the drag setting and how much pressure was on his rod. He was really something to watch.

We reached a stalemate with this swordfish. It was down around 100 feet, and it just wouldn't come up any higher. It wasn't coming up, and it wasn't going down. The Hydro Glow light in the water would let us see what we were doing when it came time to gaff the fish, but at this moment we didn't need it. So I said, "Ok, we've got to try something. Let's unplug the light. Maybe that's keeping him away from the boat." So we unplugged the light, and the fish ran off 200 yards of line straight down into the depths. And now we couldn't see what we were doing, so we plugged the light back in and Gary got back to fighting the fish. He fought and fought and the fish started to rise, but at about 150 feet it put the brakes on. By now we were five or six hours into the fight, and I said, "Unplug that light again." We unplugged the light and the fish charged back into the depths.

We were dumbfounded as to what to do. We put the light back in the boat and decided to fight him without it for a while. We fought for a couple more hours, and finally at the end of eight hours we got the swordfish up to the boat. If anybody wants to talk about what the toughest fish in the ocean is, this fifty or fifty-five pound swordfish on eight pound test, in an eight hour fight with a world class angler - that was one tough fish. And we were thrilled to catch it. It wasn't anywhere near the record, so we let it go and sent it on its way.

As a sidebar, Gary went out the following night with Tony DiGiulian and his mate Leo Lombardo. That night they caught a 125 pounder on eight-pound test in less than an hour. But what a bummer; their tournament approved line over-tested. And was Gary ever upset about that, because he always pretested all of his line. It turned out that the batch of line he had would measure, first under eight pounds, and under eight pounds again, and again under eight pounds – and then ten pounds. Then under eight pounds, under eight pounds, under eight pounds - ten pounds. There was a flaw in the machine manufacturing the line, and every once in a while there would be a spot in the span that would go over eight pounds.

217

I don't know if Gary got that record or not, but he and his wife continue to catch world records all the time.

Hiller African Pompano

One of my avid light tackle fishermen is Benji Hiller. This one time he was out on my boat with his son, Daniel. We ran down to the middle of Key Biscayne with a bunch of live herring and a couple of pinfish for live bait. In that area there are a bunch of shallow wrecks in fifty-five to seventy feet of water, so I decided to make a drift over them. On the first drift we hooked a nice cobia. We brought the fish up and turned it loose.

We set up another drift with the same baits we had out before. We got a good bite on a live herring on six-pound line. Daniel grabbed the rod and started fighting the fish. It fought and fought, and we went around in circles. It was a long drawn out fight, and I'd say it took an hour and a half to land this fish. It was a beautiful African pompano, probably thirty pounds, an excellent result on six-pound test.

We unhooked the pompano and let it go and went back to the same area. We put the same baits out again and in short order got another hit. Benji took the rod and fought the fish, and it took even longer to land than the last one. Finally he got it up to the boat and it was another beautiful African pompano. We weighed it and it was over forty pounds, four or five pounds more than the current record for six-pound test. Benji asked, "Do you want to kill it for a sheet of paper or shall we let it go in future hopes of catching it again?" We decided to let it go. So, instead of going for the recognition, we released a world record African Pompano over forty pounds on six-pound test.

We went back, and I'll be a son of a gun if we didn't hook another African pompano. Daniel caught this one. So we caught three African pompanos and a cobia. We used a grand total of five baits on an eight-hour fishing trip. By the time we landed the third pompano it was well past time to go home. We spent very little time fishing, a whole lot of time fighting fish, and only used five pieces of live bait.

We had four bites and caught all four fish. It doesn't get any better than that one when it comes to light tackle fishing.

Benji, Daniel, and Gabriel Hiller

Benji, Daniel, and Gabriel Hiller had numerous other light tackle adventures with me. One time, when we got the first bite of the day, Gabriel grabbed the rod. The fish started burning out drag with six-pound test, and up jumped a 300 pound blue marlin. As soon as he jumped the line broke, and that was the end of that blue marlin.

We caught numerous sailfish on six and eight-pound line including some very quick catches. We caught sailfish on six-pound test in just over a minute where they came jumping toward the boat, and the mate grabbed the leader, and the leader broke and the party was over. We have also fought sailfish for six or seven hours on six-pound test without winning the battle.

I remember one that we hooked and it headed south. It would go up on the reef and swim around for a while, then go down to 150 feet. Then it would swim south for an hour, and then come up on the reef and swim around. It was completely unfazed by us. It was one of our more embarrassing failures when it broke loose from our light tackle.

One of the most frustrating fish to try to catch on six-pound test are twenty-five to thirty pound blackfin tunas. It's a very hard fight with a lot of maneuvering, and it takes an hour and a half to land a typical blackfin. As all our anglers know, blackfin tunas go down deep, and they stay down. So we can't chase them down with the boat. We have to fight them, and then we can lift them and turn them loose.

The sailfish on the other hand are much more fun. They run and jump, and we chase them with the boat, wide open in reverse, then forward, and then turning around with anglers running all around the boat and the sailfish jumping; it's just a ball.

One light tackle event that comes to mind was a day in May when the weather was less than perfect. There wasn't any wind, but it was overcast and there were a lot of rainstorms around. The elements in the air were such that when we would cast a live herring out on six-pound test, the herring would arc though the air and go into the water. As they left slack in the line, the line would float up into the sky. It wouldn't sink down into the water because static electricity would actually lift the light line up into the air. That was some spooky stuff.

We caught many good-sized tarpons on real light tackle too. Those fights can be exhausting, and we have actually broken the leader on purpose on a tarpon over 100 pounds on four-pound test.

I might add that numerous fish we caught on six-pound test actually were tagged and released. We always joke about zing-pow fishing, as in zinging drags and popping lines. The truth is that the Hiller family rarely breaks a line. It almost never happens. We have some smoking hot fights on light tackle. Some the best fish fighting we ever experienced came on light tackle with Benji, and Daniel, and Gabriel Hiller. It's a family that has given me light tackle memories to last a lifetime.

Ralph Brown and Dusky

Sometime in the late 1970s my wife was looking at one of my fishing magazines. On the back inside cover was an advertisement for Dusky boats. She said, "That's the boat you need, the Dusky 256. Look at that boat, it's just perfect for you." My response was that Dusky was a mom and pop operation and that if I were going to get a boat I'd want a name brand. I put the Dusky out of my mind; but my wife would still remind me of it every once in a while.

In 1979 I was doing a lot of teaching people to fish on their own boats, and doing some private boat gigs. I received a phone call around early November from Hans DeMetz. He wanted me to run his boat while he was in town. He was taking delivery of his boat on December 22, and he wanted me to help him take delivery and set it up. Then we would fish together for about six days before he went back to New York.

I agreed and we decided to meet up at the Dusky factory in Dania. I asked how I would know him, and he responded, "I'll be the only guy driving a yellow Rolls Royce."

I said, "Well, I'll be the biggest guy in the parking lot, and I'll see you there."

I inquired as to why he had bought this mom and pop boat as opposed to a name brand. He said he had met the people at the boat show and they were really nice, and he thought they had given him a good deal. So we met up at 2:00 o'clock and took delivery of his brand new 256 Dusky with the 235 Evinrude. I ran it over to Dry Marina in Port Everglades and he drove over in his car. He opened up his trunk.

In it he had some Penn Internationals, and some beautiful custom rods, and spinning rods, and pretty much everything we needed. I rigged up all the tackle, and made sure all the reels were full of new line. We were ready.

The next day the wind was blowing fifteen to twenty with four to six foot seas. So we went out into this nasty sea and put out some live baits and caught a blackfin tuna. A while later he said, "Well, we've been out here a couple of hours. What do you think of the boat?"

I told him that if he ever wanted to sell it, I'd be interested. During his time here we fished all over the place. We would leave out of Ft. Lauderdale and run down to Haulover. We caught a lot of tarpon, and sailfish, and groupers, and sharks. We'd catch a few blue runners while we were tarpon fishing, and then we'd go out to the edge with a kite. We'd sailfish back to Ft. Lauderdale, or we'd stop and fish on some wrecks on the way in.

Fifteen months later Hans called me. He said, "Well, Bouncer, my wife is filing for divorce and I have to sell both of my Duskys." He had bought a second one and took it to New York. As the saying goes, he made an offer I could not refuse, and that became my first Dusky.

In about 1983 or 1985 I became obsessed about getting a fish around cuddy cabin. I went to Ralph Brown, who had now become my friend. I'd been on the cover of Saltwater Sportsman Magazine with the Dusky, and I think that impressed him. Over time we bonded and became closer friends. We did some tournaments together, and fished together quite a lot. I told him, "I want to buy a new Dusky, one with a fish around cuddy cabin."

He said, "Go in with one of my salesmen and figure out everything you want on the boat."

So I did that, and they worked up a price sheet and gave it to Ralph. I went to see him. By now I was doing radio shows and seminars and was acquiring something of a public image in the South Florida fishing community. Ralph said to me, "You keep doing what you're doing, and I'll keep doing what I'm doing. And this is what it's going to cost you for the boat." He handed me a piece of paper. I wasn't expecting something so generous; it was a really good price for the boat, and I bought my second Dusky. And I've had a Dusky ever since.

I have been very happy with Dusky boats. They are extremely well built, and they're great sea boats. The 256 I owned had a modified V, which is relatively flat in the back. So when we stopped to drift or anchor fish, it was a very stable platform. The bow had a deep V, which allowed me to go out comfortably into some pretty rough weather. One time when I went to Bimini on the Dusky the weather we were running in had a name. It was a tropical storm. The boat handled it well.

Another time I brought the Dusky back from Fresh Creek, Andros, a 150 mile run. I made the whole run in thirty mile an hour northeast winds with fifteen to twenty foot seas. But I never doubted that the boat could handle it. I had become Dusky's biggest fan, and when they came out with the thirty-three I had to get one.

Ralph Brown, and Mrs. (Pat) Brown, and their son Mike, used to put on tournaments in Dania Beach for Dusky owners. It was a low profile tournament where we would go out early, fish for dolphin, and fish until about one or two in the afternoon. We had to be back to weigh our fish by 3:00 o'clock. As the fish were weighed, the staff from Dusky, especially Michael, would filet all the dolphins. There would be professional cooks there from different caterers. They would be cooking fish, and hot dogs, and hamburgers, and there would be watermelon and beverages and desserts, and everything imaginable for a picnic. Then there would be buckets full of fishing swag for every captain in the fleet. There would be prizes, only one per boat, for the top three junior anglers, top three lady anglers, top three aggregate catches, and biggest dolphin. All the door prizes were very valuable. It might be a new Penn International with a rod, or a Guy Harvey shirt, or electronics. It would just be a huge party, so much fun. It was a lot of work, but I still wish it would come back someday.

I took Ralph Brown and Gary Jones from Evinrude to numerous Arthur Smith kingfish, dolphin, and wahoo tournaments up in Palm Beach. One year we walked into Holiday Inn and told them we had reservations for three rooms for the weekend. They asked our names and Ralph said, "It's Mr. Brown."

Gary Jones said, "It's Mr. Jones."

And I said, "It's Mr. Smith."

The receptionist said, "Sure, Brown, Jones, and Smith. No Garcia in the crowd?" It was pretty fun traveling that way.

We liked those Arthur Smith Tournaments. I remember one time I saw the biggest bull dolphin jump I'd ever seen, and we tried to find him to catch him, but no joy. That was a near miss in that tournament. But we did come in the money with a big kingfish one year. Mike Brown was with us one year when he and his buddy bailed us out. They caught thirty-nine bonitos one day and saved us from having to fight all those bonitos.

When the Arthur Smith Tournaments quit we didn't have a tournament to go into anymore. So I was looking for events that Ralph Brown, and Ron Widner from Evinrude, and Bill Applegate, and I could go on so we could have another fishing trip together. Well, in Bimini they had the Bimini Big Game Club Small Boat Tournament. So we said, "Let's go fish that."

So we went to fish that tournament and had a really good time. We caught some nice fish, and Ralph was so impressed with it that the next year he booked a whole week of the three-week tournament just for Dusky owners. And boy, did we have a ball. Good eating, lots of camaraderie around the grills in the evening, and lots of good fishing.

Every night we would meet at the grills. We would mix stone soup. That means one family had a salad and a snapper filet; another family had a can of corn and two steaks left. Another family might go across the street and buy peas and rice. Another guy might just have a lot of beer and rum. But everybody combined everything they had, and we had a great big cook out. It was like a covered dish dinner, but we called it stone soup.

When we started going to Bimini we developed a trophy called the Coconut Monkey. Everybody won it at one time or another. The year I won it Ralph and Mike Brown, and Ron Widner, and an executive from Mercury were all sitting around one table and drinking pitchers of Pina Coladas in plastic cups. The used dirty cups were all stacked in the middle of the table, and in my drunken state I decided all the cups were too tall. So I put my hand up and smashed down on top of the cups, and all the dregs of the Pina Coladas came flying out all around the table. Everybody at the table was covered with Pina Colada that came out from between these cups.

Ralph Brown has been a champion in my life. I can't thank him enough for years of good shared times. It has given me many excellent memories. As long as I live Ralph Brown will be one of the men I admire most in my life.

Sports Personalities

Bob Trumpy + Don Criqui
I had several trips with Bob Trumpy who was a broadcaster for the Orange Bowl on many occasions. He fished with me and his sons, and other people who were involved in the broadcast booth. They would be free from about six in the evening, so we would go out at about nine or ten. We usually fished off Haulover and caught some nice tarpon.

One time he brought along one of the production guys who sit in the trailer and pick which camera they are going to air at any time. It's a very hectic job because there are five, or six, or ten screens there, and he has to push a button and go to camera two, and then camera four, then five, then back to two. That's his job. He was a very interesting guy to talk with.

There was a light north wind and we were using shrimp and a pinfish for bait. I saw the pinfish jerk one time, but nothing happened. I thought that maybe it had gotten scared. But then as some time went by, it seemed like four or five minutes, but it may have been thirty seconds in reality, all of a sudden the rod up in the bow bent over double underneath the boat. The guest grabbed the rod and leaned out over the side, and worked his way around the bow. He had a 150-pound tarpon hooked on the other side of the boat. The tarpon ate the pinfish, swam down the beach, and went under the boat, and out the other side. When he finally came tight, the angler panicked and bent the rod over at a scary angle. But we caught the fish.

On many occasions since then I've seen a bite, and the rod just bent a little bit. I'd tell the angler to start winding, but there's next to nothing there, and all of a sudden the tarpon would be out in the back of the boat, or under the boat, or off the bow where it ate the bait, and swam right past the boat before the line came tight. It can be alarming on a dark night were visibility is so limited.

Don Criqui was Bob Trumpy's co-host in the booth. The two were as opposite as black and white. Trumpy was an outdoors guy. He had been a football player, and he was also a hunter and a fisherman. Don Criqui was a sports announcer and an indoor guy, completely the opposite personality.

One time Don brought his two sons with him and we went out of Haulover Inlet. We put the baits out for about five minutes. We hooked a big tarpon and Don fought it. The fish went around the boat a couple of times. Every once in a while we'd see someone who couldn't hold the rod any longer, bending his arm and sticking the rod in the crook of his arm, or trying to wind upside down because he can't crank anymore. Don was full of all that, but he did catch a nice 120-pound tarpon that he had mounted.

Barry Switzer

Another famous sports personality I took fishing was Barry Switzer when he was head coach for Oklahoma. We went out together several times. One of the most memorable times with him was when we rescued a sailboat that was stuck up on one of the flats. The tide was falling, but it had not gone out enough to get the sailboat in deep trouble just yet. So we threw over a line and towed it off the flats and got him squared away. The owner was shocked and thrilled to meet Barry Switzer.

We bid our adieus to him and ran down to Government Cut. I drove around for a minute by the first red marker outside the inlet. I marked a bunch of tarpons, so we dropped a bait down. We were baiting the second rod when we got a bite. We caught that fish, went back, dropped another bait down and caught that fish. Then we dropped down again. We couldn't get the second bait in the water because we hooked a third tarpon, and then it was time to go home. We caught three tarpons, one right after the other. We didn't fish; all we did was catch the whole trip. That was very memorable.

We always had good fishing with Barry Switzer, partly because he was always here for the Orange Bowl Game which fell around the first of January, and that was prime tarpon time. But give the man his due; Barry Switzer knew how to catch fish.

Anthony Munoz and Dave Rimington

Another great trip was at Super Bowl time. I took out Anthony Munoz and Dave Rimington of the Cincinnati Bengals. Anthony Munoz was so tall that when I was sitting at the helm, and he was standing next to the t-top, I couldn't see much more than up to his chin. We were going down Miami Beach, from Haulover to Government Cut. The Coast Guard stopped us, and these Coasties were so infatuated with Anthony Munoz and Dave Rimington, that they tied us up for almost an hour shooting the breeze about football with these football stars. Anthony and Dave were great with it, and the Coasties were having the time of their life.

We got down to the inlet and fished for a little while, but didn't catch anything. They had a curfew they had to meet so I had to drop them off.

As a little sidebar, that was the year that we also had riots in Miami, and while we were out there tarpon fishing, we could see all the bad things going on in Miami. It certainly was memorable having Anthony Munoz and Dave Rimington to fish with.

What an honor as it was to have all these outdoors people out there aboard my boat at different times. I can't thank the Orange Bowl Committee enough for their help in introducing me to so many of these great sports personalities.

Teachers

Teachers help make us what we are. I couldn't do a list of teachers without leaving out as many as I remembered. For all of those teachers I can't thank you enough. Believe me, in my heart I know who you are even though I may have missed you in this chapter of my life story.

That first teacher was my dad. He started me out fishing when I was three or four years old. By the time I was seven, he left me on the bank of the Osabo River in Central Michigan and told me that if I had a bite to holler. When I had a two-pound trout up to the bank, I hollered and he came and netted it, and set me up again. Again he instructed me that if I caught another one to holler. I caught another two-pound trout; I hollered, and he came and netted it. He was delighted that I caught those two two-pound trout. We hiked back to the campsite and cooked them up and ate them. It even made the Pontiac newspaper.

I can remember sitting on the dock, fishing with baloney, or hot dog, or whatever, for bluegills or sunfish while my dad and his buddies were out on the boat on the lake catching nothing. We went to Lake Okeechobee and the boat was full, so he left me on the bank. I made friends with a kid at the fish camp down at the boat ramp. A fellow came in from fishing and told us there were some shiners left in his boat and we were welcome to use them. We rowed out in the lake with cane poles and shiners, and I caught my biggest bass ever, a seven pounder, while my dad was out on the lake getting skunked again.

As I progressed, I worked on the Newport Fishing Pier and Pappy and Roland taught me how to catch pilchards to sell them to the other fishermen on the pier.

Then I went to more exotic fishing. Guys like B.J. and Wayne Conn, and Randy and Grant White, and Paul Leader; we all learned how to fish together. We fished off the pier or off the shoreline. One guy would learn something and teach the others. B.J. caught a tournament winning pompano on my fly rod while I stood there taking lessons from him.

Tommy Ribbel and Tommy Whitmore were teaching me how to fish off the bridges in Islamorada. I caught a tournament winning cero mackerel on Whitmore's rod while he was showing me how to bridge gaff.

When I got into the head boat scene Billy Miller taught me so much, as did Gene Gamon and Bill Seddon on the *Tiki II*. Hank Aldifer taught me that the direction of the current is where it is going, and the wind is where it is coming from, so north wind and north current are opposing, going in opposite directions.

Matty Tambor taught me that there were tarpon off South Beach when nobody was fishing that area. He gave me all his GPS numbers and keeps me aware of how my mates are holding up.

I got on full time at night on a head boat on Pier Five. I was working with Jim Smith. He taught me to never hold a mangrove snapper up so that somebody will have to get it off my finger. A mangrove snapper had chomped down on my finger and Jim said to hold the snapper upside down. I held it upside down and Jim whacked the lower jaw with a pair of pliers, and drove the teeth even deeper into my finger.

Tommy Salvano came down to the drift boat and asked if anybody could work on the charter boat. I went with him and he hired me. I won't say Tommy was a great teacher, but he did have me doing the job. That being said, he talked Captain Billy Ridgeway into riding along to teach both of us how to improve our bottom fishing. Billy Ridgeway taught me how to fish for Warsaw and snowy groupers, and amberjacks. He taught me how to improve my trolling spreads and a great deal about charter boat fishing and the day-to-day charter boat operation. He was one of my all time idols.

From there I went to the *Top Luck* with Captain Randy Lacey. Randy was a really good sailfish and marlin troller. He showed me how to drop back to a fish and what to look for. He would wake up on the bridge just as a blue marlin would show up. He had an intuition about it. He taught me a lot about hooking sailfish, and blue and white marlin.

Then I went down to Islamorada. Down there I was going into a whole new game. I went from blue water fishing to flats fishing. I could never have made it successfully without Sonny Eslinger. Sonny showed me some of the fine points of bone fishing, and tarpon fishing, and permit fishing. He taught me how to throw a cast net, and just one thing after another. We shared a trailer for a while, fished together, and went to dinner together. He took me to Ocean City Maryland where I was introduced to white marlin fishing. I ended up working up there for several summers. While I was up there, I met a lot of other captains who shared their knowledge with me.

All through the years, and still, I share knowledge with captain Jack Plachter. We chartered and head boat and private boat fished together, and learned a million things. As I've gone on through life Skip Smith, who I started out teaching about kite fishing, and now he has taught me so much about marlin fishing, and swordfishing, and all aspects of big game fishing. He's a super wealth of knowledge and really great to be around. In recent years I've added R.J. Boyle to that list of people who have shared their knowledge, and by sharing our knowledge we both learn as we go along.

There have been so many real great teachers. I know I've missed a bunch of them, but these were some of the guys who really got me over the top. It was so much fun to learn from them. I can't overemphasize how rewarding it is as I was growing up and learning from all these people. And then coming back from the prime of my life I get to share all these different tricks with all these captains, and mates, and clients. Teaching people how to fish, and teaching them about fishing is extremely rewarding. I've always said, "When you can't learn anything else it's time to put the nails in the coffin."

But maybe when the learning stops and the teaching begins, we can keep the nails out of that coffin a little longer. What a great life of teachers I've had, and I thank all of them for what they've taught me.

My Family Story

Dad and Mom

My dad was quite a gentleman. His name was Terry W. Smith. He was an automotive die designer, which meant he drew the designs to make car parts back in the early and mid-fifties. Our home was a farm of sorts in Pontiac Michigan, a few miles outside of Detroit. We had rabbits, and vegetables, and fruit. Our next door neighbor to the west was a polo pony ranch a half-mile down the road. The next house to the north was up the hill, probably a quarter mile away. Across the street it was a half-mile to a lake. Between our house and the lake was nothing but brush. There was nothing on the street from our house to Federal Highway, which was a couple of miles away. We lived in the country, raised some food, and had a good life.

Dad drove to his job in Detroit everyday. Back then car styles changed every year, so there was a lot of demand for people who could design the dies to make the car parts. Because of that, there was an ongoing war among several companies to get the top designers. Fortunately, our dad was very good at it.

One of the companies he worked for, Modern Engineering, said to him: "We can't offer any more money per hour. You're at the top of our pay scale. But if you'll sign a two-year contract with us, we'll pay all your moving expenses to move you to Miami, Florida. There you can fish, and play golf, and tennis all year round. No more shoveling snow."

Dad jumped on the chance, and moved on it very fast. I remember that for Christmas I had gotten my first double bladed ice skates, and my older sister got her first adult lace up skates. They were still in the boxes when we moved to Florida on January 6, 1956. We never got to use our new ice skates. They weren't used the next year when we went back for vacation either, so we gave them to the kids at the top of the hill. That was the end of our ice skates and snowy winters, but the beginning of a great adventure.

We had a Ford station wagon with wooden sides. Dad put down the back seat, put a mattress back there, and threw the four kids, the suitcases, and the dog on the mattress. Mom and Dad got in the front seat, and we headed to Miami.

We lived at the very north end of the county in the area called Norwood. It was close to Norland Elementary School, and junior and senior high school, near where the Hard Rock Stadium is today.

Dad was an outdoorsman in every sense of the word. From the time he was a kid growing up, he was collecting Indian arrowheads in Michigan. In the fall he would collect nuts. He was always enjoying the outdoors, and sharing it with his kids. He worked at his regular job Monday through Friday, but weekends were reserved for home and family projects. On one of the weekend days he did home maintenance, either gardening or working on the inside or outside of the house. The other day of the weekend was always spent on outdoor activities.

We would drive to the west coast of Florida to collect seashells on the beaches, or surf cast for snook and trout. We would sometimes head south to go snorkeling on the reefs, or diving in the Florida Keys. But mostly we fished, whether it was on a head boat, or going out on a friend's boat. We sometimes ran down to Flamingo; and other times we fished offshore Miami. I caught my first sailfish with my dad when I was eight years old.

My parents had four kids. One of Dad's great projects with my older sister, Sue, was to build a fourteen-foot fiberglass rowboat. The two of them laid it up and built this boat out of fiberglass. Then when I was about twelve, Dad and I built about a sixteen-foot aluminum runabout with a single forty-horse Evinrude outboard. We called that

234

boat *Piscatorial Cornucopia*. During construction, when the boat was upside down, I would crawl up inside and hold a steel bar up against the backside of rivets while Dad used a riveting gun to smash the rivets. I used a whole lot of cotton blocking my ears while I was inside this tin can bucking rivets and Dad was on the outside with his riveting gun.

And what trips we had on that boat. We learned to fish for dolphin offshore with ballyhoo instead of trolling feathers. Many times we went to Flamingo and caught what we then called Jewfish (they are now called goliath grouper), and sea trout, redfish, snook, sharks, and big tarpons. That boat served us well.

When my brother, Flip, was about twenty-one or twenty-two, he and my dad built a twenty-seven foot, single engine, inboard diesel, aluminum boat with a viewing glass in the bottom. That boat was called *Moon Track*. It served my dad and my sister and her kids for years. They kept it in Key Largo in the summertime and would drive back and forth. They'd go scuba diving, and snorkeling, and fishing. We'd go fishing off Miami and to all the marine events on that boat. I remember going down to the Marine Stadium to watch the firework displays. We got a lot of use out of all those homemade boats. Our dad was just a great outdoorsman, a great mechanical engineer, and an all around great guy.

But not to cut my mother short, she was the sweetest, greatest mother I could have ever asked for. Her name was Donna Jean, and she was a stay at home mom with a couple of unique fish stories of her own.

Our next-door neighbor was a car dealer, and his wife was also a stay at home mom. From time to time these neighbors would take my mom out fishing. I remember one day Dad came home and my mom said she had been out fishing with them. He asked how it went. She said, "Well it was a strange day." My dad called me into the living room to hear the story. Mom and the next-door neighbors had been trolling. They went by the buoy that was off the Newport Pier, what we call the Buoy Reef that marked the edge of sixty feet of water. They trolled by there and saw a five-foot shark. As they ran past the buoy, the shark swam over and took one of their baits and they caught it. Dad asked what kind of shark was it. Mom explained that it was really interesting. It didn't have any teeth, and its colors were unique. It was light brown on top and had a dark brown stripe down the middle of its side, and then it was white on the belly. The only thing that is perfectly described by that is a cobia; and a five-foot cobia could be in the range of fifty or sixty pounds; and they are delicious to eat.

People back then were particularly motivated to catch fish they could eat. So my mom continued to tell us that they went farther offshore, and on the way back in they went by the buoy again. They saw another five-foot shark, as they trolled by. This shark ran over and grabbed their bait, and they fought it and brought it up to the boat. And it was the same thing: no teeth, dark brown stripe down the side, brown on top, and white on the belly. Dad asked what they did with that one, and Mom explained that it was a toothless shark and they cut it loose.

In my dad's fishing career, which in salt water extended from 1956 to the 1990s, he never saw a live cobia on the line, or swimming in the water, or anything. My sister, Sue, who has also been an avid fisherman her whole life, has only seen one cobia. That one was caught by one of the guests on my boat when Sue was on a ride along because she was a good friend with the guest. My mom encountered two giant cobias and cut them loose because they just figured they were sharks and didn't want to keep them anyway.

Mom had a lot of health problems later in life and Dad would make believe she went fishing with him. Just he and the dog would go out on the boat into north Biscayne Bay. He would bait up a spinning rod with a popping cork and put a live shrimp on it and throw it off the bow of the boat. He would turn to the dog and say, "OK now. That's Mom's rod." Then he would go in the back of the boat and bounce a buck tail off the bottom with a little bit of shrimp. If Mom's rod got a hit, the dog would have a fit, and Dad would put his rod in the rod holder and go up and wind up Mom's fish. When he came home he would tease Mom and say she out-fished him.

But she would argue, "But I wasn't even on the boat!"

And he would say, "But it was your rod that caught the fish."

Mom kept a tackle box on the back of the washing machine, and that's where she would put all the hooks, snap swivels, and sinkers that fell out of our pockets while she did laundry. She ended up with quite a collection.

My mom would talk about her most traumatic story: We got up real early one day and she and Dad loaded the four kids in the back of the station wagon. They got in the front seat and we drove across Tamiami Trail from North Miami. In those days, when we went to Marco Island we could drive right out on the beach. We would go shelling, and Dad would take off to the south, and was out of sight in no time. My mother and her four little ducklings: my brother and my two sisters and I, would all be hovering around her. We'd walk at a slow pace, collecting seashells and looking at everything along the waterfront. Sometimes in the afternoon we would stop and surf cast for sea trout, or redfish, or catfish. At the end of the day Mom and Dad would put us in the back of the station wagon and head home. No seat belts, and we didn't even have the seats up. We'd just have a flat surface, and end up falling asleep on the way home.

We'd be starving on the way home and Dad would tell us not to worry, we were going to Smitty's Bar and Grill. We'd keep asking, "Are we there yet; are we there yet?"

"No, we're going to Smitty's Bar and Grill; we'll be there soon." And we would pull into the driveway and tell Mom and Dad that they forgot to stop for dinner. And they would say, "No, no. This is Smitty's Bar and Grill, because our last name was Smith. We'd get our sandwiches or whatever we were having for dinner real quick and Mom would run the bathtub for the kids.

This particular time everyone took a bath, and later on Mom came down for a bed check. She checked the girls' bedroom, and everything was good. She checked my brother's bedroom; everything was good there too. But my bed was empty. So my mom started looking for me, but couldn't find me. She opened the bathroom door and called to see if I was in there. No answer. So she continued searching around the house. Now she and my dad were beginning to panic. They checked everything again, and my mom went back into the bathroom and turned on the light. I was face down in the bathtub. She screamed, and I jumped up and screamed. It woke my sisters up, and they screamed. Everybody screamed. Thank God! I had been sleeping in the bathtub, but the water had drained. It was a fine outcome, but it sure gave them all a start. That's my mom. We sure loved her; and we sure miss her. She was just a great Polish mom.

We talk about our dad all the time because he was a true genius with photographic memory. He was beyond belief. When people ask about our mom, we tell them that our mom was just a really terrific mother. She took great care of her kids, and her house, and Dad. She was the perfect mom. We miss both Mom and Dad, but I guess they're together in heaven, and we were lucky to have such great parents.

Sue Singer

My oldest sister is Sue. She is one of those people who is always helping other people. When my little sister, Sharon, lived nearby Sue would drive up to her house every week to take her out grocery shopping. She would take her out to lunch; and the three of us would get together for lunch once a month just to catch up on anything going on in our lives, and spend some quality time together. Sue raised two children, Keith and Amber. Amber, a brilliant member of Mensa, is now with the State Department, traveling all over the world. Keith lives in Atlanta. Sue and I go up to visit Keith and his wife and children every year at Christmastime. They come down here a couple of times every year to go fishing and boating with us, and just to spend some time in Miami. Keith is married to Alex. They have a son named Jamie, eleven, and their daughter, Louise, is nine.

Sue's husband, Joe, passed away several years ago. Together they fished constantly, and Sue was the female Met Master Angler, and won the tarpon release award. She loves to fish. Several times a year Sue, and my mate Abie, and his wife, Yudith, and I will all go out fishing. The girls love to catch smaller fish like Spanish mackerel or mutton snapper, anything that will bite fast and furious. Sue loves to catch, and is an authority on sea trout. Anybody who doesn't believe it just has to ask her.

Sue keeps an immaculate home and loves to entertain. She will put on the most beautiful meals, on the most decorated tables for friends of mine, or friends of hers, or any opportunity to entertain. She is an artist at it, she loves it, and she does a great job of it.

Sue and Joe had a two bedroom, two bath condominium on South Beach, just two blocks from where I keep my boat. When Joe passed away, and my wife got tired of being married to a fisherman after thirty-five years, I was living across the bay, six miles away. We would socialize together, and go to fishing club meetings together, and go to big fishing events together, and out to dinner from time to time. Or I would come to her condo for dinner. After a couple of years of the two of us being single, she invited me to share her condo with her. So now I have one end of the house with a private bedroom, bathroom, and privacy door, and she has the other end. We share the common area of living, dining, and kitchen. Everyday I have a home-cooked meal thanks to my wonderful sister. I used to try to beat her to the washing machine but have since given up; but I still have clean laundry a couple of times a week. Sue is just the most generous, outgoing, loving person ever. I could never say enough about my fabulous sister Sue.

Joe Singer

A couple of times in this book, and in passing, I have mentioned Joe Singer. Joe was my brother-in-law, married to Sue. They met at the South Florida Fishing Club, and had a wonderful life together. They raised four beautiful children: a son named Keith, and daughter named Amber with Sue, and two sons of Joe's from a previous marriage. The whole family tarpon fished, and offshore fished together for many years. Joe and Sue fished from Alaska in the north to Venezuela in the south, and many places east and west in between.

It was kind of funny. Joe would never have an autopilot on the boat. Most of us never did, but my sister drove him to install one. They would be out fishing, and he would ask her to drive while he put the lines out. Then once he got the lines out, he'd have her fish and he'd drive. When he asked her to drive he would say, "Just go to that cloud over there." She would suppose to be driving in sixty feet of water, and all of a sudden the downrigger would be hung on the bottom in forty feet. He'd turn around and say, "What are you doing going that way? I told you to go that way."

She would say, "Well, I was watching a seagull," or "I saw a porpoise," or some silly story. They were the sweetest, most awesome couple, and I say jokingly they saved their marriage by buying an autopilot.

What a helpful guy Joe always was. My boat was in the marina right near his condo. I could call him and tell him my bilge pump was stuck, or something like that, and he would come in and fix it while I was busy getting the boat ready between my day charter and my night charter.

Joe was also quite clever and creative. I came in one morning and discovered this beautiful leader rack across the back of the inside of the t-top. I had been keeping my spools of monofilament line in beer cozies to protect them from getting tangled up, scraped up, or too much exposure to the sun. Joe had taken all my leader material and had screwed the cozies to a piece of wood, and tie wrapped the wood to my t-top. Now I had a great leader dispenser of quarter pound spools of line, and I could pull the line off the end. It was very ingenious and really handy. I still use it today.

Joe was a big part of keeping the boat running while I tended to the business of chartering. He backed me up in many different ways. He would come down to the boat and anything that could be puttered with, he would do. And in a pinch, if my boat was out of service, I could borrow his twenty-six foot boat to use for the day. Joe and I spent a great deal of time together fishing, and talking on the radio with him on his boat and me on my boat.

Along came an opportunity with a bunch of his buddies from the South Florida Fishing Club to go marlin fishing in Chub Cay. They pulled out of Haulover Inlet on a big Hatteras. Joe was in the salon, and when they were about ten miles offshore, he said he didn't feel well. He was very pale and seasick. So they turned around and brought him back.

They got to Haulover Inlet and the paramedics met him there and ran him down to Mt. Sinai Hospital. Joe had had a heart attack. They put a stent in, and over the next few days while he was recuperating in the hospital, all his buddies came in to make sure he was OK. His son flew in from out of town to be with him. It was like a giant reunion of the Joe Singer fan club.

He got out of the hospital and returned home. On Sunday he was watching Tiger Woods play golf. I called him up and told him we had caught a potential worlds record sailfish for a junior lady angler. He was thrilled about that. Fifteen or twenty minutes later my sister came out of the craft section of their house and found Joe on the living room floor. She called the paramedics and they took him back to Mt. Sinai, but he never regained consciousness.

Joe and I would get together and watch football and basketball games, or bounce fishing ideas off each other. Everybody loved him, and he was one of my closest friends. What a tremendous loss to the South Florida community. Sixty-three years old, and the picture of health, but has now passed on to better fishing grounds in the sky. He'll always be missed, but he'll never be forgotten.

Sharon Richter

My younger sister, Sharon, is the girly-girl in the family. She was always very prim and proper, and very cautious about cleanliness. It was funny; when she was a little girl and we were sitting down to dinner, we had to pull our chairs up to a breakfast counter were we ate. She would come out of the bathroom with her spotlessly clean hands and pick up her stool with her elbows, and carry it over to the counter and climb up onto the stool and eat her meal. She has always been very caring. She is more of a person who stays at home, and is quiet in her own life.

One of my favorite stories about my little sister: She knew when my dad was running our boat he would pull the plug on the inside of the back, and all the water would run out. So this one day we were anchored by Fowey Rocks Lighthouse. Sharon and my mom stayed on the boat while everybody else was snorkeling. Sharon noticed there was water in the boat, so she pulled the plug out while the boat was sitting there anchored. Of course when my dad pulled the plug, and the boat was running, the water ran out. But when the boat is stopped and the plug is pulled, the water runs in. There was a near disaster there when my little sister Sharon nearly sank the boat. I still love you Sharon, we didn't lose the boat, and we all got home safely.

Todd Richter

Sharon is married to Todd Richter. Todd has been in the gun and fishing tackle industry pretty much his whole life, and is an avid fly fisherman. We really got to know each other when Todd was running a fly shop that he and his dad were partners in. He's neat guy with a lot of knowledge about fly-fishing, and fly tying, and fishing in general.

He was a curmudgeon to be sure, always moaning and groaning about something, but we all knew that inside he was the most generous guy in the world. He was the guy who would give you the shirt off his back in a split second without ever questioning it.

He did some great fly tying for me. I learned from him that in the Bahamas a yellow and white, or an orange and white, was far more effective than almost any other color. It was based on the fact that the pilchards in the Bahamas are called Sandy Cay pilchards, and they were yellowish orange and white. From that came the Sandy Cay fly patterns. We caught a whole lot of fish with them. And Todd tied a ton of them for me and my other brother in law, Joe.

Todd, and Sharon, and my wife, and I went to Bimini together a couple of times and had some really great fly fishing adventures for yellow tail snappers, and cero mackerels, and amberjacks.

At Thanksgiving Joe Singer and his sons, and my sister Sue's son, and Todd and I would go out in the morning for some fishing while the dinner feast was being cooked. Those are trips I'll always miss. We had trips where my nephew Keith, or my other nephew Joseph, would catch tarpon right off South Beach. Or we would anchor off a wreck and catch Spanish mackerel, and amberjack, and blue runners on fly rods. We'd have one cast right after another. One time we took Keith's father-in-law out, and although he got seasick, he did catch a twenty-five pound jack crevalle.

One of the things he did that I'll never forget happened when he was dating my sister. He came over on Christmas morning and was playing with my dog, Dreyfus. I think he blew on the dog's nose or something like that, and the dog bit him right on the lip and chin. So Todd and I went scrambling around North Miami to find a doctor who would sew up his lip and chin. What a fiasco that was. But after that Todd and the dog became best of friends.

When I had become single Todd lived about a block away, and whenever I'd go to the Bahamas, Todd would go over and take Dreyfus for a walk and feed him and my cat. He is generous and outgoing, and is still happily married to my sister. They have now moved up to Sebastian and have a great life for themselves there. When it came to fly fishing or helping a friend in need, I could always call on Todd to save the day. What a great guy he is.

Flip

The three of us had a younger brother named Phillip, but to us he was always Flip. He was the adventurous one. He had every pet known to man: a raccoon, and a skunk, and a seagull. We all had dogs and rabbits.

Flip really took a beating, and it seemed he could never get a break. One day we were digging a hole out in a field and I accidentally

243

hit him right on top of the head with a shovel. Another time we were dueling with curtain rods in the yard across the street from our house, and he stabbed his sword into the ground, and the sharp end of his curtain rod cut a hole right in the palm of his hand that probably should have had stitches. Another time he and I were playing football in the back yard and I accidentally broke his collarbone. My dad said, "Oh he just bruised himself. Sit in front of the fireplace for a while. The heat will make it feel better." Poor Flip sat in front of the fireplace for hours crying his eyes out. I don't know if it was the pain from the collarbone that I had broken, or if it was the heat cooking him alive. They finally took him to the hospital and put his arm in a cast.

Flip was helping me deliver newspapers one morning and he ran over a pop bottle that caused him to fall off his bike with all these newspapers. He picked up the pop bottle and threw it down the street, and of course when he threw the bottle, the broken glass laid his hand open.

Another day I took him fishing at Greynolds Park and he fell down on the oysters and got all cut up by the sharp shells. I was sure the police were going to be looking for me for sibling abuse for all the injuries he got while we were together.

Unfortunately his worst injury happened when he was married and had a little daughter. He was going down a dirt road on his motorcycle and a farmer had maliciously strung barbed wire across the road from one Australian pine tree to another. Flip broke the wire with his throat. This resulted first of all in near death in the emergency room, and then years of surgeries for a clogged windpipe.

Flip became a crackerjack welder. He built that boat with my dad; he welded the whole thing. He raised a beautiful daughter, had a wonderful son, and adopted another daughter. He was married to two different beautiful women, two great ladies.

Unfortunately, the trials and tribulations of repeated surgeries, and with all the trials of his life, he decided it was all too much for him. He took his own life when he was twenty-seven. But what a great man he was and I really loved my little brother.

Radar Range Observer

Observers are frequently used in catch and release sportfishing. They're like judges put on each boat to make sure everything is done by the rules. The first time I ever fished with an observer was in a sailfish tournament the 1970s down in Duck Key, just above Marathon in the Florida Keys. Our angler was Van Every.

We predominantly used spinning rods with twelve or twenty pound line. We could have used eight, twelve, or twenty pound test, but the most logical way to win was with twelve-pound test, so that's what we were using.

Our observer came on the boat the first day and made himself at home. As we headed out of the harbor he came up to me and asked, "You ever see one of these radar ranges?" He was talking about microwave ovens.

I said, "No, I've heard about them, but I've never seen one."

His next comment was, "Well, I sure would like to have a radar range."

I said, "Yeah, I hear they're really nice. As a matter of fact Mr. Every has a boat being built, and he's putting a radar range on there, and he has one in his house. He knows a lot about them."

So the observer high tailed it up onto the bridge. We had cleared the Duck Key marina going out into the channel so I went up on the bridge where everyone else was gathering. The observer asked Mr. Every, "The mate tells me you got a radar range."

He said, "Yeah, I have one in my house, and I'm building a new boat, and putting one in there too."

So the observer asked, "How long does it take to cook a hot dog in a radar range?"

Mr. Every said, "Well, it takes about a half a minute to cook a hot dog."

The observer said, "Well, that's really fine. And how long does it take to make a baked potato?"

He responded, "I think a baked potato takes about five minutes, but I haven't cooked one in it yet."

The observer said, "Boy, I wish I could afford a radar range."

That was the end of the radar range conversation for a while. Then about noontime the observer came up to me and said, "So, have you ever cooked with a radar range?"

I said, "No I haven't cooked with one. I told you, the only one I know of is Van's. He has one in his house and one going on his new boat."

"Well, how much do those radar ranges cost?"

I said, "I think they're about a thousand, twelve hundred dollars."

He said, "I wish I could afford a radar range. I heard they were really good for cooking fish."

"Yeah, I wish could afford a radar range too."

He said, "I wonder if other seafood could be cooked in that radar range."

I said, "I really don't know, but I imagine you could cook almost anything in it."

He repeated, "I wish I could afford a radar range."

"I guess we all wish we could have one."

We all went back to fishing, but I had really messed up. Dude Perkins, from Dude and Harry's, was right when he told me that I needed to take these rubber squids down as teasers for sailfish in the Keys. I had laughed at him at the time, but now everybody in the tournament was doing really well with daisy chains of squid hanging from each outrigger. We didn't have them, and we weren't getting any bites.

At about 2:30 here came the observer again. Everybody was down in the cockpit with me and we were shooting the breeze. The observer came down and said, "You guys know you are mighty slow."

Van said, "What do you mean by that?"

"You all know, if I could afford a radar range, you could be catching a lot of sailfish. That's only if I could afford a radar range though."

Now it was clear. The hayseed observer was making a veiled offer to cheat for us if someone would buy him a radar range. Van was disgusted and said he thought he should go sit in the corner and learn to be an honest observer.

The next day we had a different observer, a woman. As soon as we put the baits out we caught a little bonito. She said, "Oh you gotta throw him back. You're not allowed to keep the sailfish." She didn't know a bonito from a sailfish. This tournament was definitely going downhill.

The next day was Thanksgiving. I had learned my lesson about the squid teasers so I had some rubber squids shipped into town so we could have some daisy chain teasers. I figured if we were going to use squid for teasers, we ought to have squid for bait. So I rigged up ten pounds of squid for trolling baits. And along came our observer. He introduced himself and said he had his tape measurer, and he had to measure every one of our leaders.

I asked, "You have to measure every one of my leaders? I have one hundred of them."

He said, "Yeah, they all have to be under fifteen feet."

I pulled the towel off the top of the baits and said, 'I'll tell you what, you pick out any six leaders, and if they're over fourteen feet ten inches you can measure every single one. But we're going to start with measuring six."

He said, "That sounds pretty fair." He measured six leaders and they were all under fourteen feet ten inches. They were allowed to be fifteen feet, so he was satisfied.

Finally, on the last day of the tournament we got an observer who came aboard and introduced himself, asked where we would like him to sit, and said if there was anything we needed him to do, just let him know. Otherwise he would try to stay out of the way.

On the last two days we caught some fish, but we were too far behind to catch up. The trip was a total flop with no squids. The squid daisy chains really made all the difference; but we learned our lesson too late.

Corey Wayne Leonard

Corey Wayne Leonard came to Miami from Kansas and wanted to learn to be a fisherman. He worked as a dock attendant at the marina, but got frustrated and went back to Kansas. He returned to Miami and worked as a truck driver for a road construction company, but had problems with some of he other workers, and quit the job. He was hanging around the dock because what he really wanted was to be a fisherman. So I started taking him on the boat with me. In the course of six months I think I gave him close to $10,000 to eat and to pay his bills.

I taught him to fish, and he went to sea school and got his captain's license. I was grooming him to work on the boat at night and to work on Abie's days off. He worked quite a few night trips and even some day trips by himself, and he was really getting the hang of things. I had great hope for Corey.

All of a sudden one day he didn't show up; and he didn't show up for more than a week. I had to turn down trips and cancel other trips because he wasn't there. He never came to me to tell me what was up. He just dropped off the scene.

When I talk about Corey Wayne Leonard I have to share one of my best practical jokes ever. Corey went to wash something off the deck with the saltwater wash down hose, but it didn't work. It didn't work because Corey had not flipped the pump switch on the dashboard. So he complained that the hose wasn't working, that he couldn't get any water. He was shaking the hose and the nozzle and it still wouldn't work. I told him to look and see if it was clogged. He looked at the end of the nozzle and didn't see anything. So I told him he wouldn't be able to see anything unless he pulled the trigger on the nozzle. So while he was looking in the nozzle I quickly hit the pump switch and it came on. He got water up his nose, and blew off his sunglasses and his hat. It was a cruel thing to do but I had to laugh. And how about this, eight days later I got him with the same thing.

Come on Corey. Come back to Miami. We'll welcome you with open arms. I know he's driving a truck and making good money now, but I also know his heart is in fishing. He's also a catfish and bass guide so, no matter where you are Corey, I hope you're having fun.

Rods Overboard

I've lost a few overboard, and I've thrown a few overboard on purpose. The good news is, the ones I've thrown overboard on purpose, I've managed to get most of them back.

The first time I remember losing a rod overboard I was in Flamingo fishing with my dad and one of his buddies, Dominic Torelli. We always put out a big bait for sharks and tarpon, usually a half a ladyfish or something. I had a Penn 65,on a solid glass rod. We didn't have any rod holders on the boat, so I jammed it under the wooden deck with the tip out over the side. I thought it was pretty secure. We were fishing with jig heads with shrimp on a sinker, and a short leader with a 4/0 circle hook. We were catching red fish, and trout, and sheep heads, and snappers.

Sure enough, my big bait got a hit, and I guess the rod wasn't secured under the deck too well because it went flying out of the boat. I thought my favorite rod and reel was gone. I had caught my first sailfish on it, and hundreds of other fish. I had owned for about five years, and I was really in love with it; and there it went over the side. I thought I'd never see it again. Just a split second later my dad was fishing with a ten-pound spinning outfit and he got a screaming strike. He was fighting and fighting and it wouldn't stop. We took off following with the boat, and I'll be doggone if he didn't come up with my rod. His hook was like a little 3/0 Old English bait hook, which is kind of like a semi-circle hook. It slipped right over the shaft between the reel and the handle of the crank, just a little piece of chrome-plated sleeve over a brass shaft. The hook was caught right on that. It was a miracle that it caught there. I got my rod and reel back and caught a fifty-pound shark besides. That was the first rod I ever lost overboard, and I'll be doggone if I didn't get it back.

The next rod I remember losing was on Newport Fishing Pier. We were fishing the sunrise kingfish bite using live bait. We would cast them straight out to the east from the end of the pier. We coaxed our baits to swim out by hooking them by the tail. Every time they would stop going out we would pull on them a little which would turn their nose back offshore and get them to swim further from the beach. That gave us a decent chance to catch a kingfish or bonito, or maybe a big Spanish mackerel. The pier was 1,000 feet long and I probably had another 100 feet of line out.

I had been fishing with the same bait for a while, and it was not swimming very well, so I decided to wind it up. I was holding my rod in my right hand with my thumb on the spool. I was holding the rod with just my forefinger wrapped around the butt of the rod and my thumb, thumbing the line so it wouldn't backlash. I reached over with my left hand to push the free spool lever from free spool to engaging the reel. When the reel snapped into gear the timing was perfect. At the exact moment the lever snapped, the line came tight with something on it, maybe a king or a bonito going after my bait. It headed straight east. The rod and reel flew out of my hand and didn't land until it was more than 100 feet beyond the edge of the pier. It went surfing across the water never to be seen again. That one I wasn't getting back. It was like I hit the switch on a missile. First it was a missile, then it was a torpedo, and then it disappeared from site. But what a crazy way to lose a rod and reel!

I was out night fishing when I lost the next one. I had this beautiful plug-casting outfit. It was a six and a half foot custom rod, probably a Uslan plug rod. I can't remember what kind of reel it was, but I think it was a Pflueger Supreme. We were catching kingfish using a rig that had three hooks on it. I had been caught up in a tangle of other people's lines. I leaned my rod up against my shoulder as I was trying to get my line free from another angler's hooks. Fortunately the timing was perfect, because if the fish had hit my bait while I had the hooks in my hand, I might have been hooked by these three hooks that were tangled in my line. As it worked out, I had just cleared my line, and before I even got to grab my rod, it went from leaning on my shoulder to crashing down on the railing of the boat. This gave it leverage, which pulled down on the tip and flipped the reel and the butt end of the rod probably six or seven feet into the air and right straight down into the water. So, that was my second missile launch, and the second rod I never saw again.

The only other rod I ever lost overboard myself was really stupid. I was tarpon fishing near the beach. It was just one customer and me. We had come too close to the beach and had to wind the lines in. I wound in one of the rods and went to put it in the rod holder just as I saw a big wave coming. I tried to do too many things at once. I wanted to bump the boat into gear and turn toward the wave. But at the same time I was trying to put the rod in the rod holder. As I reached around to put the boat into gear and point into the wave, I flat out missed the rod holder, missed the side of the boat, and just dropped this twenty-pound spinning outfit right over the side. Lost and gone forever.

After that I never had another rod that I personally lost overboard. I had one fisherman drop an outfit way out in the Gulf Stream catching schoolie dolphin. I never saw that one again either. Other than that, all the other outfits that went overboard, we threw overboard on purpose.

Sometimes we would have a tarpon on and it would go underneath a dock. We would clip an anchor ball to the rod, then we'd get the tarpon pulling drag really well, and throw the rod in the water, expecting the tarpon to pull the rod underneath the dock and come out on the other side. The tarpon would be pulling because they were fighting resistance, but when we threw the rod in the water, the resistance let up and the tarpon would immediately stop running. So the tarpon we were counting on to pull the rod twenty feet under the dock, would only pull it five or six feet. Then we'd have to reach under

253

the dock with a gaff and pull the anchor ball back out and pull on the tarpon to get him running again, in an effort to get him to take the rod to the other side of the dock. I had to do that four or five times and it usually worked. We'd go around the other side of the dock, get the rod and catch the fish.

We also did this sail fishing out in the ocean, and it was usually no big deal. We'd hook two sailfish on twenty-pound spinning outfits. They'd be down almost to the knot so we'd put the anchor ball on. The anchor ball is two feet in diameter and orange, so it was easy to see where it went. We'd throw that rod overboard and chase down the other fish. Once we caught it we'd go back and find the orange ball. There wasn't a lot of pressure on the fish so he wouldn't travel very far. We'd pick up the rod, unclip the ball and catch the next sailfish.

There were a couple of times we'd hook them on conventional rods. One time I threw a customer's International twenty overboard. He was shocked that I would do that. For whatever the reason, we had to throw his instead of mine. Maybe I just didn't want to have to clean mine. Bottom line is we caught those fish.

Then there was one day when nothing went right. We had two sailfish on six-pound test line each. One was going north, and one was going south. We decided to chase the one going north, and come back for the other one. So we clicked the anchor ball on and threw the rod overboard, and took off to the north. In short order I saw a boat go right next to the anchor ball, probably twenty feet away from it, and I figured for sure he would have cut the line. We landed the first fish and went back, but the anchor ball was gone. I had punched into my GPS where I was when I threw it overboard. I was looking and looking and didn't see the anchor ball anywhere. There was a stiff east wind so I just let the boat drift for a minute. Just about a mile northwest of us I saw a boat anchored on the reef. I was thinking maybe that boat could have picked up that rod and reel. It would have gone right in that direction. So, I pulled up next to the guy and said, "Hey, how you doin'?" As I said that I saw my anchor ball with my name on it in the front of his boat. I said, "Oh, I see you picked up my rod and reel and my anchor ball. Can I get those back from you?" He was fishing with our rod and reel, and our anchor ball was up in his bow. I don't think he had any plans of ever having to give that rod and reel back to anybody. We got our rod and reel back and it only had about fifty feet of line left on it. Another boat had cut the line. At least we got the customer's rod and reel back and my anchor ball.

Those are my tales of rods overboard successfully and not successfully. But it's all part of the game, and it's always fun to watch people's faces when we hook the anchor ball to the rod and reel and throw it overboard. It's been a while since I've had to do that. But I'm sure it will happen again in the future.

On three occasions I have run out of line on a reel and clipped another reel on and thrown the first rod overboard, and let the fish run line totally off one reel and partially off another. I saw that happen one time where they actually clipped on three reels and threw them in the water on a big shark on Newport Pier. But they were lucky and got them all back. That was a lucky catch.

Gary Walker, the Penn Man

I went to a Saltwater Sportsman seminar where I met up with the Penn rep, a great man by the name of Gary Walker. He had given me a great deal on all new Penn eight-pound and twenty-pound spinning rods and reels. My tackle collection was dressed to the nines. I had six brand new big spinners and four brand new little spinners.

We were on my twenty-five-foot Dusky where I had racks on the inside of the boat. I had six of these rods stored on the racks: four twenty-pound spinning outfits, and two eight-pound spinning outfits. We were fishing with Penn International twenties, and we had a tarpon on. We got it up to the boat, and I told the angler that if the fish goes under the boat, to point the rod straight down so the line doesn't rub on the bottom of the boat, and then we'll maneuver to get him back out again.

The tarpon was still pretty frisky. It came up to the boat, and then it dove under the boat. The angler pointed his rod down into the water, and the tarpon came up on the other side of the boat and flew right into the boat. So now the tarpon was crashing and thrashing all over the back of my boat. Rods were flying and banging, and it was total chaos. Finally the tarpon stopped jumping and I grabbed him by the lower jaw. We took a picture real quick and threw him over the side, and he took off swimming straight toward the beach. I hope he survived.

He left a little blood and a lot of slime and scales. The boat was a mess. I grabbed a bucket and a brush and cleaned up all the guts and slime. I was picking up rods, and pieces of rods, and got everything all squared away and took inventory. Every twenty-pound spinning outfit was destroyed. Rods were snapped in half, reel handles and bales were crushed, and the housings of the reels were totally wrecked. I started with four twenty-pound outfits, and there wasn't one in the bunch that could be fished with.

Then I came to the first eight-pound outfit and it appeared to be totally unharmed. I took the line in my hand and I pulled down and it went dink, dink – it was broken in three places. Then there was finally the last eight-pound outfit. The tip half of the rod was laying on the deck. Never to be seen again was the bottom half of the rod and the reel. Apparently the whole outfit, sans the two feet of tip, had been kicked right over the side of the boat by the tarpon. We had destroyed six outfits. The only reel that was still usable was that one eight-pound outfit, and it broke when I flexed the rod. So we ended up with one salvageable reel.

This happened during the Miami International Boat show. I was going to the show in the afternoon after the trip, so I took the broken half of the rod with me. I went up to Gary Walker, who was working at the boat show, and I said, "Gary, I think we have a problem with our rods and reels." And he was nice enough to replace all the outfits for me. But what a destructive tarpon that was!

Seasick

There have been a lot of people over the years who have gotten seasick on my boat. We've tried all the various remedies. Some work for one person, and some others work for others. Some of them don't work for anybody.

Bye Bye Ron, I Miss You

I have surely seen my share of people getting seasick. Probably the most disheartening case of seasickness I've ever had was with a really great guy named Ron, who fished with his uncle, Ben, and his two little kids. Ron never got seasick, and neither did Ben. Ron's daughter would get a little bit on the edge of seasickness, and we would sometimes change our game plan to help her out.

We were out fishing one day and, lo and behold, Ron got seasick. The saddest part about him getting seasick is we loved him. He's a great guy; he's great company, and really a pleasure to have aboard. But we haven't seen Ron since the first time he got seasick. It's quite a loss to us.

Bandar's Entourage

For many years we have been fishing with a Saudi Arabian Prince by the name of Bandar. Bandar went to school in California where he met a car dealer by the name of George, and they became close friends. Bandar and George fished with us on many occasions. Bandar loves to fish for whatever will bite. We've fish successfully for tarpon and sail. We've had some days that were tough and caught a few groupers and a few kingfish. But the stories that Bandar shares are just phenomenal. He loves to cook and goes into great detail describing what he's going to cook for us when we come to Fisher Island to join him for dinner (although we never got there). But the menus are very exciting.

Bandar, in addition to being a prince and a high level Saudi executive, was one of the most outgoing and generous people I ever met. He would arrive in the morning with his fishing partners and his staff. The staff would sit him down on the dock box and get him ready, slather him down with sunscreen, and bring enough food to last for six years on an eight-hour fishing trip.

Bandar taught me a lesson that I have tried to incorporate into my own life. Here is this Crown Prince from Saudi Arabia. He travels all over the world and meets all kinds of people. But he still calls me every couple of weeks just to say hello, ask how I'm doing, and what I've been up to. He tells me where he went fishing, and what he did here or there. He once flew me to France to learn about marine reserves. I was invited to Saudi Arabia, but that was put on the back burner because of some political unrest in the Middle East at the time. But the lesson is about how a big international figure can take the time to call, and be friendly with a South Florida fishing guide.

Bandar tells stories of racing camels and show camels. Who would imagine that a camel as ugly as they are could be worth more than a million dollars? What he explained was that when there's a camel show, each competitor might have 100 camels. Contestants who do not have 100 camels are penalized, and every missing camel detracts from the score. Top camels might be worth a million dollars or more, so imagine what these guys spend on a championship. The amounts are mindboggling.

Sometimes when Bandar showed up there would be too many people for one boat, so he and George would fish on separate boats. On this one particular trip we had three on my boat, the Prince and two of his assistants. Mario Cote took George and the rest of the entourage out on his boat.

On the first day we went out it was really rough, but nobody got seasick. The second day was about the same. Nobody on my boat got seasick, but the two assistants who went with Mario were both seasick. George said to one of the assistants, "Hey, I noticed your patch is gone." This was a scopolamine patch placed behind the ear. The medicine is transdermal, meaning it goes right through the skin and into the blood stream to help prevent seasickness.

The assistant said, "Yeah, when I took my shower last night I took the patch off.

George said, "Those patches are good for three days, and they're very expensive. You're supposed to leave it on."

The assistant replied, "Oh, I didn't know."

Then George turned to the other assistant and said, "What about your patch?"

That assistant said, "Yeah, I took mine off too." So now both men without patches were seasick.

George was a kind of a clown anyway, and he said to Mario, "You got any electrical tape?'

Mario said, "Yeah." He got out the electric tape.

"You got any scissors?"

"Yeah," He got out the scissors and gave them to George. Then George cut out two round pieces of electrical tape and told the men to stick them behind their ears. But, the placebos didn't work.

Woozy but Not Seasick

Three times in my life I've been close to seasick. One time I was on this big Hatteras in the Tongue of the Ocean. It was real rough out there when it ran out of fuel in the tank it was running on. The captain didn't know how to prime the fuel system, so I had to go down into the bilge and do it. It was stifling hot down there, with thick diesel fumes. I had to crack the return line on the generator, extract a bucket of diesel fuel, and then reconnect that fuel line. Then I had to take down the filters on the main engines and fill them with diesel. Then I had to crack the injector lines on the mains. Once all that was done, I was able to get the engines to start. There was diesel fuel all over the place and I got to feeling really woozy, but I recovered without chumming overboard.

Sick but Not Seasick

The other time that I thought I got seasick I was devastated and broken hearted. I was working on the *Soporfin*, a party boat out of 163rd Street in North Miami Beach, and I was sicker than a dog. I couldn't believe I was so sick on the boat. How could me, Bouncer Smith, be seasick? I went on for three more days with a terrible case of the flu. I was thrilled to have the flu, because it meant I wasn't seasick. That was refreshing.

Sick but With a Good Excuse

I got sick on a boat one other time. That was the time I had to have the hook surgically removed from my finger and the doctor gave me a tetanus shot. On the day after the shot I had a reaction. I felt seasick but actually it was just a reaction to the tetanus shot. My record of never getting seasick remains intact.

Porpoise

Being career fishermen, we have a lot of encounters with porpoises or bottlenose dolphins. One of my neatest encounters with one was when I was fishing with Mark Sosin. We were targeting barracudas and spinner sharks on the artificial reefs off Key Biscayne. We were using live speedos for bait. We used wire leaders with two hooks, one in the upper lip, and one three quarters of the way down on the side of the bait. We were slow trolling with a downrigger in 150 feet of water. We saw a porpoise rolling from time to time, coming up to take a gulp of air.

We eventually got a hit on the speedo. Mark grabbed the rod and started to fight the fish. It didn't run and it didn't come in. It just sat there showing just enough life for us to know we weren't hung on the bottom. Mark pulled but the fish held on. After a couple of minutes the fish came off. So Mark wound in the line and the wire leader was straight as an arrow. The hook was fine, but the bait was gone.

So we re-baited with another live speedo. We sent it down about sixty feet and started to troll back and forth through the area again. It wasn't five minutes before we had another strike. The fish pulled, and Mark pulled, and the fish pulled some more, and Mark pulled. After several minutes the fish came off. Again, Mark wound in and the leader was straight, the hooks were fine, and the bait was gone.

The next time we put it out the same thing happened again. But this time instead of pulling, the porpoise came to the surface and rolled to take another gulp of air. Now at least we could see what our opponent was as the line went straight from the rod to the porpoise. The next time we put the bait out we hooked a shark. The porpoise hung around, and I had the impression he was asking why we fed the speedo to the shark instead of saving it for him.

I can't count the number of times a porpoise has inspired our days. We'll be trolling around and the porpoise will come by and swim with the boat, or jump around, or swim under the boat, or ride the bow wave. It makes every trip extra special.

We had a recent occasion where a porpoise would have to compete with a frigate bird for our ballyhoo. The porpoise would swim on its back while playing with the bait, while the frigate bird looked for an opening where it could sweep in to eat the ballyhoo. The porpoises were feeding on these real small ballyhoos, and it would be quite the game. As the ballyhoo jumped, the frigate bird would dive. This went on and on. The porpoises would jump up to catch the ballyhoo, and as they came down they would flip back over onto their stomachs. If they were lucky they would not have their breakfast stolen by a bird.

But watching this was a real National Geographic moment. It was a show to remember and it sure had us fired up when we first saw those birds and realized we were coming up on a pod of porpoises.

263

Wheel of Meat Tournament

Over the years I became a fan of the Paul and Ron show at Big 105.9 FM. I ran into Paul Castronovo at Sands Harbor Marina for the Pompano Rodeo, and he asked me about doing a radio show with him. I said that I would love to. He asked if I was still with Mike Ranieri, and I told him that I was. He indicated that it might be a kind of a conflict, which I understood. So he asked if there might be someone else who could be on the show with him. I happened to be right there with Dennis Forgione and I said, "Here, Dennis is right here. He covers for me whenever I can't go on the show. He'd be real good for you." I introduced Paul to Dennis, and from that introduction Dennis was on the show every Friday morning for twenty years. Eventually Dennis retired from radio, and I took that spot.

I was doing the show with Paul Castronovo once a week, but I listened to him everyday. One of the games they played was the Wheel of Meat. Contestants would call into the show and they would spin this wheel in the background. I thought it was just a sound effect, but no one knew any better. They would spin the Wheel of Meat and someone would come up with an answer to some zany question.

This one year we were fishing the Miami Dolphins Football Team Spring Fishing Tournament, which raised money for cystic fibrosis. Paul Castronovo was on the Board of Directors for the tournament. I fished the tournament from time to time with different people, including Paul a couple of years. Now came the time for the tournament, and it was being held at Miami Beach Marina.

264

For the organization and the captains meeting they set a big tent up in the parking lot of the marina. The weather was horrible, pouring down rain, and windy. It was so bad it nearly flooded out their tent. But they succeeded in having a good captains' meeting with plenty of cheerleaders and football players, Hooters Girls, and just a good time for everybody. So now it was Saturday morning. We were all ready to go fishing, but the wind was blowing thirty-fives mile an hour. It was pouring down rain, so there was a question about what to do about the tournament? They decided to cancel it, but told us all to stay tuned in case they decided to fish at noontime.

We had a little powwow in the tent, talking about what to do about the weather. They asked me about it because I'm a full time fisherman. It looked like it was going to be a blow out. I asked Paul, "Do you really have a roulette wheel. Is the Wheel of Meat really a roulette wheel?"

He said, "Yeah."

This was a big fancy tournament and a lot of people had come from out of town. I said, "You have so much involved in your captains meeting and the awards dinner, what if you take the Wheel of Meat, and change it out a little; put a fifty-pound dolphin, and a twelve-pound dolphin, and an undersized dolphin, and seaweed, and broken line. And maybe we'll have a forty-pound kingfish, and a twenty-pound kingfish; we'll say we caught an old boot, and so on."

They took my idea and did it. There were four species of fish, tuna, kingfish, wahoo, and dolphin. We would make a roulette wheel of good catches, bad catches, fish getaways, and some real booby prize catches. I proposed that every registered angler could spin the wheel and see what they caught.

It was probably as much fun, if not more fun, than going fishing. Everybody was up there and couldn't wait to take their turn to spin the wheel. As it turned out, a very senior couple, Mr. and Mrs. Rudman of Hook and Tackle Clothing, won the tournament. They each caught a fifty-pound dolphin. I don't remember what else they caught. Every spin of the wheel they had was a significant catch – no broken lines, pulled hooks, old boots, or anything like that. They won the tournament and never even got on the boat. There was so much laughing and carrying on at the awards dinner with everyone spinning the wheel, just like a tournament in a normal year. It was talked about for years to come.

Then and Now

The difference between then and now is very disconcerting to me, as I believe it should be for all lovers of the oceans and their amazing inhabitants. As an example, when I was in my teens, snook were very abundant. We fished on plugs and with flies from the shoreline around North Miami Beach. Driving around in our cars, we'd hit a certain seawall or point of land, or wade into a river mouth. We caught small snook in huge numbers, and big snook in good numbers. Then, in part due to gill netting, there were too many snook being harvested. If the netters didn't take them and sell them, the snook would die anyway. Land development also had a lot to do with it, but the bottom line is that the snook population crashed. It reached the point where I wouldn't go fishing for snook myself, let alone take a charter snook fishing.

Fortunately today, due to some really good management, snook fishing rebounded. I can go fun fishing for snook, and I run lots of charters for them too. I've had charters where we caught twenty snook in the course of an evening. We caught our biggest snook ever on a charter just a few years ago. We had a bit of a hitch recently in Government Cut where the snook fishing was slow, but it was good in other areas. Today the snook fishery is in pretty good condition.

Swordfish is another very positive story. I had the worst timing in the world when I went to Islamorada to become a flats guide in 1976, the same year that nighttime swordfishing exploded. Jerry and Jesse Webb went out with Mike Carey and Billy Harrison, and they caught a couple of big swordfish. Then everybody was swordfishing while I was bone fishing on the flats in Islamorada. I missed out on the beginning of swordfishing, but got into it a year or two later. I caught a few nice swordfishes and then the fishery crashed. There were so many long lines out in South Florida that it was nearly impossible to fish. No sooner would we get our spread out than we would drift over some long liner's gear and lose all our rigs. Or if we hooked a fish, we might get tangled in long line gear and have to break it off.

Swordfishing declined to the point where there were programs to discourage people from buying swordfish in restaurants. The scientists got involved and decided that the Straights of Florida were a nursery ground, and it shouldn't be abused by commercial fishing. So the swordfish in the Straights of Florida were protected, and by the late 1990s swordfishing was great again.

In the early 2000s swordfishing was crazy. Tackle shops could not get enough big Penn Internationals to supply the market. The tackle shops were doing a land office business in big swordfishing tackle. I've gone out swordfishing at night when there were a hundred boats out there. From commercial airliners people would look down on South Florida waters and marvel at all the green lights fifteen or twenty miles off the coast. Those were the Hydro Glow lights we use to attract the swordfish.

At about the same time that daytime swordfishing was introduced to South Florida, buoy gear was introduced. The buoy gear took out so many juvenile swordfishes that had been protected from the long liners, that there was no longer a viable nighttime sword fishery. It used to be that in three or four hours at night we could get several bites and have a catch or two. With this buoy gear nighttime swordfishing has shut down. The good news is that we still have a viable daytime sword fishery. In the past couple of winters the daytime swordfishing has been phenomenal. So, swordfish are now a good news story.

But then we look at kingfish. When I was just out of high school, we would go out on a drift boat and our record was more than 300 kingfish in a four-hour trip. In less than three hours on one trip I personally caught twenty-seven kingfish. It was common for head boats up and down the coast to catch fifty, seventy-five, or a hundred kingfish on a morning trip, or an afternoon trip, or a night trip. It was just unbelievable. Then the spotter planes started going out and finding the schools of kingfish and radioing to the gill-netters. The boats would each take a part of the school while being directed by the spotter planes. A whole spawning mass would be wiped out in one day. To point out how wasteful it was, they caught so many, and the boats were so full, that the kingfish in the bottom of the boat would be crushed by the weight of the kingfish on the top of the pile. Additionally, they were unchilled, so when they came off the boat they may have been OK for chicken feed, or fertilizer, but not for human consumption. Maybe the top layer would almost be good. But then again, they would be baked in the sun while they were running back into the dock. Instead of getting top dollar of fifty or eighty cents a pound, they would sell these destroyed kingfish for a penny or two a pound.

How has king fishing rebounded? It hasn't. We go out king fishing now and there are weeks when we catch only one or two kingfish. At times in the past we would have had no problem catching twenty or thirty. We did a lot of catch and release on kingfish because many people didn't care to eat them. I don't know if kingfish will ever come back. They were so beaten up years ago that they show no signs of recovering.

Looking at bottom fish, I can remember when we would pull into the boat ramp at Haulover and unload our daily catch of mutton snappers or groupers, and people would swear we had been in the Bahamas. We'd have muttons that weighed ten, and fifteen, and twenty pounds. We'd have black, and gag, and red groupers. We had really great catches of groupers and snappers on our daytime trips. Anchored up fishing with live pilchards or pinfish, in the course of the day we'd catch eight or ten big, quality bottom fish. Now we might catch a ten-pound mutton two or three times a year. I can't even remember the last fifteen-pound mutton I caught. They just don't exist in the Miami area anymore. There are a few places very close to the spawning areas like

Key West or Key Largo where they catch some respectable muttons, but certainly not like they were in Miami in years gone by.

The gag grouper population is crashing from the Carolinas all the way to Florida because of overfishing. Guys in the Carolinas were going out and catching fish boxes full of twenty-pound gags. Now they're going out and catching fish boxes full of four pound gag groupers. The handwriting is on the wall: if something isn't done to protect these gag groupers from commercial and recreational fishing, they are going to fall off the readily available species list.

And then turn it around. The groupers and mutton snappers are disappearing, and the red snappers are over controlled. People are going out, and no matter how they rig for fishing, except for trolling, they're catching red snappers. But they're not allowed to harvest any. So fishermen are trying to catch a mutton snapper or grouper for dinner, and they are catching and releasing red snappers. They can't take them so they leave them, injured and floating over the surface, wasted for no benefit. If the managers would allow us to take red snappers, which are in abundance, we could catch one or two for dinner and then go out trolling or dolphin fishing because dinner would already be in the box.

It's a good thing the red snapper fishery is so healthy. I catch them all the time. For the last ten years I've caught more red snappers that I did in my whole lifetime before. I went from 1966 to 2000 without ever catching one red snapper in my home grounds around Miami. Now I've caught as many as ten or twelve in a day that were ten to twenty pounds. Red snappers are the one bright spot among snappers today.

Yellowtails are having problems too, so they have imposed limits. In Dade County we used to rave about catching a five-pound yellowtail. Now we're thrilled if we catch one two-pounds.

This is happening in the Bahamas too. We used to anchor on a wreck in twelve feet of water, looking at downtown Bimini, and catch twenty-pound mutton snappers. Now we catch nothing on those wrecks. Now we go to the spawning areas and, where we used to catch twenty-pound muttons, we catch five-pound muttons. The Bahamas is letting the same thing happen to their mutton snapper population that is happening elsewhere. The hopeful news is that there are some marine reserves that are targeting mutton snapper spawning aggregations, as in Key West around the Dry Tortugas where they are having great success.

And what do we need to do to improve the bottom fishing situation? We need to set aside small areas, maybe a hundred square miles, and that's only ten miles by ten miles, scattered all along the coast. So whether it's the Carolinas, or Georgia, or North or South Florida, there should be places where some population of fish can live unmolested to full maturity. Where they can lay millions of eggs, instead of hundreds of eggs, and repopulate our areas. Without those marine reserves we are going to see a continuing decline on these bottom fish.

Then we can talk about our billfish, whether it's sailfish, or blue marlin, or white marlin. All these fish are in grave danger because of international long lining. In the United States there are restrictions on hooks, and what they can keep, what they have to release, and their bait. But the international long liners are using all kinds of gear, J-hooks, live bait, shallow sets; and they're devastating the billfish population all over the world. Young men today are saying how good the sail fishing is. They might brag about catching twenty in a day. That's because they're hitting a pocket of really good sailfish, and they have refined tools for catching them.

But when I was a young man, a run of sailfish would extend from Miami all the way to Palm Beach. We would see dozens of sailfish tailing on the surface, and we'd all be catching plenty. Today we see one or two, but nothing like what we used to see. We are all much better at catching those that swim by, but many sportsmen haven't learned not to kill those fish that we do catch so they'll be there next season.

Now in a tournament, instead of bringing the fish to the boat and cutting the line at the hook or de-hooking it, some people cut the

271

line right at the snap swivel leaving fourteen feet of line hanging from the fish. Here's the point: of all the sailfish that break lines, and all the sailfish that are released with long leaders on them, I don't know any captains who admit that they are catching sailfish with long pieces of leader on them longer than the body. None. Day in and day out, it doesn't happen. That's because sailfish do not survive with long pieces of line hanging from them. These guys go back to the dock bragging that they released twenty sailfish, and the truth is ten or fifteen of them may be dying because they left the leader hanging on them. It also happens that when they fish ten lines, and a sailfish breaks off or cuts the line, and he may get away with a hundred feet or more of line hanging from him.

These fishermen who catch all these fish and release them this way for bragging rights, are actually doing great damage to the fishery and depriving future generations of a great day of sailfishing. So we can point our fingers at the long liners, but we also have the responsibility to do what's right.

A billfish should not be taken out of the water for a picture. It has been proven that most will not survive for the next week. When sail fishing, give up those ten line spreads and use a more reasonable four lines in the spread. Also, when a sailfish is hooked, bring it up next to the boat and, better yet, hold the fish by the leader and cut the leader right next to the mouth. Don't even touch the fish. That's the best way to ensure a healthy release. And that's the best way to ensure sailfish for the future. Get the best out of the fishing event, and then release them gently.

By the same token, with the shark situation as it is today, it is advisable to use slightly heavier tackle on the sailfish so the fight is over before it is even noticed by a cruising shark. A shark will attack a fish during or after the fight, so we have to move fast and with a purpose to protect those sailfish.

One other success is with the bluefin tunas. I've fished off South Florida full time for sixty plus years, and I've seen more bluefins in the last couple of years than I saw in my whole lifetime in the past. I believe that because of quotas and fishery management, we're seeing a regrowth of the bluefin population. Responsible bluefin fishery management has done a lot to make this happen. It's just amazing to catch, or even to just see, a beautiful thousand pound bluefin tuna, so let's keep that progress going.

Then and now. It's a tough picture, but we're the apex predator on the earth, and we can figure out how to keep these fish around for a long time with good and proper efforts, and everybody doing his part.

Acknowledgements

I would like to thank the scores of friends who, along with my sister Sue, have been encouraging me for years to write my stories. I enjoy telling stories, but have never submitted them to writing. I want to thank these people for not giving up on me. This book has been in my head for a long time. It's something I wished for but the thought of writing it myself was daunting. That problem was overcome when Pat Mansell offered to do the writing while I did the story telling. I think it worked out great, and I thank Pat for all his work to help make my book a wish come true. I would also like to acknowledge the beautiful work of my friend R.J. Boyle of R.J. Boyle Studio in Lighthouse Point, FL, who is an extraordinary marine artist, and was kind enough to contribute the cover graphics for the book. He willingly jumped into the project and turned my book into a work of art.

Made in the USA
Columbia, SC
10 May 2020